Choice Cuts: A Savory Selection of Food Writing from
Around the World and Throughout History

Salt: A World History

The Basque History of the World

Cod: A Biography of the Fish that Changed the World

A Chosen Few: The Resurrection of European Jewry

A Continent of Islands: Searching for the Caribbean Destiny

FICTION

City Beasts: Fourteen Stories of Uninvited Wildlife

Edible Stories: A Novel in Sixteen Parts

"The Belly of Paris" by Émile Zola: A New Translation
with Introduction by Mark Kurlansky

Boogaloo on 2nd Avenue: A Novel of Pastry, Guilt, and Music

The White Man in the Tree and Other Stories

CHILDREN/ YOUNG ADULT

Frozen in Time: Clarence Birdseye's Outrageous
Idea about Frozen Food

Battle Fatigue

World Without Fish

The Story of Salt

The Girl Who Swam to Euskadi

The Cod's Tale

The Importance of Not Being Ernest

My Life with the Uninvited Hemingway

MARK KURLANSKY

Books & Books
Press

Coral Gables

For permission requests, please contact the publisher at:
Mango Publishing Group
2850 S Douglas Road, 4th Floor
Coral Gables, FL 33134 USA
info@mango.bz

For special orders, quantity sales, course adoptions and corporate sales, please email
the publisher at sales@mango.bz. For trade and wholesale sales, please contact Ingram
Publisher Services at customer.service@ingramcontent.com or +1.800.509.4887.

The Importance of Not Being Ernest: My Life with the Uninvited Hemingway

Library of Congress Cataloging-in-Publication number: 2022930926
ISBN: (print) 978-1-64250-463-7, (ebook) 978-1-64250-464-4
BISAC category code BIO013000, BIOGRAPHY & AUTOBIOGRAPHY / Rich & Famous

Printed in the United States of America

To Marian and Talia, the real events.

"The real events that influence our lives don't announce themselves with brass trumpets but come softly, on the feet of doves."

—Josephine Herbst, *The Starched Blue Sky of Spain*

and

Nire lagun euskaldunei
(to my Basque friends*)*

Write a lot—but see a lot more.

—Hemingway's advice on writing to
Canadian writer Morley Callaghan

TABLE OF CONTENTS

A Dream Intrudes

Self-portrait of the author handlining cod on a commercial skiff
in Petty Harbour, Newfoundland, September 17, 1996

"Coevolving with the structure of the brain, language freed the mind from the animal to be creativity, thence to enter and imagine other worlds infinite in time and space."

—Edward O. Wilson, *The Origins of Creativity*

The truth is, I am a dreamer. This used to be a well-known fact about me. It was a frequent criticism. My father claimed I daydreamed in the crib. "What is he thinking about?" Mark daydreams in school. Daydreaming is not considered good. I suspect that my accusers had no idea the extent of my daydreaming. I was in an alternate universe most of the time. Only those who do daydream understand that this is a strength, not a weakness.

I enjoyed the real world, but enjoying the other one is how I became a writer. I had conversations with myself about ideas, about people, about many things, and I enjoyed these conversations with myself.

Now you may be thinking, "This is why he spends so much time fishing, because it gives him time to be alone daydreaming." That is the complete opposite of the truth. The wonderful thing about fly-fishing is that it affords freedom from thinking. It is the only time when the dream stops.

A good fly-fisher is utterly thoughtless. The mind is working, but you are thinking about what insects are hatching, what is floating in the river, where the river is swift and where it breaks into still pools. Your mind turns into nothing more than a fish brain. You try to think like a trout. Fly-fishing requires that kind of concentration. A trout is focused on survival and I assume it has no time for abstractions. Neither does a good fisher.

I fish the Big Wood in Ketchum, Idaho, in the winter when few other fishermen are there to disturb my concentration, unbothered by the beavers stripping black bark from the cottonwoods, or the elk staring down at me from the steep sage brush mountains, or even a giant moose wandering down to the river to eat willow buds. My interest is rainbow trout, as beautiful an animal as nature has ever offered.

In the winter of 2012, I had just turned sixty-three—I was watching my artificial black spikey midge drift in the Big Wood trying to lure a rainbow trout along a deep trench on the opposite bank. Maybe it would work better with a drop, a second fly—perhaps a larger dry fly floating on the surface where I could see it. Then I thought about how Hemingway fished the Big Wood with two drops, three flies in all.

Now I was lost. My mind had slipped into that other world. It is true that to be in Ketchum and never think about Hemingway is as unlikely as being in Sherwood Forest with not a thought of Robin Hood. I thought not about the rainbow trout but about the fact that only a half mile upriver along the bank, Hemingway had stood behind his house and blown his head off with a shotgun—literally nothing left of his head but fragments along the black-trunked cottonwood bank, maybe some even in the river where trout and merganser ducks might feed on it.

Then came a shocking revelation: I was older than Hemingway ever lived to be. I was now older than the grizzled old man who called himself Papa—older than that battle-worn, thinning-white-haired, stooped-old Papa ever lived to be. This made me feel quite old, realizing that the old man in all the pictures around town was actually younger than me. But it was not an entirely negative feeling. I also had a feeling of liberation, as though I had outlived his ghost. I had a whole life ahead of me that Hemingway never had.

I had post-Hemingway years—decades, I hoped.

Until then, it had felt like Papa had followed me everywhere. He was certainly an inescapable presence here in Ketchum, where every bar and restaurant had Hemingway memorabilia.

I started thinking about how many of the places that were important in my life had also been Hemingway places. I had spent much of my life not only with the ghost of Hemingway, but around people who were still obsessed with that ghost—a few had even been with the actual living Hemingway and would never forget him.

Without ever meeting him, Hemingway had often been a presence in my life. It started when I was a child and he was the most famous living writer in the world. He may even have influenced my childhood decision to be a writer. He definitely shaped my idea of what a writer

was and should be.

I did not seek out Hemingway places but came to them by coincidence. It was the Idaho Basque community and not Hemingway that had brought me to Idaho. Like Hemingway, I have felt a connection to many places in my life.

Hemingway was present in many phases of my life because the myth of Hemingway left an enormous imprint wherever he went. Few people have ever had their lives revealed to the public in myth and truth with as much detail as Hemingway. We know that the first sentence ever uttered by Ernest Hemingway was "I don't know Buffalo Bill," and his habit of creating nicknames for people dated back to his early boyhood. We know too much about his bad hygiene, what flies he fished with on what kind of tackle, how he cooked his trout, his favorite sandwich, his favorite wines, his favorite shoes.

He impacted places that have no role in my life such as suburban Chicago, rural Michigan, Key West, Toronto, and East Africa. There are places important to my life that are not Hemingway places such as New England, New York, Haiti, Jamaica, the non-Cuban Caribbean, and Mexico. But there are always those chance intersections. I recently realized that a favorite hotel of mine in Chicago, the Whitehall, was also a favorite of his, though for him in the 1920s it was a state-of-the art modern hotel on the up-and-coming Northside. For me, it is a charming old place. To its credit, this stately old gem never mentions that Hemingway stayed there, and I never realized that he did until later.

But there are four Hemingway places that have been important in my life and have kept Hemingway in front of me—Paris, where I lived for ten years; Basque Country, which I have been writing about for nearly fifty years; Havana, which I have been writing about for forty years; and Ketchum, where I have been fishing for more than a decade. Hemingway has had an impact on my life in all these places because these are places where escaping Hemingway is not easy.

When I was young, I passed up many opportunities to talk to people who had known Hemingway because I had no intention of writing about him. By the time I wanted to, few were left. I talked to Bud Purdy in Idaho, George Plimpton, and A.E. Hotchner, all of whom are now gone. And I

talked to a few Cubans with cloudy childhood reminiscences—Havana bartenders and restaurateurs who remembered him, son Patrick Hemingway, and daughter-in-law/secretary Valerie Hemingway. They were the ones who were left. I talked to far more people who never met him but were shaped by him, like a friend in Paris who named her son Bandy because that was the nickname Hemingway had given his first son. (I wasn't going to tell her she got it wrong, and the nickname was Bumby.)

Patrick wisely said that if someone wanted to know his father, the best thing was to read his letters. This is probably true. Some 6,000 of them have been located, but at the time of Carlos Baker's book they were only available in archives for scholars. In 1981, Baker published a very limited selection of letters, and in recent years there has been a project to publish all 6,000. At the time of writing this, only five volumes running up to 1934 have been published, but the plan is for seventeen volumes. Many other biographies, memoires, and accounts have come out since Carlos Baker's, including a multivolume study at the end of the century by Michael Reynolds, which seemed to score higher marks with critics. Patrick, Hemingway's only surviving son, the rare Hemingway to achieve old age, said that he thought the best was *The True Gen,* a 1988 book in which journalist/novelist Denis Brian compiled interviews with people who knew him. Patrick may be right that this is the best of the now countless books about Hemingway. Others told what he did, but Brian tried to explain who he was through interviews with those who knew him. It was written in the 1980s when this was still possible. *True Gen* shows that there is little general agreement on anything about Hemingway.

This book is different from the many other books on Hemingway because they are sagas in pursuit of the great man, whereas this is a story of the great man pursuing me. The other books tell you what he was really like, but I don't know. I never met him. There is only that deafening noise of everyone else telling me.

CHAPTER ONE

Entrances and Exits

In central Idaho, Castle Rock as seen from Rte 20
towards Ketchum, March 27, 2009

*"Il n'y a qu'un problème philosophique vraiment
sérieux: c'est le suicide."*
("There is only one truly serious philosophical
question: that is suicide.")

—Albert Camus, *"L'absurde et le suicide"*

For Hemingway, 1948, the year I was born, began inauspiciously and our assessments, no doubt, would not have matched. The night that turned to my most fateful year, Hemingway and other celebrities were at the Sun Valley Inn in Ketchum, Idaho. The inn was made famous by excellent skiing and by inviting celebrities to stay there for free, giving it the cache of a place where celebrities hung out.

There was a New Year's Eve Party. The party reunited old friends Ingrid Bergman and Gary Cooper from the 1943 movie *For Whom The Bell Tolls*. The Cooper-Hemingway friendship was even older than that. The actor was one of the writer's closest friends. Cooper was a Montana outdoorsman and the two spent a great deal of time hunting and fishing in Idaho. Hemingway had chosen both Cooper and Bergman for the film.

The first edition of the book has a photo of Hemingway writing it at the Sun Valley Lodge. The film was one of the silliest of the many Hemingway disasters in Hollywood. To begin with, director Sam Wood, who cut his teeth on Marx brothers movies, had become a fanatic right-wing anti-communist. He put a clause in his will that his heirs had to swear they had never been Communists before they could inherit from him. Hemingway had been inspired to write the book out of sympathy for the leftist Spanish Republic's doomed fight against the Fascists. Though the script was written by Dudley Nichols, a leading film writer at the time, Wood removed all political content from the script, insisting that it was a love story that would have worked just as well if the leads had been fascists. In so doing, he removed the larger meaning from the story. Gary Cooper has a ridiculous death scene in which he drowns in Hemingway speak. In the book, they speak convoluted English that is supposed to seem like Spanish. "I am with thee," he says in his farewell to Maria. But

in the movie, he explains more about how he is we and he does not exist except that he is with thee. It goes on, catastrophically. Still, the film was nominated for eight Academy Awards and Greek actress Katina Paxinou, probably deservedly, won Best Supporting Actress. Hemingway knew that it was a ridiculous movie, but it was also a significant box office success.

Five years later at the Sun Valley New Year's Eve party, Ernest, in his uniquely Hemingway style, turned to Ingrid Bergman at midnight and said "Daughter, this is going to be the worst year we have ever seen." He offered no clear explanation for this prediction, quipping when asked that his "limited command of English" made it impossible to explain. This might have been a reference to the strange English in *For Whom the Bell Tolls*. Hemingway loved ambiguity and it was often not certain what he was saying. Bergman simply insisted that it would not be a bad year for her. It wasn't for me either.

For a few years after 1948, I was not thinking much about being a writer, but by 1956, my mind was made up. I don't remember exactly how this came about, but in 1955, when I entered Mrs. Long's third grade class, my desk was moved to the hallway because of my bad behavior. I must have done more than daydreaming but that is all I remember. I did not "act up" very much. To be abandoned in the hallway was to have been a terrible punishment, because most people do not like being left alone. A recent study by the University of Virginia and Harvard showed that most people would prefer to be given a meaningless task rather than to be left alone with nothing to do for even as little as six minutes. But I never felt this way. During class time, the hallway was quiet and empty and I was left alone with my inner dialogue, my imagined worlds, and my ideas. It was there, at the age of eight, that I decided to become a writer.

I wrote a novel (which I hope will never surface anywhere) called *The Coming of the Tiki Fish*. Some may say it was prescient that it was a book about a fish.

Why did I decide to be a writer? I cannot say how much I was influenced by Hemingway, whose reputation had recently reached new heights with a book about a fish. In 1955, the previous year, he had won the Nobel Prize in Literature. The Nobel citation asserted that the award

was at least in part, "For the influence that he has exerted on contemporary style." This is irrefutable. We all write a little differently because of the influence of Hemingway. He changed our taste in literature—those who admired him and those who didn't.

Once I decided to be a writer, the image of Hemingway was very important. Who could think about being a writer in 1956, or even today, and not think of Hemingway? As a third grader, like many adults today, I had an idea of what Hemingway was about without having read anything he had written.

Our childhoods had little in common. We were both middle class. His father was a small-scale family doctor, and Hemingway grew up in a home of books and music and art. My father was a small-scale family dentist, and I grew up in a much smaller house of books and music. We both had numerous siblings.

But Hemingway grew up in an affluent suburb of Chicago in a large house and I grew up in a blue-collar industrial suburb of Hartford in a small house. His family was deeply involved in the Christian religion with no drinking or swearing allowed, and claimed an ancestor, Jacob Hemingway, was the first student at Yale in 1672. The family was proud of both its English and American roots. I came from a family of Jewish immigrants where drinking was definitely okay. If I had been invited to dinner at the Hemingways', it would have been like the famous scene from the Woody Allen movie *Annie Hall*, where he has dinner with her family and imagines he looks like a bearded Chasid.

Our homes did have in common a central role for classical music, which was played constantly. And concerts and music lessons were part of both our lives. Both Hemingway and I played the cello—he even played in his high school orchestra. I only discovered this coincidence a few years ago. And while he dropped the cello early in life, I still have one at the ready next to my desk.

In an interview with George Plimpton in 1954, Hemingway said:

I used to play cello. My mother kept me out of school a
whole year to study music and counterpoint. She thought
I had ability, but I was absolutely without talent, We played
chamber music—someone came in to play the violin; my
sister played the viola, and mother the piano. That cello—I
played it worse than anyone on earth.

Typical of the Hemingway love of hyperbole, he never took a year off to study music.

According to Madelaine "Sunny" Hemingway, a younger sister who was close to him, Ernie was once asked, "what contributed to your success?" He answered, "I owe it all to the idle hours I spent in the music room playing 'Pop Goes the Weasel' on my cello."

His tale of family chamber music struck me because my mother suffered us with the same fantasy. She played piano, one brother and a sister the violin, the other brother flute and piano—she was forever trying to put together a torturous ensemble, which I generally avoided. It takes a deep feel for music, yours and the others, to play chamber music. And there wasn't a genuine lick likely to emerge from the bunch of us.

I have always been curious about what impact music had on Hemingway. His mother was a serious musician who might have had a professional career as a classical singer. Their house had an acoustically engineered music room. In his adult home, there were always records with a considerable variety of styles including classical. He played classical music for dinner guests. He also listened to a classical music station on a Zenith portable radio. In fact, classical music and jazz were frequently heard from the Hemingway house in Cuba. He played Bach, including guitar renditions by Andres Segovia, and, ever the modernist, Igor Stravinsky. He also liked Louis Armstrong, Oscar Peterson, and Frank Sinatra, and Fats Waller made him smile. As with his reading, his music tastes were eclectic.

But in the same 1954 Plimpton interview, Ernest was asked about "literary forbearers" from whom he had learned. Some of the writers, such as Dostoyevsky and Chekhov, would be on my list, though most aren't. He also named a number of painters, including Cezanne and Gauguin.

But also stuck in the list were both Bach and Mozart. Was he just making a point about great composers or was there something deeper, I wondered? He did say to Plimpton, "I should think what one learns from composers and from the study of harmony and counterpoint would be obvious."

The reason I wondered this is that I have always believed that Bach was the root of modern creativity. Without Bach, Jimi Hendrix would never have done his riff on "The Star Spangled Banner," nor would Miles Davis have created *Kind of Blue*. Oscar Peterson, a Hemingway favorite, was strongly influenced, whether the pianist knew it or not, by Bach. Theme and variations, *Toccata and Fugues,* impacted the poetry of Alfred Tennyson, T.S. Eliot, and certainly Allen Ginsberg. And it affected the way we now write. I play parts of his first Cello Suite several days a week, but I know that I will never master it. My left hand will never have the dexterity for his sixth suite, and I would be lucky to master the first. Even without the finger dexterity, the ability to understand what he was doing is an enormous insight into any form of composition.

Hemingway told *New Yorker* writer Lillian Ross in 1950, "that he had learned a lot from Bach, that in the first paragraphs of *A Farewell to Arms* 'I used the word 'and' consciously over and over the way Mr. Johann Sebastian Bach used a note in music when he was emitting counterpoint.'" Bach used repetition and variation so fluently that it is sometimes even witty. A good musician can't help but smile playing the unwrapping of some Bach variations.

Bach could weave five parts, all of different moods and colors, driven forward by a relentless rhythm. This influenced Mozart and Beethoven, but also Motown, Miles Davis, and Jimi Hendrix. Bach wrote themes and variations that he played against the theme, and then variations on the variation. Musicologists have said that his counterpoint was both horizontal and vertical.

Writing is about establishing rhythm, and rhythm is often established by repetition. If a writer seems flat and without appeal, the problem is usually not that he does not use the right words, as is often believed, but that the writer is arrhythmic. The writer must find and establish the rhythm of his work, which is why a writer should never listen to music

The Importance of Not Being Ernest

while writing—then someone else's rhythm gets picked up. When a writer like Hemingway can immediately pull you in with his voice, it is the rhythm that does it. It can be like Bach, or the rock beat that immediately pulls you into a Motown song. It has to be there, and even in the worst of Hemingway it is always there. Hemingway understood that repetition creates rhythm. Sometimes he credited Gertrude Stein with this influence and sometimes Bach.

The idea that Hemingway understood this about Bach, one of my pet theories, is very exciting to me. I confess that all my life I have fantasized interviewing Hemingway and that one of my questions would be on the influence of Bach. Interviews are serendipitous things and the question might have fizzled away—or it may have yielded something fascinating. Hemingway usually tried to give questions their due.

He never completely forgot about the cello. In fact, the older he got the more it came up. In *Across the River and into the Trees* he wrote, "Her voice was as beautiful as Pablo Casals playing the cello." In *Islands in the Stream,* at the end of his life, he described a fishing line tensed up by the pull of a fish as "taut as a tuned cello string." In another posthumous novel, *True at First Light,* he describes a leopard's sound as "A noise like the C string on a bass viol." But a bass viol doesn't have a C string, it is the lowest string on a cello.

• • •

It is not that I ever thought that we were cut of the same cloth. I was a Jewish New Englander, he was a Midwestern wasp born a half-century before me.

But once I decided to be a writer, I hoped we would develop other attributes in common. Hemingway, unlike any other writer at the time, was regularly in the news. He was constantly being photographed and written about. Growing up in the 1950s, there was not much chance of escaping him. He was the times we were living in. Nelson Algren wrote, "Of many American writers who represented their own times, Hemingway alone made his times represent him."

And so writing or reading or hearing about Hemingway was inevita-

ble. In 1959, Algren began his funny and unpredictable book, *Notes from a Sea Diary: Hemingway All the Way,* by stating:

> An essay on Ernest Hemingway was a labor to which I felt compelled. Everyone else was acting so compulsively I had to do something compulsive too or I wouldn't get invited to any more parties.

In the 1950s, famous writers, even Nobel Prize winners, were constantly asked for opinions on Hemingway, even before he won his own Nobel Prize. William Faulkner, the 1949 Nobel Prize winner, was frequently asked his thoughts on Hemingway. On a trip to Japan in 1955, describing what pleased him about the face of a peanut vendor, he wrote that she looked like "she never read Faulkner, she neither knows nor cares why he came to Japan, nor gives one single damn what he thinks of Ernest Hemingway."

Hemingway was in Spain with bullfighters, in Venice with good wine at fine hotels, in East Africa killing large beautiful animals. I did not want to necessarily do any of these things—I certainly didn't want to kill beautiful animals in Africa.

Hemingway, hence, a writer, was someone who went places and did things. That was my idea of a writer's life, the kind of life I wanted. So very early in life I knew what I wanted to do and how I wanted to live my life.

Hemingway was not my only model. I loved the beatniks, and the idea of aimlessly driving around America and writing a novel on a roll of toilet paper was also a draw. Wearing a beret and not fitting in had an appeal too. They too invented their own kind of writing. When I was very young, my sister Ellen, only a year older but knowing I loved beatniks, gave me a copy of Lawrence Ferlinghetti's *A Coney Island of the Mind.* This book was a huge and lasting influence because it showed me that there are no rules. Hemingway also made up his own rules. Once you are free to do that, your own voice is released, let out of its cage, and you can be a writer. That is why it is important not to spend too much time studying writing.

· · ·

The first blow to my Hemingway fascination, the first of many Hemingway coincidences in my life, was on July 3, 1961, when I was twelve years old.

Every summer, my parents, my sister, my two brothers, and I packed into an enormous Buick and rode around America for six weeks. The car was so big that not only were all six of us seated comfortably—the front had a middle seat in those days—but its cavernous trunk held luggage for six for a month and a half with extras, such as my father's brown leather case that he always called "the typewriter." When we arrived at a motel he would say, "Mark, take the typewriter case in." I was happy to do it because it seemed a writerly thing, though in reality, as I knew perfectly well, the case was my father's bar, containing two bottles and some glasses for his end of the day. This too was a writerly thing to do.

Being on the road with my family was not like Kerouac. It was domesticated Kerouac, but still a little exciting. Swimming pools were still a novelty, especially for us in the Northeast. I only knew one person in my neighborhood who had a pool and they never invited us over. The best thing about these trips was that we always stayed in motels with swimming pools. We swam our way around America. We saw a lot of towns because the interstate highway system had not yet been built. I examined these distinct towns, noted their different architecture and the fact that breakfasts got larger as you moved west, and more and more stuff was piled on a hamburger. But I was not sure I could ever get anything to write about this way.

In the beginning of July, we were in Idaho on our way to Seattle where my parents had friends from when my father had been based there during the war.

In the morning, my father picked up a local Idaho paper with a very large headline.

Hemingway was dead. The paper said that he had accidentally shot himself with one of his shotguns.

My father, in that slightly weird way he had of talking, said, "Accident, my foot. He killed himself."

I pointed out angrily that he had no way of knowing and the newspaper said it was an accident. My father pointed out that Hemingway was a lifelong expert with firearms, and an expert could not accidentally shoot himself in the head with a shotgun.

Of course, my father was right, and the true story quickly emerged. But I did not speak to my father for hours for the off-hand way he asserted that Hemingway killed himself. Why would he, when his life was perfect? This was not how the ideal life, the perfect writer's life, was to end. But at this point I had not read much Hemingway and I didn't know that Hemingway always insisted that all true stories end badly.

CHAPTER TWO

A Writer Must Escape

First sign of spring, Champ de Mars, February 20, 1994

> "Through the back streets
> Of all my memories"

> —Lawrence Ferlinghetti, *A Coney Island of the Mind*

When I was a teenager, I knew that I could not yet be a writer or live a writer's life. Even Hemingway, in his affluent suburb of Chicago, a city where literature flourished, had not achieved that. But I was growing impatient.

Hemingway, like many Midwesterners, knew he would have to escape the Midwest at the first opportunity. New Englanders did not feel that way, which may be why New England lost its dominance in American letters.

Writers would even move to New England, but no one was going to escape to my hometown. Instead of wanting to escape a handsome Chicago suburb like Hemingway, I dreamed of escaping Hartford's ugliest suburb, Newington, in what was often known as "the grea-er Har-ford area." Among the many things the area did not have was the letter "T" in its local accent. I liked to joke that we couldn't afford consonants.

At the top of my street, I could catch a bus and in a few minutes be in downtown Hartford, which also had very little to offer except for the homes of two literary giants, Mark Twain and Harriet Beecher Stowe. I was always perplexed that they chose to live in Hartford. Newington was an industrial area and most of the people who lived there worked in factories. The factories made small components for the larger factories in Hartford. Newington didn't even have the important factories. If you wanted to study music, if you wanted good Italian food or fresh fish, if you wanted to shop for fashionable clothes, you went into Hartford, because Newington had nothing. It did not even have a synagogue.

My father was from Boston and my mother from New York, both places we visited often, and I could never understand why we ended up in Newington. Of course, they did not come from desirable ends of New York or Boston—South Bronx and Quincy. But such places had standing because New York and Boston had standing. Newington, the Quincy of

Hartford, had no standing because Hartford had none. In any event, T.S. Eliot was right when he wrote "Home is where one starts from." It is not where you end up. It certainly wasn't going to be for me.

In the meantime, I read and I wrote. I wrote poems and stories and novels. If a teacher assigned some writing, I would turn in sixty pages—with illustrations. They seldom seemed pleased.

For school I read Hawthorne, Melville, Jack London, Mark Twain, and James Fenimore Cooper. *The Scarlet Letter*, which to me was about the price of nonconformism, particularly moved me, and I still regard it as one of the high points of American literature. But I liked them all, especially Jack London.

On my own I also read poetry. I read Hemingway's fellow modernists—Ezra Pound, T.S. Eliot, Marianne Moore, H.D., and William Carlos Williams. I struggled to understand Pound, but I knew he was important—Hemingway had said so. But he never took hold of me the way some of the others did, the way T.S. Eliot did, drifting out his own language and images in a rhythm so embracing that you could instantly memorize it and replay it in your mind, like the words to a popular song.

> Let us go then, you and I,
> When the evening is spread out against the sky
> Like a patient etherized upon a table;

It is believed that language is older than music, so maybe music is an outgrowth of poetry and not the other way around. It is significant that Eliot called his poem to J. Alfred Prufrock a "love song."

But then I also read the Beats starting with Ferlinghetti, who was so early he was really a pre-Beat. Though completely original, he in many ways resembled Eliot with his irresistible rhythm and his own images and words.

Johnny Nolan has a patch on his ass
Kids chase him
thru screendoor summers
Thru the back streets
Of all my memories

Ferlinghetti's words also stick because they too are songs.

Allen Ginsberg also thrilled me, making words so succulent and expressing ideas that at times seemed too rich to digest. This was written in 1956, the year I declared myself a writer, though I probably read it some years later.

I saw the best minds of my generation destroyed by
madness, starving hysterical naked,
Dragging themselves through the negro streets at dawn
looking for an angry fix

I read this poem, "Howl," because of the attempt to ban its publication. I admired this. Shouldn't all writers produce work that someone wants to ban? I was seduced by the music of the words even when I did not completely understand their meaning. It seemed to me that the best of poetry should not be completely understandable, that it expresses a truth that we can sense but is slightly beyond us. Once at a reading at UCLA, an audience member who did not understand a William Carlos Williams poem he had just read questioned the poet. Williams answered, "I didn't ask you to understand anything, only to listen."

Hemingway, also a rebellious modernist, believed this of his fiction—that everything should not be clear, that some things should be left for the reader to figure out. This was his love of ambiguity. In his 1954 interview with George Plimpton he said, "I always try to write on the principle of the iceberg. There is seven eighths of it under water for every part that shows." This is the kind of idea that writing students and writing teachers love. But it is not easy to do unless it is your normal way of operating. The hidden seven parts have to be completely developed in the writer's mind and then the part that shows has to quiver with all that stuff underneath.

I had not yet heard the phrase "iceberg," but I admired Hemingway's ambiguity and hoped to some day learn how to be ambiguous. But striving for ambiguity is essentially absurd, like trying to be beguiling.

I started writing poetry and when I was in college, I gave readings in seedy cafés in New England and the Midwest. Yes, this seemed a hip thing to do, but more importantly, in my mind, it was my first work as a professional writer. It was not diminished because I was usually not paid for these presentations. I have always thought that poets are the most honest writers because they do not work for money. Shouldn't we be a little suspicious of writers such as Hemingway or myself who have appeared on bestseller lists?

· · ·

I had the good fortune to come from a generation that had no YA books available. Once you moved beyond children's books there was nowhere to go but adult books. Now you could read the *great* books. It was exciting. You didn't have to completely understand them to enjoy them—the modernists said that you weren't even supposed to completely understand their work. I decided to identify the great writers one by one and read their entire body of work. If the author was worth something, you needed to read their entire body of work. I did this with Dostoyevsky—all those dark and intense scenes, life about to erupt. And I did Tolstoy—storytelling larger than opera. I was disappointed that Tolstoy did not have Dostoyevsky's intensity. It was only after having lived some years as an adult, going back to Tolstoy, that I appreciated how well he understood people.

But I started with the two greatest living American authors, John Steinbeck and Ernest Hemingway. There was also Faulkner, but for some reason he didn't speak to me. As an adult, I came to understand that he was a bold experimental modernist and, like Hemingway, some of his most engaging work was short stories. But he was not one of the muses of my youth. There were many things in all these books that a boy in his early teens could not quite grasp. I have gone back and read some of Steinbeck and all of Hemingway and found much that I had missed the first time. But there is always a thrill to the first time.

I began with Steinbeck because my parents gave me a copy of *Cannery Row*. I loved the richness of the characters and the sense of being in a kind of community I had never known. The canneries were connected to a California sardine fishery and the book awakened in me a fascination with fisheries that has never left.

Then I went on to the rest of Steinbeck, or at least everything he had published—he was still living and writing at the time. He seemed the most American writer, and though he seldom left California, his books and the people he met always felt like a trip across America.

Literature at its best is a political conspiracy; not a diatribe, but an experience that inevitably leads to certain political conclusions. I pondered a great deal after reading *The Grapes of Wrath* and was left with ideas about the importance of a social conscience. They were ideas that would probably have emerged anyway. There were two kinds of people—fruit pickers and fruit owners—and it was pretty clear which one you wanted to be.

Then I went to Hemingway who I had already been admiring without having read a word of his. This is too often the circumstance with Hemingway fans. I was once in the gift shop of the Hemingway house in Key West and a woman turned to me—I don't know why—and asked what souvenir I thought she should buy. I asked if she had read Hemingway and she said that she hadn't. I pointed to a shelf of his works and said, "You should read some of these, it is all that matters." She walked over to the shelf and to my pleasure selected several to read. I hope she enjoyed them.

Of course, as a child I was making the mistake of focusing on his novels and nonfiction books. The best of Hemingway is his stories, and he had already published quite a few excellent ones before his first novel. I began with *The Sun Also Rises,* a truly awful title, but I wasn't being critical at the time. Hemingway was particularly difficult because, although he was considered quite scatological for his day and his mother complained that he was writing dirty books, he was quite careful and vague about sexual matters, not wishing to be too explicit. This left young readers unsure of what he was talking about. Do girls sometimes worry about where the noses go when they kiss as Maria did in *For Whom the Bell Tolls*? I didn't

know. In *The Sun Also Rises*, I could not understand the nature of Jake Barnes's problem—something about a war injury, or why he and Bret couldn't just go off and be happy together.

But Hemingway, despite many great flaws of temperament, seemed to have an irresistible magnetism as a person, and an irresistible magnetism to his writing. When you start reading Hemingway you do not want to stop. I learned this best many years later when I was teaching a nonfiction writing class at Bernard Baruch College. Part of the bargain-priced New York City college system, my students, honor students, were extremely bright, hard-working children of immigrants—really the best of New York. I gave them many pieces to read and as an experiment, I decided to give them the worst of Hemingway, *The Dangerous Summer*, which was written in 1959 and 1960 for *Life* magazine. He wrote 120,000 words, which in book form would have been nearly 500 pages; even in three weeks of excerpts, *Life* could only run half of it. It is about the competition between two leading bullfighters in Spain. In 1985, Scribner, forever in search of a new Hemingway book, published 40,000 words. And that is the book I assigned to my class. It still goes on too long, contains absurdly sexist observations, and did not seem to be the kind of book that would appeal to young twenty-first century men and women. He dwelled too long on the physical appearance of young women, and not even in a particularly interesting way like the descriptions of men. The matador Luis Miguel Domingúin was "a charmer, dark, tall, no hips, just a touch too long in the neck for a bullfighter, with a grave mocking face that went from professional disdain to easy laughter." There was Hemingway, the keen observer. He then goes on to describe Domingúin's sister "very dark and beautiful with lovely face and she was beautifully built." Easy, Hem.

Later he writes of the festival in Pamplona. "It's a man's fiesta and women at it always make trouble." Such attitudes, fortunately, would not appeal to my young students.

They loved the book. They liked it better than Orwell on the Spanish War, or C.L.R. James's great book on cricket, or numerous other carefully selected examples of nonfiction. Hemingway got to them. He was irresistible. Something about his voice, the man who knows, the intelligence

and depth and wit never fails to seduce.

Flaubert said, "An author in his book must be like God in the universe, present everywhere and visible nowhere." In Hemingway, the author was God-like and all-knowing. However, more flawed Hemingway-like characters keep popping up, like Jake Barnes or Nick Adams.

Even when he is at his worst, he has great insights, a rapturous gift for description, and a sonorous sense of rhythm. Antonio with his cape made "the long, slow endless passes that were like some deep music that only he and the bull could hear. He could always break my heart with the cape…" so that even if you have no interest in bullfighting (which would be most people), he could convince you that something was there. He could have you with descriptions like "Antonio was calm and relaxed as a leopard resting under the sheet on the bed."

This was probably true of him as a person, which explained why, despite sometimes saying horrible things and behaving horrendously, it was hard to stay away from him. His sense of irony could be bitter and caustic, but it could also be genuinely funny. Once asked what an appropriate epitaph for his grave would be, he said, "Pardon me for not getting up."

Hemingway seduced his readers like almost no other writer.

• • •

After being a youth enthralled by his celebrity and later a teenager disillusioned by his death, I finally did the only thing that mattered and started reading him.

Some novelists only have one novel in them, and then their first novel is the great one. But writers destined to create a real body of work are often their worst in their first novel. But reading *The Sun Also Rises,* I think at age thirteen, he got to me.

The book made more sense to me as a kid than as an adult. In both good and bad ways, this book is the young Hemingway. The book has an enthusiastic, irresistible energy that none of his later books do. It is full of this here-I-am-living-in-Europe thrill. This "what-café-do-we go-to-now" adventure. It was all gripping for an early teen that had never been to Europe. The characters are supposed to be in their mid-thirties, which is

completely believable when the reader is thirteen, although even then I never understood the way they acted. All of this getting drunk and saying mean things and getting into fist fights. Later as an adult, I realized that these characters were acting like a bunch of kids. They were created by a kid. The pen and ink drawing on the original book jacket tries to show a much older Hemingway than the youthful, ruggedly handsome man in the photographs of the period.

But even as a kid, and a bit foolish, Hemingway seemed to know about life and about people—he had the observations of a much older man. Though childish, there was a certain grey-haired wisdom to him. In fact, he started calling himself "Papa" at only age twenty-six. It was originally the nickname of a wealthy American friend in France, Gerald Murphy. Hemingway's wife Hadley liked it and started calling her younger husband "Papa." It caught on very quickly. Hemingway also liked Murphy's affectation of calling women "daughter." Hem, as he got older, called women with whom he was flirting "daughter," which is odd because middle-aged men trying to attract younger women generally don't emphasize their age difference.

Hemingway never wanted to be young and was always much older than his years. "Don't we pay for all the things we do, though?" observed Jake Barnes. I had no experience to confirm if this was true. And I'm still not sure. But at the time I assumed it was true because Hemingway always seemed like a man who knew. I pictured the old white-haired, white-bearded man I had seen in the newspapers, even then older than his age. But he had written these things at twenty-six. He seemed to know a lot about things of which I knew nothing, like the observation, "It is awfully easy to be hard-boiled about everything in the daytime, but at night is another thing." Could I ever grow into the kind of man who could make such observations?

I did not see the shortcomings of *The Sun Also Rises* until years later. I saw its virtues immediately. Hemingway had lived up to the myth and this was my favorite book. But it did not even prepare me for my response to the next Hemingway book that I still remember as the single greatest reading experience of my life.

One day my parents asked me how I would feel about going to a "prep school."

I had never heard the term and had no idea what a prep school was. Kids in Newington didn't go to prep school. I soon learned that it was a special school for rich kids. Some of these kids were interesting. Some were just rich. They certainly disproved Fitzgerald's theory that the rich were special interesting people.

I soon learned some actually wanted to be writers. It only took a few weeks for the school to take an interest in my writing. Incoming students were asked to submit writing to a contest. I won with a short story and was invited to join the staff of a literary magazine. All of us on the magazine wanted to be writers. This was different than Newington, where the most celebrated literary accomplishment was a poem a friend of mine got published in the school newspaper. He was expelled from school because if you read down the first letter of every line, it formed a vulgar sentence cursing at the school principal. This is the only piece of writing by a Newington student I can recall ever being discussed.

The first day on the eighteenth-century campus was unusual. Not only was it the first time I lived away from my family, which, though I had no bad feelings about any of them, seemed like an exciting possibility—maybe the first step toward becoming a writer. But the other unusual thing was that I had a room to myself. It was a small room, only wide enough for a single bed, but it was the first room I had ever had to myself. At home I always shared a room with my twin brother, Steven, with whom I had almost nothing in common. Let's just start with the fact that he was very tidy and interested in clothing.

When they dropped me off, my parents told me to go out and make friends. Classes didn't start until the next day. The school had also told me to "go out and make some friends." People always tell kids to do this, as though they were some kind of adolescence diplomats skilled at this sort of thing.

I went to my room—my own personal private room. I started to unpack. My mother had given me a Hebrew National salami and some

chocolate-chip cookies—a perplexing cuisine. I had brought a copy of *A Farewell to Arms*, one of those Scribner paperbacks with the gray and charcoal wood grain cover design.

I sat on my bed and opened the book. I read "book one."

"In the late summer of that year, we lived in a house in a village that looked across the river and the plain to the mountains."

Many years later I came to understand that one of the jewels of Hemingway's genius was his opening lines. I read on to find out more. I never even learned the name of the lead character, Frederic Henry, until page seventy-four when he is wounded and a nurse asks him for it.

At the end of the day, never having moved from my bed or even looked up, deep in Italian World War I, Milan, and the Lake Country, places and events and lives I had never seen, Catherine was dead and I read, "It was like saying good-by to a statue. After a while I went out and left the hospital and walked back to the hotel in the rain."

Surely this was Hemingway's greatest book. How could he ever be better? He never was, except maybe in a few short stories. I had never been so moved by a book. I did not make any friends that day; I went to the dining hall for dinner and was assigned to a table where most of the students were Spanish-speaking and had no interest in me. It didn't matter because I was so lost in World War I Italy and Frederick and Catherine that I had no desire to talk to anyone. However, I did learn my first sentence of Spanish: "*Pasa la mantequilla, por favor.*"

• • •

Part of what drew me to this book was that it was profoundly anti-war. It was the summer of 1963 and I was thinking a lot about war. I had already been interested for several years in the anti-nuclear weapon movement, which had the logo later adopted to mean peace and then, even later, displayed everywhere to mean nothing.

This was a story about people who walked away from war. They simply decided not to participate anymore. Hemingway came back to this idea in other work. The best opening line he ever wrote, one of the best in all literature, was the opening of "In Another Country," a short

story he published two years before *A Farewell to Arms*. It begins, "In the fall the war was always there, but we didn't go to it anymore." Wasn't that the best thing to do with war? Just don't go to it.

He was determined to be that rare writer who told the truth about war. In 1942, as the United States was entering World War II, he collected an anthology of war writing called *Men at War*. He wrote in the introduction that he had collected the book for his sons. "This book has been edited in order that those three boys, as they grow to the age where they can appreciate it, and use it and will need it, can have the book that will contain truth about war as we can come by it, which was lacking to me when I needed it most."

World War I was his war and he went to it foolishly; World War II would be his sons' war and he hoped they would approach it more soberly. My father had been in World War II, and my uncle, and the fathers of my friends—the whole generation. Soon there would be a war for my generation, and I did not think that the World War II generation had told us the truth. I thought it would be in this place called Vietnam, though I still was not sure where that was. I had an older next-door neighbor who had already gone to Vietnam with the Marines. Was I actually going to go there and kill people? Why? Or would I, like a Hemingway character, walk away? I would have to figure this out because it was surely coming.

Growing up in the aftermath of World War II, I had very negative feelings about war. But I felt alone. *A Farewell To Arms* was the first anti-war book I ever read. The first evidence that others, grown-ups, even veterans, had these same sentiments. In *A Farewell to Arms*, most everyone hates the war and recognizes patriotism as a sham. They have a condition Hemingway calls "the war disgust." One soldier says that people who see war realize how bad it is and adds, "There are people who are afraid of their officers. It is with them the war is made... We were all cooked. The thing was not to recognize it. The last country to realize they were cooked would win the war." This, in fact, is a fairly accurate description of how World War I ended. But it seemed that it would never end. Once wars start, they have no end date. Frederick asks Catherine, "Where will we live after the war?"

And she answers, "In an old people's home probably."

With the word Vietnam coming up more and more, I was struck by Hemingway's hatred of war, notable because, though he was never a combat soldier, he was often associated with war. One character said that people go crazy when they understand how bad war is.

I grew up secretly nursing such thoughts, but I never heard others, especially someone with Hemingway's stature, saying it. In his 1948 introduction to the reissuing of *A Farewell to Arms* he wrote, "I believe that all the people who stand to profit by a war and who help provoke it should be shot on the first day it starts...." And there it was. I was convinced that had Hemingway lived, he would have actively opposed the Vietnam War. He would have been one of us.

• • •

Hemingway had difficulty deciding on the ending to *A Farewell to Arms*. He knew what happens. Catherine dies. What should he say after that? In his papers and letters, forty-seven different endings have been found. There may have been more. There was the characteristic Hemingway irony about death. He wrote, "That is all there is to the story. Catherine died and you will die and I will die, and that is all I can promise you." That is not the ending I would have wanted at age fourteen and a surprising ending for an author who was only twenty-nine. But he was probably shaped by his father killing himself with a handgun while he was writing this book. Deeply disturbed, he had denounced the act as cowardly, which was what his father had always said about suicide. But then Hemingway told his younger sister Sunny, she recalled, "I'll probably go the same way."

The photo on the back of the book shows still a young man, one of the last pictures with an unscarred face. I could not yet understand Hemingway's old man side. Some endings are religious about everything in God's hands. Some of his proposed endings were strange, such as, "See Naples and die is a fine idea. You will live to hate its guts if you live there. Perhaps there is no luck in a peninsula." *A Farewell to Arms* is not even set in Naples.

Being Hemingway, he said that working on it made him happy.

"The fact that the book was a tragic one did not make me unhappy since I believe that life was a tragedy. And knew it could have only one end."

I was struck by this comment, these comments that Hemingway often made. Was the source of his greatness his tragic view of life? I did not have that view and maybe that would always keep me from greatness. It certainly would keep me from ever being Hemingway, but I was not unhappy about not being unhappy.

Once I put the book down, I did keep thinking about it and I wanted to talk about it. But nobody else had been reading it. Everyone else had been out making friends.

Hemingway said the ordinary get an ordinary death. He wanted out of Oak Park and, so clearly, he didn't want to be ordinary. Who does? In my summers I worked on commercial fishing boats or on the docks. My best fishing job was on a forty-five-foot, wooden-hulled lobster boat that had been built years before in Bath, Maine. The boat had no stability in open ocean and violently heaved from side to side. It took several days to master standing on my feet. Since then, I have been able to stand on any kind of pitching deck. You also had to master the craft of over steering to starboard and then to port in order to chart a straight, and therefore fuel-efficient, course. We set lobster pots in open ocean off Rhode Island. I hauled 200 feet or more of line with three water-soaked wooden pots at the end. I didn't know much, but I was strong.

Those summers gave me a lifelong love of commercial fishing and commercial fishermen. I go out whenever someone will let me. The last time was on a drift netter in the Gulf of Alaska. This is a one-person boat and the drift netter I had gotten to know in Cordoba, Alaska, happened to be a woman which, in Alaska, is only a little rare. She was hesitant to let me go out with her until I told her that I had worked in the North Atlantic. She hauled the nets, and I slid the salmon into the hold to be iced. She later said that what she enjoyed about working with me was how happy I was, how much I seemed to enjoy the work. It's true.

When I first started doing this at age seventeen, I knew this was something I would be writing about. There is nothing ordinary about fishermen, except maybe their meat and potatoes diet.

Hemingway never went to college. He liked to say that he was going to Princeton but couldn't because his mother took all their money to build a new house. This was another Hemingway fabrication. He did not have the patience to delay his career for four years and decided to be a newspaper reporter instead. Like most reporters, he loved it for a time because he got to meet interesting and important people and get into difficult places. Newspaper people usually didn't go to college, and even sometimes made fun of people who did. A number of my favorite writers, such as Jack London, did not go to college. To me it was more disappointing to realize that the Beats, despite their rebelliousness, were all college products—in fact, Ivy Leaguers. Ferlinghetti, Kerouac and Ginsberg all studied at Columbia University.

I was sliding more toward the Hemingway model. I probably would not have gone to college at all if it were not for the Vietnam War. Hemingway went to war instead of college, and I went to college instead of going to war. I realized that Hemingway and many other great writers were shaped by going to war. I thought about that briefly. I would have learned a lot in Vietnam. Maybe I could have gone as a medic, like Hemingway did. But that was still participating in the war effort, and it seemed to me that my generation should finally say no to war. I think Hemingway might have agreed.

In any event, it didn't matter what he might have done. I was not going to help kill peasants in Southeast Asia without any valid reason to do it. There are better ways for a writer to learn about life.

College actually is worth doing for a writer. What you don't want to do is go to school to learn how to write. Although I sometimes succumb to requests to teach writing, I always quote Isaac Bashevis Singer, the Nobel Prize winning Yiddish novelist. He taught at the University of Miami and one day I asked him what he taught there. With his Yiddish inflection he replied, "I teach what can't be taught."

Writing, if it is any good, is too personal an endeavor to be taught by someone else. Always be leery of anyone who claims that they can teach you how to write and particularly leery of a college that claims to be "a

writer's school." In fact, look out for all literary advice including what I am now telling you.

In 1929, Hemingway advised a starting writer, "If you want to make a living writing I would say that it is easier to make it almost any other way." But he said that if you had to do it, "the only thing is to write, and no one can help you."

If you are a writer you are on your own. You write alone and though you can occasionally take advice, ultimately you are the only critic that matters. If you are not any good at criticism, you are in trouble. In Hemingway's Nobel Prize acceptance speech this compulsively social writer, who liked to travel with a crowd and dined with large numbers said, "Writing, at its best, is a lonely life. Organizations for writers palliate the writer's loneliness but I doubt if they improve his writing. He grows in public stature as he sheds his loneliness and often his work deteriorates. For he does his work alone and if he is a good enough writer he must face eternity, or the lack of it, each day."

As far as I know, this is the best piece of advice to writers Hemingway ever offered. Hemingway told the truth of what it is like to be a writer—it's an endless struggle. But if you love your craft, as Hemingway did and I do, it is not an unpleasant struggle. Nothing feels better.

He said that "writing is something that can never be done as well as it can be done," and any honest writer knows this. No matter how good a day you had, you always walk away from the desk thinking that somehow it could have been better. That is the torture of writing. The rest of it is mostly joy. I love writing and it always makes me feel happy to write despite my imperfection. No matter how bad life gets—an illness, a death, a war—I have always been able to make myself feel better by sitting down and writing something. And this was true even when I was boy.

If you go to college, study something else. Study biology or physics, or Kierkegaard or Kant, or become a doctor like the modernist poet William Carlos Williams. I studied theater. I intended to be a playwright and wrote and had several plays produced. But I never studied playwriting. Fortunately, there was no such program. I studied acting and directing, and this taught me how to make aesthetic judgments. This is essential to the writer facing eternity alone. When I teach writing, I mostly try to

hone this skill of making judgments.

Of course, I also learned valuable skills from writing plays such as how to tell a story, create a character, build a scene, and write dialogue.

Deciding to be a playwright meant going to New York. But it turned out that when the Selective Service said "college deferment," they meant it literally—that your military service was deferred only to the end of college. While I was in college, they established a lottery system. Based on your birthday, you drew a number from one to 365. If your number was in the three hundreds, you wouldn't have to go. In the high two hundreds, you probably wouldn't either. Even in the low two hundreds there was a chance. My number was 12. I received my draft notice on the day of my last college final exam. It seemed they were watching.

I reported to the train station in Hartford, an old peeling wooden station built to send young men to death with the Union Army. We were taken to an induction center in New Haven. My only certainty was that I was not going to participate in the war in Vietnam. I supposed I would end up in Canada, but this worried me because I was not certain of the opportunities for playwriting in Canada.

Those people Hemingway mentioned who had not figured out how bad war was, the people he said were used to make war, were an increasingly rare breed. Most everyone on the train to New Haven was trying not to go in. Some were trying to pass as gay, though they would have been more convincing if they didn't try. One was feeling very sick from the fifty eggs he had eaten because he was told this would give him a disqualifyingly high albumin count, (though neither he nor I knew what albumin was).

It seems that the military only rejected people who wanted to go in. When Hemingway had volunteered for World War I, he was turned down for bad eyesight. Yet somehow, though they were not outright rejecting people on my day, the only one who was taken on the spot was a small meek man who had been the junior high school bully. In those days he was much bigger than everyone else. He had tried to hit me with a baseball bat because I got a varsity letter in baseball and he didn't. But he failed to keep growing; eventually, most everyone was bigger than he and he became quiet and meek, like a bad guy who had been disarmed.

What was I going to do? I would tell the truth. I walked up to an extremely tall man in a white Naval uniform. I still remember word for word what I said: "Listen, I consider what you are doing to be completely immoral, and I refuse to participate in anyway."

He gazed down at me not looking angry or surprised. He looked bored and rolled his eyes, and in a monotonous voice said, "Conscientious objector, line three."

Line three was very long and then it was many months before my hearing was scheduled. It went badly. If you were not a Mennonite or a Quaker, they tended not to believe you. Of course, some of the leaders of nonviolence, like Martin Luther King Jr., did not come from a "peace religion," while Eisenhower was raised Mennonite. But they were rigid thinkers, those draft board officials—"Minds like beds always made up" was William Carlos Williams's description of such thinking—and I spent several years on the verge of moving to Canada. Today I wish I had, but then it seemed like a drastic step.

There were no jobs for me in America because they looked at your draft status and mine said that I would soon be either in Toronto or the Mekong Delta. Fortunately, I had worked my way through college on a scholarship doing lighting and could get jobs doing lighting and other technical work in small theaters.

When I was in college in the 1960s, theater was experimental and original. That was why I got interested in it. But by the 1970s, it was not. I belonged to a group of young playwrights, and we were given tickets to all the Broadway shows. I saw about thirty a year and I rarely liked any of them. Broadway was heading for what it has become: glib entertainment for tourists.

My playwriting career was slowly building with a few small productions. I even won a prize for a radio play that awarded enough money for my first trip to Europe. I was still only in my mid-twenties, approaching the age when Hemingway would become a star. Of course, if I didn't it would only mean that my career was developing slightly more slowly than Hemingway's had. That was acceptable. College had slowed me down.

But the problem was that if I was not going to write the kind of thing that would ever go on Broadway, what was the point of being a playwright?

Then came a play called *Poor Murderer,* by the Czech playwright Pavel Kohout. Directed by a major talent, Herbert Berghof, and starring a well-recognized Broadway actor, Laurence Luckinbill, this was a surprising, original and intriguing play—the sort of play I had been hoping to see on Broadway. It is about an actor playing Hamlet who thinks he may have killed the actor who played Polonious. It is a play about the edge of madness. Prague, the home of Kafka and Rilke, has always fostered boldly experimental writers. Since the Soviet Invasion in 1968, playwrights, including both Kohout and Václav Havel, had been at the forefront of a nonviolent resistance to the Soviets. The play got excellent reviews but small audiences. Clive Barnes of *The New York Times* wrote an article titled "Hope for Drama on Broadway?" in which he noted that *Poor Murderer* was a test of whether serious, challenging theater would have its place on Broadway.

No, it would not. The play folded in little more than two months. This finally convinced me that I had no place in theater. I had recently married and my wife, Virginia, had one of the most wonderfully adventurous spirits I have ever known. She was always ready to tear it up and try something new. It was her idea that I would be better suited for journalism than theater.

I started writing occasional stories for newspapers and magazines. I also returned to my first love, short story writing. For Hemingway and Fitzgerald, short stories had been a way of earning a living between novels. They had a genius for it, especially Hemingway. His short stories were his best writing. But in my time, major magazines were not buying quality fiction for good money. There were small literary magazines, whose honorariums were as meager as their press runs. There did not seem to be much of a future in this. I only wrote a few and sent them around. The only one that was ever published—my best, "Red Sea Salt," the offbeat tale of a food critic who loses his sense of smell when he falls into a hole—was finally included in my 2010 short story collection, *Edible Stories.*

In the short term, I had far more success as a journalist and fifteen years later, a fairly well-known correspondent, I was in Prague interviewing some of the dissidents who had stubbornly led the way

to a post-Soviet Republic and I wanted to talk to Pavel Kohout, now an important political leader. I wanted to tell him about the impact his unjust failure had on my life.

But as soon as I pronounced the words "Poor Murderer," his eyes lit with excitement. He told me about how much the triumph on Broadway meant to him. He was in prison for having signed an anti-Soviet statement and to cheer him up, his friends would visit him and report on the success of the play. They probably read from the favorable reviews—Barnes in the *Times* and Brendan Gil in the *New Yorker*—but did not tell him of the poor turnout or that the play closed in a shorter term than his prison sentence. I was not going to be the one to tell him now.

• • •

When I started in journalism, it seemed clear that you did not want to start in New York or Washington because they had too many journalists. I tried San Francisco. Virginia was happy to move to San Francisco. She was always happy to move. I worked for a new deluxe magazine, *San Francisco*, which was supposed to be a kind of West Coast *New Yorker*. It lasted about as long as a Czech play on Broadway.

Then I started thinking that if an American wanted to reinvent himself, Europe was the place to go. This was a Hemingway idea, but it was also a Henry James idea. It was an old American idea and perhaps the only move I ever made directly inspired by Hemingway. But when I got there, I found there were too many Hemingways, and Paris was where I learned how important it was to not be one of them.

CHAPTER THREE

The Grass in Paris

A lunar eclipse over Place Pigalle in Paris, April 4, 1996, 1:30 a.m.

"…by the time I got to Paris, nothing remained but empty napkin-rings on the grass."

—Nelson Algren, *Notes from a Sea Diary:*
Hemingway All the Way

It was as neat a public relations coup as any dead writer has ever pulled off. In the ten years between when Hemingway died and when I showed up in Paris, Papa somehow became a bigger star than ever. Had he not, the ghost of Ernest might have vanished rather than persisting in my life.

The first big event was another Hemingway book, *A Moveable Feast,* published in 1964, three years after Hemingway's death. Hemingway's younger friend A.E. Hotchner claimed he was with Hemingway having lunch at the Ritz in 1956 when the hotel informed him that they had a trunk of his from 1928. Hemingway had no memory of this trunk but was delighted to discover a pile of notebooks in it that he had handwritten in the 1920s about his life and his friends.

A Moveable Feast is Hemingway's most romantic book. It showed him with far more love for his first wife Hadley than for his second Pauline. This upset the Pauline wing of the family, who produced a revised more pro-Pauline edition in 2009. Most readers prefer the first version, but the real love in this book was neither wife but Paris.

Though only middle-aged, Hemingway was feeling old and looking back on a time when he was young, which, I suppose it could be said that is what I am doing right now. In a 1932 letter to Ezra Pound, Hemingway wrote that he was not going to write memoirs "until I am convinced over a period of years that I am unable to write anything else."

Hardly any American, certainly no American writer, can think of Paris without thinking of *A Moveable Feast.* In the mid-sixties we all became obsessed with the literary life in Paris—not Hadley versus Pauline, but hanging out with F. Scott Fitzgerald, Ezra Pound, Gertrude Stein, and all the others. It was the greatest assemblage of American letterers, and Paris seemed the perfect place for it—more perfect than earlier clusterings in Greenwich Village, Provincetown, or Boston. Why American literature

should take place outside the US is difficult to explain, but many American writers for centuries have thought this way. Certainly, Hemingway did not originate the idea of American writers moving to Paris.

I am not sure if it was conscious or unconscious, but in the back of my head (maybe every young writer's head) was the line "If you are lucky enough to have lived in Paris as a young man, then wherever you go for the rest of your life, it stays with you, for Paris is a moveable feast." The authenticity of the line is not certain. Some think Hotchner paraphrased the line from something Hemingway had said, and others have even suggested that it was lifted from Camus's *The Stranger*. But the line resonated with the youth of the 1960s: Yes, I am a young man.

In 1970, with the posthumous Hemingway clearly established as a superstar, he came out with a new novel, *Islands in the Stream*. This was an edit by Mary Hemingway and Charles Scribner of a manuscript Hemingway left behind. They cut a 997-page unfinished trilogy into a 528-page novel. Critic Malcolm Cowley once wrote, "Going back to Hemingway's work after several years is like going back to a brook where you had often fished and finding that the woods are as deep and cool as they used to be." Then in 1971, Scribner published *The Nick Adams Stories*. Nick Adams was a partly autobiographical character who appeared in many of Hemingway's early short stories.

Ten years after that dark day in Idaho that I thought was the end of the Hemingway story, it became clear that Hem would go on and on, perhaps with no end. Apparently he left boxes of manuscripts, and we could keep getting new Hemingway for years even though he was dead.

• • •

In April 1917, when Woodrow Wilson entered World War I only months after being reelected on a promise of keeping us *out* of war, Hemingway, like many young Americans, started thinking about joining the military. In October, at age eighteen, he wrote his older sister, Marceline, from his newspaper job in Kansas City that he wanted to join the Canadian Army because they were "the greatest fighters in the world. "He explained to her, "I will go, not because of any love of gold braid glory etc., but because

I couldn't face any body after the war and not have been in it."

This generational peer pressure is how wars are made. There could be no wars if young men were not convinced that going to the war was the responsibility of their generation. Louis Bromfield, who went on to be the bestselling American writer of 1920s Paris, told his mother when he volunteered, "It is better to be killed, than to miss the greatest experience of your generation." These statements reminded me of my father who, in 1942, was exempted from service as a dentist but volunteered anyway. He told me, "This was what my generation was doing, and not to experience it would be not being a part of my generation." My father never understood that I was free of that lunacy because, though many disapproved (including my father), I believed that opposing the war was my generation's experience. "How could I face anybody after the war" and have not opposed it?

Apparently, the Canadians did not take Hemingway, and his next plan was to join the Marines with three friends or wait until he was nineteen and try to be an aviator. In January 1918, he was debating with another sister, Madelaine, about which branch of the service had the uniforms that were most "snappy." Wars are fought by kids.

Hem was turned down by the military for bad eyesight. By March 2, he was saying that he intended to volunteer as an ambulance driver for the American Ambulance Service in Italy. He wrote excited letters to his family that he would get the rank of Lieutenant and be issued an Italian officer uniform! At first, Hemingway was thrilled that enlisted men had to salute him, but he had to return the salutes, which in time proved tiresome. I remember my father, an army officer, telling me that he used to duck down empty alleys to avoid saluting.

Hem was sent to New York to await embarkment. Another unlikely Hemingway coincidence: he was billeted in the Hotel Earle on Washington Square. As a high school student more than forty years later, I used to love going to New York, wandering Greenwich Village like a young writer should, hearing readings in coffee houses, going to off Broadway theater, drinking in artsy bars (the legal drinking age in New York was only eighteen, and apparently by the age of sixteen I could pass). I always stayed at the Hotel Earle, not because Hemingway had stayed there—I

didn't know that—but because it was only four dollars a night and it was in the right neighborhood. At the time, there was also a rumor that Bob Dylan had briefly lived there. Today, it has all been dressed up and renamed the Washington Square Hotel, and rooms must be booked many months in advance. That's what's happened to New York.

In 1918, Lieutenant Hemingway was among the troops that marched up Fifth Avenue and were reviewed by Woodrow Wilson. The young officer was thrilled.

At the beginning of the war in 1914, it became obvious that thousands of lives could be saved if ambulances could rush the wounded to field hospitals. The roads would be rough and a 1914 truck was a crude vehicle. The mangled survivors screamed as they were rushed over the pitted terrain to the hospitals.

It is remarkable how many who would later become famous, especially writers, were ambulance drivers. In addition to Hemingway, E.E. Cummings., John Dos Passos, Archibald MacLeish, Louis Bromfield, Malcolm Cowley, William Somerset Maugham, Charles Nordhoff, Robert W. Service, Hugh Walpole, John Masefield, Dashiell Hammett, and Harry Crosby were all ambulance drivers, as were composers Maurice Ravel and Ralph Vaughan Williams and future filmmakers René Clair, Jean Cocteau, William Wellman and Walt Disney. There were also artists, such as later Hemingway friend Waldo Pierce. A few, like Dos Passos, entered as pacifists opposed to the war. But that was certainly not Hemingway.

Everyone had their own experiences that later informed their writing. Poet E. E. Cummings spent three months in a French internment camp after having been falsely accused of espionage, and his first book, *The Enormous Room*, was a novel rich in character portraits about that experience. Hemingway's unique experience was getting blown up while distributing chocolate bars.

Hemingway traveled through France on his way to Italy and reported to his family that "Paris is a great city but not as quaint and interesting as Bordeaux." He was sent to the Dolomite Mountains in northern Italy. He spent three weeks there, but bored with the lack of action, he volunteered to go to the Piave where the Italians were pushing out the Austrians, and deliver to the soldiers in the front chocolate, postcards, cigars, and

cigarettes. He felt that he could do more good if he went right up to the frontline trenches with his packages. The command gave him a bicycle. For six days, he pedaled around the trenches delivering chocolate while seeing men blown apart, limbs thrown asunder by shells and mortars. This made a lasting impression. In the trenches, shells would come in and you would be alright but then, he wrote, a direct hit and "your pals get splattered all over you."

After only six days distributing chocolate and cigarettes at the front, on July 8, 1918—a date he would remember all of his life—an Austrian trench mortar exploded near him. The explosion was so enormous that it knocked him unconscious and buried him in earth. An Italian soldier standing closer to the explosion died instantly, another had both legs blown off. A third was severely wounded and Hemingway slung him over his shoulder and carried him to safety in the face of machine gun fire. When he got to safety, he was so soaked in blood that he was given little chance of survival. But then it was realized that most of the blood came from the soldier he had carried. Hemingway said he had no memory of any of this and was informed of events the next day when he was told he was to receive a medal. The 200 pieces of shell and a few machine gun bullets were all in his legs, mostly the right leg and foot. Two large pieces were lodged in the knee. He was taken to a good hospital in Milan and received excellent care. The leg was saved, the shells removed, and after weeks of operations and crutches, he was up and walking.

For a time, he was in intense pain and would whistle to let it pass. He was tormented by nightmares for the rest of his life. His leg never completely healed and he famously wrote at a standup desk, not because he was too vigorous to remain seated, as was commonly supposed, but because it was painful to keep his right knee folded for long periods of time.

But his letters home were full of the excitement of being overseas, the pleasures of Italy, and how he was becoming fluent in both French and Italian. He was celebrated as the first American to be wounded on the Italian front. He wrote a lot about this celebrity status, though in reality he wasn't the first. The first, the forgotten Edward Michael McKey, had been wounded in the same canteen service distributing in the front, at almost the same spot, three weeks earlier; he was hit by a shell and had

died of his wounds. Hemingway did not write about that and avoided talk of death and spoke very little about pain, less about the terror, and nothing about nightmares. This bravado continued for some time, to a certain extent all his life.

It is like the 1915 song about a rest station in Armentieres, Belgian for fighters on the French front:

> You might forget the gas and shell
> But you'll nev'r forget the Mademoiselle

In reality the gas and shell were never forgotten, but the Mademoiselle was what you talked bout.

I know this exercise. My uncle who was clearly traumatized for life from the five months—December 1944 to May 1945—in a misbegotten outfit that suffered horrendous casualties with an ill-conceived poorly armored antitank gun, blasting their way from Belgium across Germany to meeting the Red Army on the Elbe, had lots of stories about life with the French, the calvados they drank in the basement, how they drank tea with the Russians. There was nothing about the horrors that plagued him.

Hemingway returned on his crutches to America. He tried to purge himself by trout fishing in his old Michigan haunts, amused everyone with tales from Europe. He found work as a reporter at *The Toronto Star*, which paid by the word and after a time agreed to pay him by the story with expenses in Europe. He gave a range of stories, from color features and humor pieces to serious political analysis. This was exactly what I did for a number of newspapers when I first moved to Paris. In fact, we once did almost the same feature, on the French Royalist party. They were less entertaining when I did it because they had shown themselves to be anti-Semites and Nazi supporters. The Comte de Paris, the pretender to the no-longer-existent French throne, was the first person I ever interviewed in another language. I had just arrived, and my French was still shaky, and it is a difficult thing to interview someone who makes little sense with an uncertain grasp of a language. You keep asking "Is this really what he is saying?" He explained to me that he had to support the Nazis to stand up to the British who he said had killed "the flower of French aristocracy"

in an eighteenth-century naval engagement in Brittany.

On the ship to France, Hemingway claimed to have boxed with a prize fighter named Cuddy who, records show, was fighting in the US at the time of the crossing. Hemingway was in the process of making himself a fictional character.

He was always a skilled hustler. In 1921, he met Sherwood Anderson in Chicago, *the* person for a young writer to meet in Chicago. Anderson was one of the most important fiction writers at the time and had recently taken his first trip to Paris. He changed the course of Hemingway's life because up until then, Hemingway's dream was to take his fiancé, Hadley, and move to Italy, which he liked to call "wopland." All his life, Hemingway had an unfortunate habit of trying to be colorful by using tasteless pejoratives. Despite many Jewish friends he referred to them in letters as "kikes" with disturbing frequency. And did his friend Marlene Dietrich really enjoy being constantly referred to as a "kraut"? Anderson urged Hemingway to move to Paris instead of Italy and furnished him with letters of introduction to Ezra Pound, Gertrude Stein, bookseller Sylvia Beach, and a leading columnist for the *Paris Tribune*, the local edition of their hometown *Chicago Tribune*, Lewis Galantière. So he started with connections to important people.

In Paris, with his letter of introduction, he walked into Shakespeare and Company, introduced himself to Sylvia Beach, who wore mannish suits and a masculine haircut, said he was a wounded war veteran and lifted his trouser leg to show her the scars. Sylvia Beach had wandered to Paris without a plan, became the lover of Parisian book seller Adrienne Monnier, and opened her own bookstore. Like Monnier's store, Shakespeare and Company was also a lending library, and Ernest loaded up with classics—Turgenev, Dostoyevsky, and Tolstoy. Hemingway, never modest in ambition, considered such writers to be his real competition.

The extraordinary phenomenon of Paris in the 1920s wasn't just that Hemingway was there. There was an unprecedented gathering of talent. Novelists such as Fitzgerald, James Joyce, Gertrude Stein, E.E. Cummings, Robert McAlmon, Ford Madox Ford, Hilda Doolittle (H.D.), Djuna Barnes, and composers such as George Antheil and Erik Satie, painters such as Joan Miró, Juan Gris, Pablo Picasso and Georges Braque

and sculptor Constantin Brancusi. What gave this particular importance was that they were all part of a common movement—modernism, which involved many others such as poets T.S. Eliot, Wallace Stevens, Marianne Moore, and William Carlos Williams.

Modernism was not unique to Paris. In fact, Hemingway was introduced to modernism in Chicago. Sherwood Anderson, Carl Sandburg, Ring Lardner and Theodore Dreiser were all interested in modernism. Ernest had befriended both Anderson and Sandburg. He always knew how to meet the right people.

London had its modernists, including the American T.S. Eliot, the Bloomsbury group, which included writers Virginia Woolf and Duncan Grant. So was writer Ford Madox Ford, who was born in London but associated with the Paris movement. There were also Berlin Modernists, and the great Black literary movement of the early twentieth century known as "The Harlem Renaissance" was also a modernist movement.

Modernism had a great deal to do with World War I. After the pointless slaughter of an estimated thirteen million or more with an additional twenty million wounded, perspectives changed. These figures do not even include the psychologically damaged. Many could not help but view the world differently, less romantically. Painting would look different, music would sound different, poetry and other literature would have a completely different feel. Virginia Woolf wrote in her 1927 *To The Lighthouse*, "The war, people said, had revived their interest in poetry."

These changes began even before the war with painters like Picasso and Matisse and poets such as Ezra Pound. Gertrude Stein, a wealthy heiress who moved to Paris in 1903, wrote many of her most important modernist works before the war. But the movement grew with anger about the war. By the 1920s, modernists, including Hemingway, were on a mission to change literature. They worked together in Paris to publish and promote each other. Hemingway, like all of them, considered himself an avant-garde writer. In fact, all his life he saw himself that way.

Gertrude Stein was older than most of the modernists. She was only two years younger than Hemingway's mother. She was not particularly successful as a writer, and she often self-published, which she could easily afford. When she could find a publisher, her work sold very little. But

she advised everyone—painters, writers, musicians—so that her voice, rather than her work, was at the center of the modernist movement. She was a self-appointed expert with advice for everyone. She once told Paul Robeson that he shouldn't sing spirituals. Some valued her advice other didn't. Hemingway did. When he told Jed Kiley, who owned both a night club and a literary magazine in Paris in the 1920s, that she advised him, his response was, "Holy smokes, I thought. A chump is a chump is a chump," a parody of her "a rose is a rose is a rose" from a 1913 poem, "Sacred Emily."

The book that defined modernism, that presented a new language, a new way of writing, and left modernists all over the world from Paris's left bank to the Harlem Renaissance awed, was Joyce's *Ulysses*. It is an outrageously original book. It is about one day—June 16, 1904—in his native Dublin.

Nothing historic is recorded. The characters seem more ordinary than heroic. The language, like all good prose, has a strong rhythm, almost like poetry. Sometimes it resembled the unorthodox poetry of Ezra Pound—really the two anchors of English language modernism, though Joyce certainly ignored Pound's distaste for adjectives. Joyce could accomplish in one adjective (sometimes an invented composite word) what would take another writer an entire paragraph of description. He loved onomatopoeias, including the sounds of food being slurped, and used whatever languages might be helpful—German, French, even Yiddish. His language does not come off as a device, a revolutionary modernist conceit. Instead, it is the naturally flowing language of thought. Everyone soon wanted to copy a variation of this.

One hundred years later, if it were published today, readers would still be struck by its newness and originality. But after excerpts were published in 1920, how did the publishing world respond to this dazzling display of genius? No commercial publisher wanted to touch it because he used bad words—the F-word, even the C-word. Pretty fucking stupid of publishers.

So Sylvia Beach decided to publish it in 1922—a hefty 730-page tome on handmade paper. With a sewed binding, it had a thin teal-colored paper cover and came in a box. She printed 1,000 copies and the first 100

were signed. Who has those and what are they worth today?

Gertrude Stein had tried to be a pioneer, but never had a moment like the publication of *Ulysses* or the response to Hemingway's early books and, to her frustration, literature was moving beyond her. But Hemingway still championed her and got some modernist publishers to take her on. He even admired the way she made no effort to be commercially successful. He often admired commercial failure, as well as experimental writers who did not worry about sales.

But he did not want to be the creative original starving for his art, which Stein wasn't anyway since her family was wealthy. He might never write anything as ground-shaking as *Ulysses,* but he wanted to sell more than 1,000 copies. He wanted it all—to be an original inventor but someone who earned a handsome living at it.

In one of the best summaries of the faults and virtues of Stein, Hemingway said that she "disliked the obligation to make her writing intelligible" but that "she had discovered many truths about rhythms and the use of words in repetition that were valuable." Hemingway learned from this. He thought the nearly unreadable prose of Stein was brilliant and he championed it. He also recognized that he was out to create something far more readable, because he was at heart a great storyteller. But he saw them as artistically kindred.

Composer Virgil Thomson saw the potential of Stein. In 1934, he presented a plotless opera, *Four Saints in Three Acts,* in which Stein's libretto simply used words as sounds for counterpoints to music. Hemingway could never have done that because he was driven by a need to use words to communicate. The opera—this is the part that always amazed me—opened in Hartford.

To Hemingway and many modernists, the movement was about simplifying images the way painters had turned to simpler lines and purer colors. Hemingway once held up a piece of bread to *Atlantic* editor Robert Manning and said, "Raisin bread is alright, but plain bread is better." At the end of his life, while being examined by a psychiatrist, Hemingway challenged him to take any sentence in *The Old Man and the Sea* and rewrite it with fewer words. He claimed that it could not be done. That was one of the goals of his writing.

Shakespeare and Company was housed behind a dark blue, traditional Paris storefront at 12 Rue de l'Odéon. This was an old concept in bookstores, a kind of literary clubhouse, that is not really seen anymore because today's bookstores pay for their expensive real estate or close. There were earlier examples like the Peabody Bookstore in downtown Boston in the nineteenth century that nurtured Hawthorne and Emerson. Lawrence Ferlinghetti tried to make City Lights in San Francisco such a place. These stores supported writers and were places to discuss ideas. It is not clear if Sylvia Beach earned a living. If a writer did not have money to buy books, she would loan them. She promoted young modernists and pushed the small press publication of Hemingway's first book, a short story collection.

George Antheil lived in an apartment above the bookstore. He was an imaginative and unpredictable genius, famous for his ballet that used airplane propellers and electric bells. He worked with Ezra Pound on a number of musical pieces. In the 1930s, his music became more conventional when he moved back to the US and started composing Hollywood themes. He appeared to have become predictable but then, during World War II, he paired up with actress Hedy Lamarr to invent a remote guidance system for torpedoes.

Even before Hemingway had accomplished anything, Stein, Beach, and Pound were all impressed with him. Even before he had his writing, he had his charisma. He was astonishingly good looking, as Stein quickly noted. He was funny and charming, and he knew it. But there was something else. Most everyone had a sense that this new young generation, born as the centuries changed and forged by the Great War, was something entirely different. They were the first post-Victorian generation, and they didn't give a damn about Victorian rules. The women cut their hair and wore their skirts short. They drank and often had casual sexual relationships. They all seemed determined to break with the past in any way possible. Their parents were outraged. Hemingway's father, according to older sister Marceline, boasted that in his hospital the staff had agreed to fire any nurse who bobbed her hair, and he further declared that he would never tolerate short hair on any of his daughters.

Ernest Hemingway, the hard-drinking son of a teetotaler family,

was typical of his generation. Like me, he and his contemporaries had a strong sense of belonging to a special generation—Gertrude Stein's label of "a lost generation" only denoted her inability to understand them. I remember older people saying similar things about my generation and for the same reason. As he wrote more, it became clear that he was their spokesman. The new generation recognized him as one of their own and older generations, such as Gertrude Stein's, recognized that he represented that new school of thought. When *The Sun Also Rises* was published, it was an instant success because it was embraced by people of Hemingway's generation, people in their twenties who thought that this was a book that expressed what they were about. Hemingway's parents hated the book.

He was movie-star beautiful, and no one seemed to mind that he was slovenly and poorly presented. All his life people commented on his disheveled style. His third wife, Martha Gellhorn, was particularly bothered by his unkempt appearance, describing him on first meeting as "a large, dirty man in somewhat soiled white shorts and shirt." Upon meeting him, Jed Kiley described Hemingway as "a big fellow. About twenty-five, I thought. He needed a shave and a haircut. And his sport coat looked like he had slept in it."

The young modernists were all in it together, supporting each other and contemptuous of artists stuck in the old-fashioned way. Hemingway and Fitzgerald express sarcasm for the work of Louis Bromfield, a fellow ambulance veteran who lived in Paris and had bestsellers and even a Pulitzer Prize in the 1920s. Some biographers say they *were* jealous of him, but they celebrated modernist successes. Bromfield was no modernist. Hemingway also turned on his mentor Sherwood Anderson, the man who gave him his start. He thought Anderson's 1925 *Dark Laughter* was a silly and maudlin book, and against the advice of friends, wrote a book mocking it: *The Torrents of Spring*. Why a writer who had accomplished very little would write an entire book just to poke fun at a book by his accomplished mentor is one of those strange Hemingway things that is hard to understand. One of those typical ironies, *Dark Laughter* became Anderson's only bestseller.

The Paris modernists constantly advised each other privately and

criticized publicly. They would get their friends to review their books. Stirring up literary controversies was also effective. "It is people talking for and against a book that sells it. Not advertising..." Hemingway wrote to his father in 1925.

Hemingway famously consulted with Stein and Fitzgerald, but in reading his collected letters it becomes clear that the writer he felt closest to, at least in those early Paris years when Hem was unknown, was poet Ezra Pound. Pound, younger than Stein but fourteen years older than Hemingway, was an original. Well-educated with a master's degree and part of a PhD from the University of Pennsylvania, he was interested in helping talented young writers in an effort to reshape literature. He was what in the sixties would be called counterculture. His lifelong relationship with English woman Dorothy Shakespear did not stop him from engaging regularly in extramarital relations, which she seemed to accept. He dressed in odd clothing that looked like he had made them himself. He brilliantly reimagined poetry, rewrote the rules, and had a startling impact on Hemingway's generation.

Pound criticized and helped with rewrites for many younger writers including Hemingway, and the two became close friends. Hem even gave the poet regular boxing lessons, which were fun because Pound stood no chance of winning, and Hemingway really wanted to win. He said that Pound had "the grace of the crayfish," a stinging observation from a man who famously lacked grace in boxing, tennis, and most any sport. He had power but no grace.

Hemingway had been obsessed with boxing since he was a child and invited friends over to spar. It was apparent that Hem could only beat people who didn't know how to box. Gregory, the family iconoclast and the only truly natural athlete in the family, questioned George Brown, the professional trainer who coached Hemingway for twenty-five years and became his close friend. Brown laughed off the suggestion that the author could stand a chance against a professional boxer. "A person cannot put into practice what they've been taught unless they have good conditioning and reflexes, and your father didn't have either," Brown told Gregory. He could only beat opponents who knew nothing about boxing. He would cheat, use dirty tricks, anything to try to win. Then he added,

"But outside of the ring, for most of his life, he was one of the finest men I have ever known."

In a novel by Colette, the boxing instructor tells his pupil, "You wouldn't make a good boxer because you are mean." I did some amateur boxing, training at the 92nd Street Y in Manhattan and enjoyed sparring with friends. No one ever got hurt. That was the sport. But Hemingway was too mean to be an amateur and too clumsy to be professional. Hemingway announced in a letter to Pound in 1925, "It is fun to knock somebody cold." Why would anyone want to box with someone with this attitude? But Pound was famously crazy.

Pound had a profound impact on Hemingway's writing. The demand of newspaper cable writing is often credited with leading him to his lean style, but it was Pound who told Hemingway to use fewer adjectives. Was that just advice, or was it good advice, or was it very good advice? Modernists especially dislike the word "very."

When Pound reworked another writer's work he usually cut it. So did Stein and Fitzgerald. Fitzgerald advised Hemingway to cut the first page of his story "Fifty Grand," and much of the opening pages of *The Sun also Rises,* accusing Hemingway with that peculiar Fitzgerald gift for words of "elephantine facetiousness." Modernism meant stripping down to the essentials. Perhaps it was Pound who came closest to a motto for modernism when he said, "Make it new."

• • •

France in the 1920s was shaped by the trauma of war. Every day of the war, an average of 893 French soldiers were killed and 2,745 wounded. Fifty-two percent of the French soldiers mobilized for the war were killed or wounded. Paris in the 1920s was far from gay. There was an atmosphere of bitterness and cynicism, especially toward a government that had led so many people to slaughter. To reject warfare in France was to reject French history because for centuries, the nation had been engaged, nearly continuously, in war. The new generation that had fought World War I was finally saying "enough!" They were even more openly anti-war than my generation. Even Pound, later a pro-war fascist, was anti-war

in 1920 when he wrote in a poem that men went to war "believing in old men's lies." Anti-war was part of the modernist creed.

1929, the year that *A Farewell to Arms* was published, was the greatest year for anti-war novels. The veteran of the German trenches, Erich Maria Remarque, published his book from the German point of view, known in English as *All Quiet on the Western Front*. In its first year and a half, it was translated into twenty-two languages and sold 2.5 million copies. But there was also *The Middle Parts of Fortune*, published anonymously in 1929. Like Remarque's book, this was written by a veteran of the trenches: Australian-born Frederic Manning. Hemingway found the book to have such a profoundly realistic description of warfare that he ritually reread it every July for the anniversary of his wounding.

In his first book published in America, a collection of short stories called *In Our Time*, Hem tells the story of a combat soldier from World War I returning to Oklahoma and finding it extremely difficult to relate to anyone. He starts inventing lies about the war, but this only makes him feel worse. Then there was *A Farewell To Arms*, and in 1933 he wrote "A Way You'll Never Be" about a brutal battle on the Italian front. Slowly we realize that the hero, Nick Adams, has become completely unstrung and cannot sleep at night. It is one of Hemingway's best pieces of writing.

It may partly be that the attitude of the times freed him to express what he was really feeling. But he was also expressing what his generation was feeling. It is not by chance that his book was titled *In Our Time*. Hemingway consciously wanted, as most of the modernists did, to be a chronicler of his time and his generation.

• • •

One of the reasons that the Paris Hemingway lived in could not be found when I got there in the 1970s is because a lot of it never existed. In pursuit of a good story, Hemingway liked to make things up. Both Hadley and Ernest claimed they had been poor in Paris, but Hadley had both an inheritance and an annual trust fund. It did not amount to great wealth, but with the cost of living in Paris at that time and Ernest's additional journalism income, they were a long way from starving.

The truth is that Hemingway liked the romance of being young and poor and happy together. But there is a built-in warning: Only people with money find poverty romantic.

In the 1920s, an American could live extremely well in Paris on very little money. This is why they were all there. It wasn't just artists and writers who were moving to Paris—thousands of Americans were coming to enjoy the strong dollar, an escape from prohibition and from a prudish, repressive American society. Many of the modernists, including Hemingway and Joyce, were attacked, even banned in America for using words that were in common vernacular but publicly described as "filth."

In Paris, one dollar could buy ten or twelve francs—at times even more. When I moved there in the 1970s, a dollar was worth less than four francs, at one point down to the historic low of three. In December 1921, he and Hadley settled into the Hotel Jacob on Rue Jacob in the Sixth arrondissement, a picturesque neighborhood that has become one of the most expensive in Paris. Their usual dinner place with three courses and wine cost twelve francs. Their hotel also cost twelve francs a night, which was about a dollar. Acceptable wine cost about a nickel, and a bottle of good rum was fourteen francs a bottle. The spending power of the dollar continued to rise. By late 1925, a dollar would buy twenty-six francs and French prices had not increased.

Hemingway's letters home were full of prices showing how inexpensive life was in Paris. In 1923 when they moved to Toronto to have their first son, with Hemingway working as a *Toronto Star* reporter, he bitterly complained about the high cost of living. Although Toronto was not a particularly expensive city, he compared it to life in Paris. He wrote Sylvia Beach, "It is impossible to live here. I make about the same as in Paris but here an apartment costs 18,000 francs a year." He repeated the same complaint to Gertrude Stein and added that a beer cost seventeen francs a bottle.

In 1922, the Hemingways settled into an apartment in the Fifth, the Latin Quarter at 74 Rue du Cardinal Lemoine. It came furnished with a nice kitchen, a dining room, a large bedroom, and a working fireplace, as well as maid service. The maid prepared dinner every night and they could request any French specialties they heard about. All this cost 250 Francs a month, at the time about $18.

There was a grand piano in the living room and Hadley, who always loved playing, used it for two or three hours every day while Ernest wrote. On the ground floor of this building (or by some accounts, the one next door) was a bal-musette, a Paris entertainment from the 1880s that remained popular until after World War II. It was a crowded dance room where an accordion played tangoes and bourrées. The bourrée is a French dance that goes back to the seventeenth century. Bach included them in his cello suites. It remained a popular form used by Paul Mc-Cartney and other later popular musicians. Today, you can sometimes hear an accordionist playing one for coins on a Paris street. The other instrument—the musette, which resembled a small bagpipe—has almost completely disappeared, as have the bals themselves. The windows would steam up, but the music went out to the street and heads could be seen inside musically shifting and circling. Hemingway said the accordion music was never intrusive and he enjoyed it in his apartment.

This one was closed by the time I got there and there were very few bal-musettes left, mostly toward the outskirts of the city. I remember one in the tenth and another in the nineteenth. They were a blue-collar thing and the blue collar was vanishing. It is a part of the defining life of Paris that is now completely gone. In the seventies, there was still a blue-collar population in Paris. The closing of the Les Halles central food market in 1971 was the beginning of an exit that took a few decades. Paris's blue-collar had their own accent and their own dialect. It was a nasal sound heard in old movies with Jean Gabin but seldom heard on the street anymore. Yes, sounded like "whaay." They had their own uniform, the *tenu bleu*, a bright blue overall worn by all Paris workers. In the mornings, cafés had a row at the bar of men in *tenu bleu* downing shots of calvados before starting their day's work.

• • •

The Hemingway version at times stretched credulity. He was, after all, more of a fiction writer than a journalist. Poor young Hemingway, he tells us, was so desperate for food that he killed pigeons in the Luxembourg Gardens to eat—surprising that he didn't know they were doves,

which are less edible than pigeons. It may be a true story because for some reason, Hemingway just loved killing birds, any birds anywhere. But he didn't need them for food. He could have just had the meal his $12-a-month maid cooked, reportedly excellent. Hadley said the pigeon story was a creation of his "active imagination." Hemingway embellished, or you might say that he lied a lot. He was born for fiction. He could never resist improving a story. He was the embodiment of that old newspaper joke, "Don't let the facts get in the way of a good story." When he was five years old, he told his grandfather he had stopped a runaway horse. The grandfather predicted either fame or infamy for Ernest because he was such a wild liar. As an editor on his high school paper, having a hole to fill one week, he wrote about a boys rifle club that didn't exist. Throughout the year he kept writing about it, adding the names of friends. At the end of the year the yearbook wanted a picture, but he was the only boy who had a rifle so he managed to gather enough shot guns so they could all pose for a photo of the make-believe rifle club. At nineteen, he wrote his family while on a trip to New York that he was marrying Mae Marsh, a movie star that he appears to have never met. He also claimed to have had an affair with Mata Hari, the spy who was executed in 1917. He returned to Oak Park from Italy with fabricated tales of his adventures as a combat soldier.

All his life he exaggerated his World War I experience. He served in the American Red Cross for about a month, of which only a week was in a combat zone, and spent a total of seven months in Europe. It is also not true that he had an aluminum prosthetic kneecap, which he often stated. And there were many more stories. He claimed he covered a Turkish Greek war that he did not arrive at until it was over. He also did not liberate the Ritz Hotel in 1944, as he often said.

• • •

If you are a young writer and you move to Paris, you have little chance of escaping Ernest Hemingway—also little chance of capturing him. This was not a complete surprise. I always believed in making my own luck, and I was a young man, so why wouldn't I go, even though I clearly

understood that this was not to be the Paris of Ernest Hemingway and the 1920s?

I certainly had no illusions that Paris in the 1970s was anything like it was in the 1920s. Virginia and I had visited Paris several times before deciding to move there, so we knew what it was and was not. And even the French culture that we had known, now that we were finally there, seemed to be fading away. We saw the last of the steamy bal-musettes and ever fewer Calva guzzling men in *tenu bleu*. Jean Renoir, son of the impressionist painter, the great film director whose works such as *The Rules of the Game*, *Grand Illusion*, and *La b*ête *humaine* seemed to define prewar France, died. Jean-Paul Sartre, the epitome of the French intellectual, died. Lucienne Boyer, the melodious cabaret singer, whose chocolate-rich ballad, "*Parlez-moi d'amour*," became anthem for the romance of Paris, also died. It seemed it was all fading away.

What astounded me when I moved there was how many Americans were there who really thought they would live in 1920s Paris.

Paris of the 1970s was nothing like Paris of the 1920s, though the seventies were more like the twenties than they are like the Paris of today. In the 1920s, with a huge influx of Americans following the high dollar, Paris started showing its first signs of Americanization. American bars, bars that served cocktails, began to appear on both the right and left bank. These shallow intruders annoyed Hemingway. In 1922, he wrote an edgy satirical takedown on the visiting Americans for *The Toronto Star* magazine. It began, "The scum of Greenwich Village New York, has been skimmed off and deposited in large ladlesful on that section of Paris adjacent to the Café Rotunde." When I was there, I resisted a strong urge to write a similarly nasty piece. It was no longer people trying to be hip and counterculture in Montparnasse but candidly bourgeois moving into the Sixth and destroying its *quartier populaire* charm as they reduced Parisian magic to a search for the most ridiculously expensive restaurants. Today there would be little point in moving from New York to Paris because they are so alike. Big cities are becoming the same with high rent, no working class, and the exact same shops. Paris in the 1970s was still a distinctly French, sometimes charming place, where neighborhoods were laced with curious little shops.

The Paris I arrived in didn't even look like the one Hemingway knew in the 1920s. Paris was an ancient northern city with gray and blackened walls. André Malraux, who in the 1920s was an avant-garde leftist writer, somehow became right wing De Gaulle's culture minister in the 1960s and started cleaning up Paris. There was blond or crème-colored stone under the black, so by the time I arrived, Paris was a completely different brighter color—a sweeter and less tough city.

• • •

The problem with the Hemingway tale of poverty is that he also enjoyed oysters and Sancerre at La Closerie des Lilas. Later, when I became more established as a journalist, I too ate oysters and Sancerre at this restaurant at the end of the Boulevard Montparnasse, where the oysters were in baskets with the busy shuckers in the outdoor café part. In my early days, I used to watch the shuckers from the sidewalk and dream. And, yes, Sancerre is *the* wine for these fine de claires from the Oléron— Hemingway was invariably right about such things. But at first, none of this was in my budget or that of most of the Americans I knew—not fine de claires, Sancerre, or the Closerie—because my wife, unlike Hadley, did not have a trust fund.

But there was good food to be found for very little money. There was still a working class living in Paris, and so there were restaurants for a worker's budget. And the government guarantees certain items at low prices because they are the rights of every Frenchman. Number one is a baguette, that long thin loaf of bread whose name means stick. The obligation of government to make certain that everyone can have a baguette is deeply imbedded in French culture and the government guaranteed that the white baguette would always remain cheap.

So baguettes were my only bread. Sometimes I would content myself with only a demi-baguette, which was a matter of centimes.

The government also insisted that every café and restaurant had to make available "*un quart rouge*," a quarter liter of red wine. The type of red wine was left to the establishment's conscience, but there were many inexpensive red wines sold by the liter. And so we only drank red wine.

White wine with fish was a phony rich man's conceit anyway.

The price of a small espresso, *un express*, was also guaranteed. *Café crème, café au lait*, all had prices carrying the full weight of the low dollar value. An espresso and a small pastry became my breakfast and it has remained so for more than forty years.

There was a small restaurant in the Fifth where, for about eight dollars you could get a salad of grated celeriac (a root not to be confused with celery, even though they are the same word in French) and lamb brain (veal brain was too expensive) in a beurre noir sauce, a small wedge of camembert or the blue cheese, Fourme d'Ambert (neither of these ancients were the original raw milk version but the cheaper industrial cheeses), and a piece of apple tart or crème caramel. And of course, *a quart rouge*.

Such a restaurant was a splurge, especially compared to Casa Miguel in the Ninth run by Maria Codina. If Paris is no longer Paris, it is because there are few people anymore like Maria Codina. She was a Catalan who fled her socialist home in Barcelona in 1939, she said only hours before Franco's fascist troops arrived. She moved to Paris with her ideals intact. The idea behind her restaurant was to provide food for people who did not have money. She began by serving paella for 2 francs 50, which was about fifty cents. By the time I arrived, a meal at Casa Miguel cost five francs, which was about one dollar, red wine included. "There are some people who cannot pay more than five francs for a meal," she used to say.

Sometimes a snack was as good as a meal, when you are young enough not to consider nutrition. A ham and gruyere with good Normandy butter on a baguette at a café was not terribly expensive and a pleasant occasional splurge. If you were hungry near the narrow winding maze of streets of the Latin Quarter near Saint Michel, there was always a hot beignet fried to order in the North African stalls. Fresh from the fryer on a cold day, this was a feast. I have never been able to eat a cold donut since.

• • •

In those days it was difficult not to think of Hemingway when in Paris. I know that it was difficult because after a time, I really tried. If I told a Parisian that I was an American writer living there, the inevitable

The Importance of Not Being Ernest

response, with a smile and even a touch of enthusiasm was, *"Mais oui! Monsieur 'Emingway!"* This quickly gets tiresome if you like to think you are doing something other than imitating a dead writer. It was Paris that really cured me of Hemingway. But it didn't matter. He was never going to leave me in peace.

I gazed out from the Pont Neuf at the head of the Île de Cité, which, as Hemingway said, was "like the sharp bow of a ship." It always reminded me of a ship's bow, and I am pretty sure that it would have even without Hemingway. Hemingway wrote of men fishing there with long rods. I could see that the two islands had divided up the river and forced the fish into this narrow stretch until it reached a visible current and was shot back into the main river.

It was clearly the right spot to catch fish and I would have liked to have fished there. In Hemingway's day they caught *goujon*, mudfish, a kind of small catfish, which he said were delicious. Certainly better than the pigeons. But they were gone now. Before Hemingway's time there were sturgeon and salmon leaping on the Seine in Paris. I can imagine walking across the Pont Neuf and seeing an Atlantic salmon leap into the air or the prehistoric monster head of a sturgeon. But now all the fish were gone. The Seine was barren like the Hudson and the Connecticut—like all the rivers I had lived on. Some day I would like to live in a city on a live river.

Virginia and I found a cozy room in a hotel in the Fifth Arrondissement. It was very cheap, though not by Hemingway's 1920 standards in the same neighborhood. We decided to live there for a while. It had extremely bright floral wallpaper, suggestive of what at the time was called psychedelic, and when I opened my eyes in the morning it made me feel dizzy as though drifting through floral space. The hotel was ancient, but I suspect the wallpaper was not.

Two pleasant young Portuguese people kept the rooms clean. Portugal and Spain were impoverished dictatorships, not part of the European Economic Community, forerunner of the EU, and so they provided underpaid unskilled workers for France. The two had found pornographic magazines left behind in some of the rooms and spent a great deal of time admiring the pages. They were lonely and always happy to talk in very

broken French. But they kept the rooms clean.

We had picked this neighborhood because it was one of the few we knew from our brief visits. Our first morning wandering in search of a café, about a block from the hotel, we found ourselves on Rue du Cardinal Lemoine and we remembered that name from having read Carlos Baker. Number 74 was a peeling gray building with a narrow stairwell and a toilet on each landing, a building much like our hotel. We looked up to the fourth-floor windows and almost imagined a youthful Hadley and Hem looking down at us. Today there is a plaque marking the building. But with much of "the lost generation" still living in the 1970s, maybe still lost, there were no such plaques in those days.

We found a neighborhood café at the Place de la Contrescarpe. Hemingway wrote about this little square but said that he avoided the café, which he called "the cesspool of the Rue Mouffetard." He described it as a foul place, frequented by evil-smelling drunkards. That café seemed to be gone and was replaced by a modern establishment, not very interesting, consumed by the curse of orange plastic that seemed to be gripping Parisian cafés. But it was a pleasant location where people in office dress came for a morning café. There were only a few workers in *tenu bleu*, muttering nasal sounds, and knocking down Calva. They were what remained of Paris's past, but the café was mostly the future: affluent middle class on their way to work and occasional tourists. We really couldn't have afforded this café if an espresso was not price fixed.

In the 1920s, however, strapped for money, Hem rented another room in the same neighborhood, on the sixth floor of 39 Rue Descartes, for writing. Sometimes he wrote at the Closerie des Lilas, or so he later said. Some biographers say he had a small walk-up on a sixth floor on Rue Mouffetard. They could both be right at different times.

Mouffetard is one of my fondest early Paris memories. One fall afternoon I was out exploring in the Thirteenth and crossing over to the Fifth, and I saw in my map book, which I always carried, that Mouffetard would lead me up to Contrescarpe. It was a narrow winding and fairly steep uphill street, and it had a huge market on the sides. There was every shape of cheese looking like the model of a gray, beige, and white Asian city of new architecture, and there were brightly colored fall fruit such as

thick grape bunches from the center of the country, figs from the south, and green gage plums and rosy little mirabelles. A Paris street market was as reliable as a calendar, and you always knew the week by the food being sold. Cherries alone could be a half-calendar year, from the first that came up from the Mediterranean in the spring to the summer cherries of the hilly Burgundy wine country, until English cherries foretold the fall.

Being fall, there were wild boars with coarse fur hanging upside down, and haunches of deer and chubby hares like rabbits on steroids hung to unfurl huge floppy ears, and pheasants brighter than blooming flowers, and taupe pigeons—real pigeons from the countryside ready for roasting or stewing in a salmi. Later when I had a kitchen and more money, I learned to cook game and specialized in a stew called *civet* in which the game was stewed in red wine with the onions (from which the dish gets its name) and wild mushrooms and chestnuts, which are also seasonal. It is flamed in brandy, finished with cream and then fresh blood, which you can buy from the butcher on the day the game comes in, quickly and gently thickened in the sauce so that it ends up the color and texture of chocolate sauce. But on this first walk through the market I could only dream of such dishes. The real pleasure of Paris was not the restaurants but the food I could cook at home.

The fish glistened and were arranged in a pattern like an impressionist painting, with big flat turbots and leaves of slick white sole and red sea monsters from the Mediterranean, silver salmon, sleek pike from the Loire, and a 300-kilo indigo tuna from Basque country waiting to be cut up.

The days are short in Paris in the fall. It had been overcast day to announce the setting of the sun that had not yet been seen, the clouds separated into opaque purple smudges on a bright orange and pink streaked sky—the last of afternoon light making the food below glow. Many Paris days ended like this. The aproned vendors in blue, their ruddy faces lit by the warm lights, hung over the stalls to display the food, were shouting out their offers in raspy nasal calls I could not understand.

Hemingway's approach to learning French was the same as mine—talk to as many different people as possible in bad awkward French, and with each conversation, the French improved. No matter the linguistic

shortcomings, he never hesitated to plunge in. Neither did I, although I had a fairly good vocabulary because I had a high school education in French literature and could read quite well. My first French novel was *Colomba,* a story of feuding in Corsica, by nineteenth-century novelist Prosper Mérimée, more famous for having written the novella *Carmen.* I bought French classics in paperback for a franc or two at the book stalls on the banks of the Seine. I noticed they also sold cheap French editions of Hemingway's books, but those I read in English. I learned about Balzac and developed a particular admiration for Zola. I bought a cheap copy of *Germinal,* about a coal miners' strike—*The Grapes of Wrath*, seventy years earlier. The stalls were also filled with posters and pamphlets from the recent student uprising in May 1968.

At the time I was reading Zola's *Le Ventre de Paris*, which is set in the now-closed Les Halles market, and Zola described market scenes such as I found on Mouffetard. I loved this book but when I tried to get it for Virginia and other English language readers, the translation did not capture it at all. Many years later I translated it myself, *The Belly of Paris*, so that you could now enjoy it. I like to say that it is the best book I have ever written, but of course I didn't write it.

Once I got to Contrescarpe, I quickly turned left down Cardinal Lemoine and over to Cujas where our hotel was, up a few flights of stairs. "Come on," I said to Virginia," I want to show you something beautiful!" In a letter home to a friend, the future wife of John Dos Passos, Hemingway wrote, "It is so beautiful here that it hurts in a numb sort of way."

For a brief instant I felt like Mouffetard was my discovery but soon realized Hemingway described it correctly as "that wonderful narrow crowded market street which led to the Place Contrescarp." Damn it! I was getting tired of finding that everything I discovered had already been discovered by Hemingway!

Once we left the hotel and moved to apartments with kitchens (although at first a very small kitchen with two electric burners and no oven, later much larger facilities), I adopted the habit of starting my day at the local street market. Every neighborhood had one: Rue du Seine when we were in the Sixth, Rue Lecourbe when we lived there in the Fifteenth (an outstanding market because unlike the Sixth, this was a very bourgeois

French neighborhood with few expatriates and well-heeled Parisians who demanded quality), or curving Rue L'Epic when I lived in Montmartre.

The vendors had the kinds of strong flushed faces that Rembrandt loved. They had a toughness, though Paris tough is nothing like New York tough, and it took a while to realize that people who speak French can be tough, especially when they speak it through their nose. Some, like the woman who sold charcuterie on Rue Lecourbe, were actually beautiful. And she had a more refined accent as she said "*Monsieurdam.*" Charcuterie is a delicate trade even if you are stuffing hot blood in intestines and such things.

The fish always looked like it came out of the water the night before. It was a tremendous *faux pas* to touch anything—poke a fish flank, inspect a gill, smell a melon. The vendor carefully chose each pear, each cheese. Their skill and knowledge was a source of great pride. They knew when you finally bit into the Anjou pear it would be juicy and tart at the same time and overflowing with pearness. Or the brie would flow with perfect ripeness. The *fromagère* or fromager would hand select the exact cheese to your liking. Did you like a spring Roquefort or a fall Roquefort? This was the week for Époisse, no not this one, she rested it after a gentle squeeze. No this is the one. I wondered why American vendors did not have the same pride. Perhaps it is because in America, jobs are always temporary and in Paris, they are a career.

If you kept going to the same stall, the vendor would know you and get better at selecting exactly what you like. They did not offer a lot of information about themselves. Like good journalists, they found out more about you. A Parisian was evident by the accent, but sometimes you could spot vendors from other regions. If he fussed over the Reinette apples, selecting the perfect ones for your *tarte tatin*, he was probably Normand.

The wine shops were where they really gave themselves away. In Paris, in shops, bars, or homes, the wine of choice is rarely the famous grand cru, unless the person is from a famous region. Most Parisians favor the wine of the region from which their family comes. With the magnetic power of the big city, few people are many generations Parisian; they came from somewhere else in France, and that is the wine they drink.

Vendors would quickly detect a foreign accent, which sometimes

meant just not from Paris. I would tell them that I was an American. They would ask what I was doing here, and I would tell them that I was a writer. That was a mistake because ever after they would address me as Monsieur 'Emingway. I wonder how they had addressed Hemingway.

$$\bullet \bullet \bullet$$

If you knew these things, the ghost of Ernest Hemingway was everywhere. When I lived in the Fifth and Sixth, I enjoyed the walk across the Jardin du Luxembourg, always replanted for the season so that it had autumn colors in autumn and spring colors in spring but was always in bloom except for the rare snowstorm, which is when it was most beautiful of all with glistening domes on the heads of all the statues. But on that spectacular walk, I could not forget that this was the walk Hemingway used to take to Gertrude Stein's apartment.

Sylvia Beach was forced to close Shakespeare and Company by the Germans in 1941 and never reopened. After the war, a veteran named George Whitman, a thin, bearded man with the look of a nineteenth century poet, opened a bookstore along the Seine in the Fifth Arrondissement with the same idea, sponsoring and nurturing writers and loaning them books and offering a place for writers to meet. But for this to work, the store had to foster a movement such as Peabody with New England Transcendentalism, or Beach with the Modernists, or Ferlinghetti with the Beats.

For a while in the 1950s, George Whitman appeared to be resurrecting Shakespeare and Company. Sylvia Beach gave Whitman her name, Shakespeare and Company. He was hosting and encouraging important Beat writers. The Beats, unlike the modernists, had an artistic reason to be in France. They were great admirers of French writers, especially Charles Baudelaire. Though Baudelaire lived in the first half of the nineteenth century, he seemed surprisingly relevant to mid-twentieth century rebel poets. He wrote about the evil and degenerating effect of the emerging Industrial Revolution and he wrote in a free form verse, one of the first to do that. The formlessness was embraced by modernists but was the absolute bedrock of Beat poetry. Also, Baudelaire appears to

have invented the word *modernité* for the obligation of poets to capture the changing values in contemporary urban life. He may have been either the first modernist or the first beatnik.

But the Beats left either because the economy wasn't right, or France did not lend itself to this kind of counterculture. Yet they centered in San Francisco, which, though little discussed, was also dominated by a wealthy bourgeoisie in large homes far from North Beach.

For me, it would have been very different had they stayed. The departure of the Beats was really an end to American literature in Paris. When I got there, Paris seemed to be nurturing writers who instead of changing literature were trying to imitate it.

It had not struck me then in my youth and inexperience, but now, familiar with the world of fiction writers, it is odd how few of the writers at George Whitman's store were women. Women dominate the contemporary fiction world. But these people were not contemporary. I also suppose women writers were not interested in being Hemingway. There were numerous women modernists they could have emulated—women played a major role in modernism. But these newcomers were not fascinated by modernism, only Hemingway. They may not have even realized that he was an experimental modernist.

It seemed that most of these would-be literati had already read *A Moveable Feast* and were now settling down with George Orwell's *Down and Out in Paris and London*. Most of the copies of Orwell in the store were dog-eared. These books went through reader after reader without anyone buying the book, Orwell's story of living in seedy hotels, eating almost nothing but potatoes, and struggling with thirty francs a week to spend on drinking, going to cheap bistros where the crowd sang "The Internationale," the anthem of world communism, or sometimes even "*La Marseillaise*," the more right-wing French national anthem. Orwell lived life on a more elemental level. Hemingway tried to, but also always wanted to drink Sancerre.

Orwell's book was not about the literati—Fitzgerald, Stein, or Pound. It was about the bottom rung of Parisian life, who lived in the kind of hotels and cramped apartments that most of us lived in. There was the man with the glass eye who denied it. There were tales of dope fiends, of

old debauchees who frequented hotels in search of pretty pageboys, of thefts and blackmail. Personally, I loved the story of a maid who stole an incredibly valuable diamond ring from the room of an American woman. Police thoroughly searched the hotel and all of the staff was searched for days every time they left the hotel. It was never found. The maid had a lover who worked in the hotel bakery and he baked the ring into a roll that stayed in the bakery until the search was given up.

Orwell described something closer to the experience of these new writers. It was as though you had to be Orwell for a time in order to one day become Hemingway. But the life of *A Moveable Feast* may have never truly existed. It was oddly uplifting from a writer who insisted that all stories end badly. Maybe he would have changed it if he had finished it.

I soon learned not to spend much time at the bookstore. It seemed like a recipe for failure. But we did come away with two friends. The first was Hank. When we first met him, on a visit to Paris before we moved there, he already seemed fairly old. A retired newspaperman from Chicago, he was in fact from Oak Park, where Hemingway also grew up, and more than anyone I have ever known, he seemed smothered by the inescapable ghost of Hemingway. Perhaps it would have been liberating for him to realize that he was already older than Hemingway ever lived to be. This didn't occur to me because I thought of Hemingway as an old man. But he was almost Hemingway's generation, so it might have occurred to him. I think being of that generation was part of what drove him. He felt he was far behind and only had a few years to make it up.

As a young writer, he had a short story published in *Esquire* and Hemingway had a story in the same issue. This seemed like an auspicious beginning, but he had to earn a living, and he spent all those years on the newspaper desk in Chicago without ever getting around to his next work. Now he was retired, living in Paris and at last working on his first novel, which, naturally, like Hemingway's first novel, was to be set in Pamplona.

He, of course, liked to see himself as an expert on Spain because Spain was very important to the Hemingway image. He traveled there and became conversant in such Hemingway subjects as bullfighting. You could actually be extremely knowledgeable about Spain without knowing anything about bullfighting, but neither Hank nor Hem saw it

that way. Hank had bullfighting anecdotes like the time he saw the great El Cordobés, at the time, the highest-paid bullfighter in history. Manuel Benítez Pérez was his real name and he was extremely popular for his theatrical flourishes. While the crowd was wildly cheering, the man next to Hank turned to him and said, *"Ese bufón,"* that clown. Hank often told that story because to him it was an insight into Spain.

When we met, Hank wanted to tell us where to go in Spain. Franco was still in power and so Spain was not well known. France did not have relations with Spain, and it took considerable time to get across the border. It made Spain exotic. Hank took maps from the store and marked them up with a pen (also from the store) and explained that it was alright because George was a friend of his.

He lived in one of the smallest apartments I have ever seen on the top floor of a building on Rue de la Ferronnerie, iron works. In Paris, the higher floors had the cheaper smaller apartments. In better buildings than this, the small top floor apartments were for the maids, the *chambre de bonne,* who took care of the larger apartments below. But this building probably never did have maids.

I had many American friends living in such maids rooms six or seven stories up. In New York, upper floors tend to cost more. A penthouse is a New York concept made popular there in the 1920s. Ironically it is based on a French word meaning "appendage," though the French rarely built them. But in Paris, where elevators at the time were a rarity, the larger better apartments were on the lower floors where you did not have to climb to get there. Hemingway lived on upper floors. Gertrude Stein, with her family money, had a ground floor apartment. All of the five apartments I had in Paris were upper floor walk-ups. Some of them, like the sixth-floor studio in Montmartre, I don't think I could live in today. They were steep winding steps. You tried not to forget anything when you left.

Hank's was in an old part of Paris where the workers in the Les Halles market had lived. Apartments were available because Les Halles was gone and the workers were leaving. There was a large hole where the famous market had been and the city was arguing about its fate. Eventually it became a shopping mall that hardly anyone liked, but in that moment,

it was a lost neighborhood in the heart of the city. Because it had been a worker neighborhood without distinction, no one bothered to rename the narrow streets after great men, and so they kept the original names after crafts and commercial activities. La Ferronnerie, the iron works long forgotten, was only famous because it was where King Henri IV was assassinated in 1610, stabbed to death. I wonder why he had been there? They say he just got stuck there on the narrow street in a traffic jam.

Hank's apartment was barely big enough for a single bed and had no space for a desk. But there he would work on his first novel, which no one could dissuade him from titling, *A Kiss in Pamplona.*

He may sound like a ridiculous man, but he was thoughtful, a keen observer, a sensitive man, a great man to converse with, and Virginia and I loved him. Maybe he could have been a good writer if he had taken care of his instrument. You have to do that. Writing is like playing a musical instrument, you have to always practice and test your skills. On one of his long walks through Paris—he had time and he loved the city—he slipped a long letter under my door. It warned me not to write for newspapers for too long or it would ruin my writing. That was also Gertrude Stein's advice to Hemingway. In a 1954 interview in Cuba with George Plimpton, Hemingway said newspaper work will not harm a young writer and "may help him if he gets out of it in time." I only recently found this quote, but I knew the truth of it when I started writing for newspapers.

A lot of newspaper people feel that way. Newspapers impose a rigid formula. It used to be even more rigid than it is today. There is the lead, the nut graph, the body, throw in a few good quotes, and that is the 800 words. I always felt that if I could just come up with a good lead, the rest of the story would fall into place very quickly.

This does not develop creative expression, which is why the prose of many fine journalists, if stretched to book length, induces real pain. I would have to decide when it was time to leave newspapers before I became one of them. But for now, I was just trying to earn a living with writing.

Many important novelists began on newspapers, even Mark Twain, though he quickly gave it up for an opportunity to be a steamboat pilot. There is no doubt that he gained more as a writer on the steamboat than

he had on the newspaper.

In 1926, Hemingway divorced Hadley and married *Vogue* editor Pauline Pfeiffer. Hadley, though brokenhearted, went on to have a long and happy marriage with Paul Mowrer of *The Chicago Daily News,* who was in 1929 the first winner of a Pulitzer Prize for foreign reporting. Like many journalists, he was not happy with his lot. He wanted to be a poet. He gave up journalism, wrote six volumes of poetry, and in 1967 became the poet laureate of New Hampshire.

William Kennedy, who became a major American novelist, started in newspapers and journalism. Kennedy, with his characteristic clarity, saw exactly what was good and what was not about newspaper work. On the positive side, "[I] gained entry to worlds I had no right to enter, learned how to write reasonably well and quickly." This is exactly what I loved about it. But he saw the problem: "What I was left with was the voice of literary objectivity—a journalistic virus, that paralyzes the imagination and cripples the language."

It has always been said that Hemingway's lean, truncated prose was the product of his newspaper work, but he wrote his copy in a literary voice. If you look at his newspaper stories, they are fluffy by newspaper standards. For example, covering Mussolini at a conference in Lausanne, Switzerland, in January 1923 for *The Toronto Star*, his lead was:

> In the Château de Ouchy, which is so ugly that it
> makes the Odd Fellow's Hall of Petroskey, Michigan
> look like the Parthenon, are held the sessions of the
> Lausanne Conference.

I can hear my old foreign editor at the *Chicago Tribune*, Howard Tyner, one of my favorites, shouting, "You just wrote a thirty-word lead!" and one that had little to do with the story. If I had written newspaper articles in Hemingway's expansive cablese, they would have been, as they used to say when copy was on paper and they had such a tool for discarding it, spiked.

Hemingway said that he had "given up journalism" and was not writing anything that anyone in America wanted to buy. This was only

partly true. He did earn money writing articles for his old paper, *The Toronto Star,* and others. I also was writing articles for newspapers here and there and could see that this was a difficult way to earn a living.

I moved to Paris without letters from a celebrated writer introducing me to important people. But I did have agreements with a number of foreign editors without Paris correspondents who said they would buy good copy from Europe. I did not have a lot, but I did have some experience. I did not arrive in Paris prepared to be a European correspondent. For one thing European correspondents were well-dressed and I had very little clothes. I had a pair of corduroy pants, a Harris tweed jacket, some dress shirts and ties. You always have ties because they never wear out. But my shoes did, and shoes were expensive in Paris. I had a pair of closed toe sandals that if worn with socks almost looked like shoes. My clothes were extremely baggy because before moving to Paris I had been working as a pastry chef and had gained a lot of weight. But on my low-budget French diet, satisfying because the food was so good, I became quite thin.

French government buildings all say *"Liberté, Égalité, Fraternité"* on them to remind you that this is the post-revolution government. They need this because, inside and out, they look like royal palaces. It is not comfortable walking in the gilded hallways with baggy corduroys and sandals. Seated at interviews I appeared to be looking at my notebook but was mostly staring at my feet trying to decide if my sandals looked like shoes and whether it was noticeable.

There were other problems. Once Virginia and I had an apartment, we had no telephone. At the time, many Paris apartments (especially the cheaper ones on the upper floors) were without telephones. A phone could be ordered but it would take as much as a year to get it. So I worked at the phone bank at the neighborhood post office, popping *jetons,* telephone slugs that could be bought at the window, into the phone for each call. This meant when somebody was not in you could not leave a number for a call back. I could only ask when would be a good time to call back.

Often, I was told, *"Il est en réunion,"* and I would think, *oh those French, they live well.* Réunion is an island in the Indian Ocean, that, instead of giving up, they made a Département of the French Republic and was now a favorite vacation spot. But after getting this response

more than a dozen times and wondering why everyone was going there, I remembered that *reunion* also means meeting. *Il est en reunion*, he is in a meeting, which was probably a standard brush off.

• • •

I was in Paris about the same short number of years after the end of the Vietnam War as Hemingway had been from the end of World War I, but without the literary response. This is why the Shakespeare and Company of the 1970s did not hold nearly the interest of Sylvia Beach's shop in the 1920s.

But the war still had an impact. The French were not in the American war, and the French war in Vietnam, also disastrous, was a distant memory. The Algerian war had ended more than a decade ago. Many of the veterans had become Paris policemen and bitterly persecuted North African immigrants, a tension that would explode years later.

Vietnam had also left its mark. The city had many Vietnamese refugees from both the French war and the American war. The Vietnamese who sided with the French, or sided with the Americans, and were able to get out, were a far more bourgeois bunch than typical Vietnamese. They owned small restaurants or little charcuteries that served delicate Vietnamese specialties.

And there were the Americans; many were people like me that had opposed the war and were relieved to be finally out of the US. I had a friend who was a deserter. He received French political refugee status and was living permanently in Paris. We used to go to rural France on weekends and teach the farmers anti-war songs. They did not understand English and only enjoyed the idea that they were singing some kind of trendy American rock. I always remember the time my deserter friend and I went to a small village in the vineyards of Burgundy, hilly country, soft and cozy with thick greenery, and one evening amused a few local farmers, who spoke not a word of English, by teaching them to sing Country Joe and the Fish. "And eets one two tree, vaat ar vee fighteen four?"

This was the anti-war that I knew well. But from down the hall at the little Hotel Cujas came the real war. At night I would sometimes hear

someone screaming. It sounded like shouting. But then it would often end up just being screaming. I had seen my loud neighbor a few times in the stairwell, a quiet, friendly man. He was tall, blond, athletic looking, and about my age. He was the type that people always call "American-looking," like someone who had been captain of his high school football team in a town with no immigrant history.

One night when he was particularly loud, I decided to knock on his door, thinking he might need some kind of help. Struggling veterans from World War II to Vietnam were not new to me. He answered the door looking like he had just stepped out of a deep swimming pool with no towel. I recognized immediately how Hemingway had described Frederic Henry in *A Farewell to Arms*: "I woke sweating and scared and then went back to sleep trying to stay outside of my dream. I woke for good long before it was light and heard roosters crowing and stayed on awake until it began to be light. I was tired and once it was really light I went back to sleep again." Hemingway might be describing himself. Hem's letters make references to nightmares and insomnia. Of all the young Americans I was to meet in Paris hoping to be Hemingway, this one may have come the closest.

He invited me in looking a little confused but happy to see me. He sat on the edge of his bed and I sat in the chair. Shaking only a little, still sweat-soaked, his eyes did not look so much unfocused as focused on someone else in the room who I could not see.

His name was Stanley and he came from one of those American places, Oklahoma. In Hemingway's story "Soldier's Home," Harold Krebs delays going home to Oklahoma after the war because he cannot adjust to hometown life again. Stanley was not yet ready to go back to Oklahoma either.

Once Stanley started talking, his sweating stopped, and he became more relaxed. For him, talking was better than sleeping.

I often talked to him at night. This dialogue between the combat veteran and the war resister had a natural flow. I have often had this experience with Vietnam veterans. They enthusiastically attended readings for my book on 1968. I think they enjoy talking to someone who does not want to make them heroes.

We did not talk about what he thought of my refusing to go nor what I thought of his going. He did what he thought he had to do, and I did what I thought I had to do. I learned Stanley had been a sergeant in the Rangers, an elite light infantry combat unit. He said that he had lost a number of his men because they would stand up and fire their automatic M-16 in fire fights. They had seen actors doing this in movies, and though they were trained not to do this, he said, "How many weeks of training and how many years of movies?" They called it "John Wayne-ing it" and it got his men killed. His voice expressed the curious irony of this, but to see how he felt about the men he lost, you had to look deep into his bright-looking eyes.

I don't think that Stanley had any more enthusiasm for the war than I had. Like me, he was drafted. The difference was that he did not refuse to go. They called him and he went. He did what he was supposed to. Put into the infantry, he volunteered for the Rangers because he thought that he would have a better chance of survival being in a small, highly trained group. His original large infantry group took a great many more casualties.

I don't know if he wished he had refused. He found it interesting that I had. When I was in college, I lived in a poor white neighborhood of Indianapolis, and not going to college, the boys from the neighborhood were sent to war right after high school. Before they left, I could see how scared and sad they were, and I would tell them that they should refuse to go. They would just smile at me with that "you-crazy-fuck" look. A year later they would come back looking ruined and would chase after me on the street to say, "You were right." I didn't want to be right. I wanted them to refuse. But, like Stanley, none of them did. What a different world it would be if everyone would refuse.

Stanley elected to join his outfit on a mission just before his tour ended—one last mission. This is almost always a mistake, but he was in a small reconnaissance group, a group leader, and he could not make himself stay behind as he was expected to do. He offered few details about this last mission and I did not press for them. Clearly the mission went badly. Some died. He was wounded, though I am not sure how seriously. Whatever happened, he relived it every night. He never described the

nightmare or the last mission to me. My uncle never described any of his combat experiences either, nor did friends of mine who went to Vietnam. There is no point in telling someone who has never been in combat. They wouldn't understand. Just keep the stories upbeat.

Stanley's ambition was to be a high school principal and for some reason I was sure that this was what he was meant to be. He would be a great high school principal. But he was not ready to go back and, in the meantime, there was something he had to try—and this was the moment when he started talking about Hemingway. He had to live in Paris and try to write. If that didn't work out, he would go back to high school in Oklahoma. He certainly had experiences to draw on—Stanley had seen a great deal more combat than Hemingway. But I always knew he was going back. People who have alternatives rarely become writers.

Stanley wandered the city, as we all did. Paris is one of the great wandering cities. There is even a French word for such a wanderer, a *flâneur*. We were all *flâneurs*. I wandered looking for food and literary sights—not just Hemingway, but Zola and Hugo, who were both writers I greatly admired (though Hemingway said that they were "both lousy writers"). I visited historic sights also, like the spot where King Henri was done in. Fellow American *flâneurs* were more dedicated "Lost Generation" tourists.

But Stanley looked for Vietnamese establishments. He loved these places and spent hours in them. He was intrigued by a cuisine he had eaten very little of when in Vietnam. And he loved talking with the people. He said that he never really talked very much with the Vietnamese during his year there. With wide-eyed astonishment he declared, "They're really nice people!"

Not all of them were. Like George Orwell when he was down and out in Paris, I used to pick up extra money by teaching English. Mostly I taught affluent housewives preparing for their big trip to *Amerique* next August. I also had a bartender at a gay club who wanted me to translate songs like The Village People's "YMCA" into French. "Do whatever you feel. What does this mean?" But I also taught a Vietnamese family whose dream was to eventually move to the US and so they wanted to learn English. There were two sons and a daughter—pampered, unbearable

teenagers whose only understanding of the National Liberation Front was that they were mean people who took away their toys. No English lessons for the mother. She had never even been taught French and spent all her time in the kitchen; I have to admit, she prepared wonderful dishes.

I taught the children in their large apartment, on a low floor. But the father wanted to be taught in various cafés in the Sixth or Seventh, an intriguing neighborhood when I first knew it but now increasingly fashionable. He showed up for his lessons in a suit and tie though as far as I could find out, he had no work, and therefore no reason to be dressed for business. He espoused a kind of intolerant nationalist dictatorship that could best be described as fascism. Between such ideas and unapologetic racism toward Black and Arab people, he was so offensive that café managers kept asking us to leave. I used to think, *This is for whom the US wanted me to fight and kill, while his sons and daughter would do nothing.* In fact, the three of them made clear that they thought I had some obligation to defend them while they had no intention of doing anything for their national defense. Teaching the four of them was a reliable part of my income, but in time, I simply couldn't bear to teach them anymore. I don't think they understood why and even offered more money. He also never understood why we kept being kicked out of cafés.

Stanley did not go to George Whitman's. I don't think he could relate to those people. I am not sure he could relate to me or to anyone who had not been wounded in a firefight. We moved out of the Cujas to a small inexpensive apartment in the Sixth. Inexpensive in the Sixth sounds completely unimaginable today, but it was a tiny upper floor walk-up. Hemingway had also moved from the Fifth to the Sixth but a different part, above a sawmill. A sawmill in the Sixth arrondissement seems incredible. But sawmill was part of Hem's lore. His son Jack recalled that it was a cabinetmaker and even included a showroom.

We were near Sylvia Beach's bookshop, which you could not walk by without thinking of Hemingway, Joyce, and that group even though it was no longer a bookstore. When Hem was with Pauline, they used to attend mass at the Saint-Sulpice church a block away from our apartment, although going to mass is not how we tend to think of Hemingway in Paris. But Pauline was a serious Catholic and she drew him into the

Catholicism of the dusty domed Saint-Sulpice.

We lost interest in the new Shakespeare and Company filled with people more interested in being writers than actually writing. They were so engrossed in the Hemingway myth it seemed they were awaiting his return. But we did befriend one writer, Chris Gilmore. He was a tall man with long blond hair who had been a journalist for a brief moment with Associated Press and worked at being large and colorful, and more or less succeeded. That he had Hemingway in mind as his role model became apparent in conversation. He was full of stories about his adventures in North Africa, escaping the law, going to prison, the gold bricks he hid by soldering them to the chassis of a car. They were good stories though frequently not believed. The thing that was different about Chris, what made him special, was that he had an actual book contract. It seemed doubtful any of these other writers ever would, but Chris had sold a novel about his hometown, Atlantic City, to Penguin. It was full of Chris's kind of storytelling, set in the 1920s, prohibition and racketeering.

He left for New Jersey to promote his book and I thought that would be the last I ever saw or heard of him. It was, but that was only because I was no longer a habitué of Shakespeare and Company. Many years later I discovered that he did come back to Paris, moved into a room in George Whitman's bookstore, was declared "the writer-in-residence," gave frequent readings there, continued to travel and tell stories, and wrote a few more books, including a little noted biography of Hemingway. He died in his early sixties.

I lost track of Stanley too, but I hope he became a school principal and I hope he found peace. I know that he went back to Oklahoma, got a teaching job in Shawnee, and wrote a number of books of Oklahoma interest. He assembled a book about Oklahoma Vietnam War veterans. Apparently, he had twice been awarded Bronze Stars, which, not surprisingly, he had never mentioned to me. He wrote his parts well enough for me to think he could have been a writer. In relaying his experiences, he did not mention one word about that last mission that had kept him sweating at night. Years later when I read the book, I could see that being back in Oklahoma had changed him. He referred to his fellow veterans as "heroes," something he never would have done when I knew him. And

he wrote that he had thought of including a draft dodger, but then added, "But I couldn't find the heart for it." We all have to make our peace as best we can.

When I first went to Paris, I was writing fiction. I had already written a novel based on my experiences in commercial fishing. Following the dictum that a writer should write about what he knows, I wrote about the only thing I knew. I suppose it was as good as first novels by young people are. I came close to selling it twice, once even to Scribner's, Hemingway's publisher. If I had sold my first novel in my early twenties to Scribner's, I might have become lost in the Hemingway myth, like my friend Hank, but it fell through. Both times the deal fell through, probably because I had no agent. I didn't know I needed one. I needed an F. Scott Fitzgerald to introduce me to a Max Perkins. I am grateful. Had I sold it, I probably wouldn't have gone to Paris. I would have written more novels without knowing anything. Young novelists usually don't know enough to write a novel. Compare Hemingway's first novel, *The Sun Also Rises*, with his second, *A Farewell to Arms*.

In Paris I worked on a second novel. I wrote it by hand at the café in Contrescarpe—not to be picturesque, but because I really couldn't write in the room at the Cujas. It was the wallpaper. It was quiet enough in the café. Just the workers in blue downing calvados and honking in low persistent voices like a gaggle of feeding geese, "whaay, whaay, whaay."

I never sent that novel out. I also wrote some short stories that I did send out, but they were rejected. I did write one good story that was reworked and published years later. Everything else I have thrown out. You learn from Hemingway to destroy everything you don't want to see published. The role of short stories has completely changed. Writers used to produce them as a way to earn money between books. Today, they are done for the love of them, and like poetry, they seldom earn money. I have always loved, more than anything else, writing short stories. In time I would get back to them. For now, I was a journalist.

I liked writing by hand and later typing it up. The physicality of writing by hand keeps you focused, "in the game" as they say in baseball. I stopped because I was doing less fiction and more journalism. Typing was faster and journalism is all about speed. Also, I could write at home

because I no longer lived with loud wallpaper. And the Associated Press let me use their machines to send to their member newspapers. The machines punched holes in a tape, and you could rerun the tape and the story would magically reappear on the screen. There was a way of wrapping these tapes round your thumb and little finger into figure eight roles. I had a drawer full of these figure eights.

I became more affluent as a journalist so that I could have oysters and Sancerre at the Closerie. I reported a lot from Spain but other places in Europe too, and sometimes Africa or Asia. In truth, Europe did not have a wealth of great stories. There was the movement against nuclear energy and there were periodic violent anti-Semitic attacks. There were occasional odd stories like the Mayor of Amsterdam calling out tanks against squatters. The most important story was the unification of Europe, and while the implications were huge—peace between Europeans for the first time in their history—the actual stories such as negotiations on Common Agricultural Policy were difficult to make exciting.

France only provided me with one good story. In May 1981, we all gathered around televisions after the polls closed on a national election and within minutes the results were given—socialist François Mitterrand was elected, the first leftist President since the 1950s. It was at last the triumph of the movement to overthrow de Gaulle by youth and workers in May 1968. Huge crowds formed at the Place de la Bastille. It was a triumph of the Revolution, the Liberation, and May '68 all at once. People climbed lamp posts and waved flags and marched through the streets arm in arm singing "The Internationale."

De Gaulle, who established a new form of government with a new constitution, had made the President of France the most powerful executive of any western democracy. Now for the first time, a leftist held this post. He brought Communists into the government, established a guaranteed income for all Frenchmen, nationalized certain industries, freed television and radio so the state no longer exclusively controlled broadcasting, and many other changes, even eliminating the official list of government-approved baby names that prevented parents from giving nontraditional names or Basque, Breton, Catalan, or Alsatian ones.

It was a great story for a time, but the changes only lasted about two

years, whereas the Mitterrand government lasted fourteen.

I started writing for *The International Herald Tribune*. Although *The Washington Post* and *The New York Times* owned this paper—the latter would eventually destroy it—for many years it had its own identity. Those of us who wrote for it understood that we had a more sophisticated readership than American papers. Among the contributors was an old-time correspondent, Waverly Root. Only four years younger than Hemingway, about the same age as Hank, he had retired from being a foreign correspondent and wrote a food column and numerous food books. I never met him because he never came into the newsroom and a messenger picked up his copy, which seems quaint today. Root wrote what I call anthropological food writing. It was not just the food but its history and its impact on culture and society. He was not the first one I saw do this. The French had been doing this since the nineteenth century. Basques and others in Spain and Italy were doing this. What was the importance of pizza to Naples, the historic importance of salt cod in Bilbao, or paella in La Huerta? How did these things happen and what did they mean?

There is also an abundance of great food writing in fiction. Hemingway, despite a love of food and drink, was not a great food writer. Too much "the food was good and so was the wine," to quote from *The Sun Also Rises*. Several times he gives instructions on cooking trout: "The trout are crisp outside and pink inside," he wrote in *The Toronto Star,* "and the bacon is well done—but not too done. If there is anything better than that combination the writer has yet to taste it in a lifetime devoted largely and studiously to eating." Typical of Hem, this sounds like the revelation of a septuagenarian but was written by a young man. He usually described food to talk about his favorite dishes like raw onion sandwiches in *Islands in the Stream*, but seldom to set scenes or describe characters the way other fiction authors have. He does with black beans, rice, and fried bananas in *The Old Man and The Sea*. And there are various raw fish Santiago eats to keep up his strength.

But Hem did not write revealing food scenes as do some Chinese writers. Just as I was developing my food writing in 1983, Lu Wenfu came out with the novella *Gourmet,* which I found in a Paris bookstore translated into French as *Vie et Passion d'un Gastronome Chinois*. This tale of an

obsessed gourmet tells us not only a great deal about the food of Suzhou, but about his character and life in twentieth-century China. It was not surprising that the French were one of the first to translate this book because there is a tradition of food fiction in France with Zola— probably the most outstanding of numerous examples. Balzac, who I could also buy in paperback on the *quai* for two or three francs, interpreted the setting of a table and went into digressions about how boring an eel pâté was, how you could be cheered by a fat carp. Flaubert, Maupassant, and Proust too all understood the value of writing about food.

Tolstoy, one of Hemingway's idols, was also a great food writer. The sad life and loves of Anna Karenina unfold in a series of lavish meals, which reveal the character and the vain life of Russian aristocracy.

James Joyce was a great food writer. One of his most famous short stories, "The Dead" is set against a large, elaborately described feast and we get to know the characters by watching them eat. My all-time favorite introduction of a character in a work of fiction is from *Ulysses*:

> Mr. Leopold Bloom ate with relish the inner organs of beasts, and fowls. He liked thick giblet soup, nutty gizzards, a stuffed roast heart, liver slices fried with crustcrumbs fried hencod's roes. Most of all he liked grilled mutton kidneys which gave to his palate a fine tang of faintly scented urine.
>
> Kidneys were in his mind as he moved about the kitchen softly...

• • •

The truth is that I came to Paris with far more experience in food than in journalism. Back in New York as a playwright, my income was sporadic. And until the war ended, my legal situation was very precarious and few people would hire me. Like many people in theater, I turned to restaurants; unlike the others, I thought it would be more interesting in the kitchen than waiting on table. I had no training but a natural ability,

and I could learn quickly. I started out as a "salad chef" (though chef is supposed to mean boss, everyone in America is a chef) in a fashionable Soho restaurant that catered extravagant midtown office parties. I went on to be various other kinds of chefs and eventually became the sous chef in a start-up restaurant in the Village near the Hudson, one of the first restaurants in that waterfront neighborhood.

Then I was hired by an expensive but mediocre French restaurant in Nantucket. America is a haven for mediocre French chefs. There are also very good ones, but most Americans do not know the difference, so a chef who would have no standing in France can be a star in America because he is French. This one was dedicated to maintaining the standard of French mediocrity so that anytime you varied from the standard recipe or the standard dishes that were on his menu, he would say, "This is not how we do it in France." Fortunately, I was hired away by an American restaurant on the ground floor of a colonial house in which the family lived. I would get in at five in the morning, give cream to the family cat and dog who were always waiting for me (and of course, truly loved me), and by noon I would have a wagon of desserts to offer lunch customers. But I could flee the customers, ride my bike out to the moors—Nantucket used to have wide open wild brush and flower moors before the island got filled with too many houses—and, balancing my surf casting rod in one hand, ride out to the beach to spend the rest of the day catching (or not catching) striped bass.

This was my best cooking job, but cooking was not something I wanted to do. Journalism was supposed to get me out of the kitchen. But cooking also gave me a background that other journalist didn't have, so that when I was sent somewhere for a package of stories I could always include one food story. These were not restaurant reviews but stories about food and the people who produced it. I knew how to talk to food people. When I learned that the celebrated boulangeries of Paris were struggling to find young people to take up the craft, I visited my local baker to ask about the problem. When I told him that I used to be a baker, he invited me to report to work the next morning. I arrived at four in the morning. Between mixing and rolling, I never stopped moving. If there were a few free seconds, they were for sweeping the flour off the floor.

By afternoon I don't know how many tens or hundreds of baguettes I had made, but I was certain I did not want to come back for Day 2 and I understood the problem.

As a number of contemporary French and American writers have discovered, restaurants are a great source of fiction material. There was the misogynous Chinese dishwasher who menaced waitresses with a meat cleaver; a kind and gentle West African dishwasher whose most valued contribution was that he turned the kitchen into a French-speaking shop because he spoke no English. Periodically, we would get tipped off and have to hide him from immigration authorities. The man who dreamed of opening a French restaurant only to be forced by his Jewish mother to include her various pickled products on the menu; the Italian restaurant where I pretended to be Marco and only kept my job because I was supposedly Italian; the owner who stepped in the ratatouille on Provençal night. What a shame Hemingway never worked in restaurants.

So it is not surprising that Waverley Root quickly gained my attention. He was not always accurate, but he had great style, humor, and grace and made reading about food worthwhile. He may have had as great an impact on me as Hemingway. There was little of this kind of food anthropology in America, and when it happened it was regarded as an innovative wonder. In 1965, Eleanor Clark won the National Book Award for her beautiful study of belon oyster producers in Brittany, *The Oysters of Locmariaquer*. It was always about European food. Americans seemed to discover food in Europe as though Europeans had food and Americans merely ate. Even Root wrote mostly about Europe. Or maybe, like me, they simply discovered food writing in Europe. I thought that Americans needed this kind of food writing and I did it for *The Herald Tribune*, US papers, magazines, wherever I could. *The Herald Tribune* had a French accountant and when I came in with my expenses, he used to address me as "Monsieur Gourmand," which is a French joke. A gourmet knows food, but a gourmand just eats a lot of it.

In 1997 when I came out with my book on cod and reviewers started crediting me with a different approach, I had been doing this for twenty years.

All totaled, I spent more time in Paris than Hemingway. As I got

older, I felt his presence less and less, though the French still always said "Ah, Monsieur 'Emingway" when I told them I was a writer living in Paris. Spain became the only really good story I had in Europe so that even as I was escaping Hemingway in France, Spain would bring him back.

CHAPTER FOUR

The Patent-Leather Soul of Spain

Sunset on the bay, San Sebastián, 10 p.m., June 29, 2014

"Tienen, por eso no lloran,
de plomo las calaveras.
Con el alma de charol
vienen por la carretera.
Jorobados y nocturnos,
por donde animan ordenan
silencios de goma oscura
y miedos de fina arena."

—Federico García Lorca, *Romance de la Guardia
Civil Española*

("They do not cry,
they have skulls of lead
and souls of patent-leather
riding down the road.
Hunched in the night,
where they go they command
silence of dark rubber
and fear of fine sand.")

—Federico García Lorca, *Ballad of the Spanish Civil Guard*

I probably first started going to Spain for the same reason as did Hemingway. If you lived in France, Spain was easy to get to and incredibly cheap. When I first went there it was so cheap that I used to think, *This must be what it is like to be rich.* And it had very few tourists. This was also true when Hemingway started going there.

In 1924, Hemingway reported a vacation including round trip train fare cost him $250. Adjusted for inflation, it may not have cost me much more. In Spain, I don't know that prices were much higher than in 1924. Dinner in Madrid—with ham, shellfish, a fish course, a roast, and dessert, with excellent appropriate wines for each course, and if you wished, a

fine Cuban cigar afterward—was only a few dollars. Angulas, tiny baby eels caught in Basque rivers, were served like a large plate of spaghetti for a couple of dollars. Today, a small appetizer of them is more than twenty dollars. The assortment of very fresh seafood was dazzling—a sole or a hake or a turbot cost very little. Spain was dark and depressing, quiet, with people afraid to speak. The last fascist country—but the food was superb.

My first sight of Spain was from Saint-Jean-de-Luz, a Basque tuna fishing port on the French side. Beyond the rich and rugged Basque mountains in France were sharp blue peaks, and these were Spain stabbing the sky like a dangerous mystery. Spain was exotic, shunned by many and a little difficult to get into. It was also completely associated with Hemingway. He was one of the few supporters of the Republic who did not boycott Franco's Spain.

• • •

In the early 1920s when young Hem decided to take a trip to Spain, Gertrude Stein suggested that he take in a bullfight. She herself was an *aficionado* and had even written a poem about the matador Juan Belmonte. Hemingway later wrote in *Death in the Afternoon* that without a current war to go to, this was an opportunity to study "life and death."

From the first bullfight Hemingway saw, Spain to him was almost entirely about bullfights with time out to eat great meals and do a little fly-fishing in the north. To treat bullfighting as the heart and center of Spanish culture would be like saying that America is all about baseball. Actually, I might argue that baseball is more central to American culture than bullfighting to Spain. I have had many Spanish friends over the years but, with the exception of one matador, none of these people were interested in bullfighting.

Hemingway's argument to all of this is that bullfighting is not a sport. He said it was a tragedy. It really is a kind of theater, and a bullring resembles an ancient amphitheater. The English language term "bullfight" is a complete misnomer. In Spanish it is a "running of the bull." There is no fight, no contest. The bull dies. It is the ritual killing of the bull and it

is about being brave and dying well—the bull, not the matador. The bull is the tragic hero. The real name of the bullfighter in Spanish is *matador*, which means killer. The matador is not supposed to be harmed, though the fact that he is in danger heightens interest. His function is to kill the bull, hopefully with artistry.

The matador has the grace and theatricality of a dancer and the skills of an athlete. The closer he comes to the deadly horns, the more exciting. Some perform classic moves with great dignity; others are hams showing off to the public, which to some is insulting to the bull. But like an actor, if a ham is skilled enough, he will have a following. Some matadors like El Cordobés were great hams. But since it is a ritual about death, matadors tend to see themselves as high priests and often speak about death—even though with penicillin and today's medicines, matadors, though often gored, rarely die. Bullfighting has its place in Spanish culture because the culture is often fixated on death. García Lorca, the Spanish poet from Andalucía, wrote much about death, almost foretelling his own assassination by the Franco side in the Civil War at age thirty-eight.

Hemingway, always a remarkable autodidact, was able to sound like a true expert on bullfighting after a few years of visits. He could do this on most any subject that interested him. In *Death in the Afternoon* he wrote, "A great enough writer seems to be born with knowledge. But he really is not; he has only been born with the ability to learn on a quicker ratio to the passage of time than other men...." I am not sure that this is a necessary characteristic of a great writer, but it was true of Hemingway.

His time in Spain was increasingly centered around the bullfighting world and remained there for the rest of his life. He even brought a matador to work with him when he was a correspondent in Madrid covering the Civil War.

He started in Pamplona, the capital of Navarra, but he also liked to fish for trout in the Irati river in the north. This is a traditional, very beautiful part of Basque country, with white and stone house villages of narrow streets wedged into the green foothills of the Pyrenees. Hemingway liked to fish and enjoy picnics there and so did I. In *The Sun Also Rises*, Jake and Bill catch trout there after the festival. In real life, he went fishing before the festival. Afterward he was writing in a fever. He

didn't catch any fish on that trip, which made me feel better because I also failed on the Irati. But it is one of those rivers where just being there is good enough.

Because Pamplona is Basque, he always tied Basques to bullfighting. But this is not really true. He might have noticed that while there were major rings in Pamplona, San Sebastian, and Bilbao, a large part of the Basque population didn't go. Bullfighting came from southern Spain, and the Basque passion was a hardball made much like a baseball. Traditional Basque family-owned companies jealously guard the actual construction. But if you take one apart and take a baseball apart, you will see the similarities. The hardball is either flung with a large basket, a *jai alai*, a smaller one, *cesta de la punta*, or the most popular in Basque country, bare-handed. Today in Basque Country, bare-handed matches are televised. It takes considerable body power to fling a hardball against a wall with enough force so that it will pop back like a ping pong. This is actually the most popular Basque sport played in stadiums and small-town clubs called a *Trinquete*. Every Basque town no matter how small has at least one of these courts. As for the rest of Spain, the national obsession is soccer (in which Bilbao is also a major competitor).

Navarra is slightly different from other Basque provinces because in the tenth century it became a kingdom, originally the Kingdom of Pamplona, to resist Arab expansion. It is the only monarchy in Basque history. The Basques did not have kings. By the time Hemingway arrived, Pamplona was still Basque and the area of Navarra north of Pamplona and across the Pyrenees into France has remained Basque-speaking and traditionally Basque. But the plains that stretch south of Pamplona to Aragon and Castile have become mostly Spanish. The Ebro is supposed to be the border, but traveling from the Rioja, if you crossed the Ebro at Logroño in the direction of Pamplona, you would not feel that you had entered Basque country until you got to Pamplona.

In the Fiesta of San Fermín in Pamplona the first week of July, townspeople dress in traditional Navarrese clothing. The processions, dances, and other folk activities are of Basque origin. When Hemingway discovered it in 1923, it was a traditional Basque folk festival enjoyed by locals, though Hemingway brought a small contingent of foreigners with

him every year. Some might say that was the beginning of the end. Others say Hemingway put Pamplona on the map.

While there is bullfighting in Basque country, even on the French side, it is unusual in a Basque folk festival. I have attended many rural festivals and they feature wood chopping contests, rope tugs of war, and boulder heaving, but no bulls.

I don't think Hemingway attended such festivals. If he did, he didn't write about them. He went to bullfights. Although his name is often associated with Basques, I wonder how much he connected with Basque culture. The Basques are not so much colorful peasants with wine skins as they are in *The Sun Also Rises*. Famously, they are industrialists and bankers.

Hem liked fly-fishing for trout in Basque rivers with an artificial fly called a McGinty that imitates a dead bee. It is an old-fashioned fly not tied or used anymore. I have tied a few out of curiosity but not done well with them. You have to find a river that has dead bees floating in it. He claimed that Spain had the best fishing in Europe. Most of these rivers have been ruined (by those famous Basque industrialists), though a few are coming back.

· · ·

Hem's life radically changed after he divorced Hadley. Catholic Pauline turned him to Catholicism. He was not completely comfortable with the idea of organized religion, but he said that this was clearly the best one. They had two more sons. They left Europe and settled in Florida where he turned from an avant-garde intellectual among the milieu of new writers, poets, and painters, to a wealthy celebrity in the company of other affluent men who hunted and fished expensively.

He was leaving behind many of his Paris friends. A few friendships survived. His relationship with Dos Passos did not disintegrate until the Spanish Civil War. But he had grown distant from Pound, who was spending too much time promoting Italian fascism, and he had increasingly less contact with Fitzgerald. Hem's relationship with Gertrude Stein faded as his own reputation grew. In *A Moveable Feast*, he implies that his falling

out with Stein had to do with discovering her sexual preference, but he had long known this. More likely the falling out came from a growing envy of Hemingway's success. Stein was Hem's mother's generation and took in Hemingway as a young man. Hadley always maintained that Stein was extremely jealous of Hemingway. Gertrude liked to tell people that she had made Hemingway, but he was far more successful than she was. Many of the young talents she had hosted with a twinge of condescension far eclipsed her, and she started to become bitter. She would lecture them about how money and book sales were unimportant. Hemingway would politely agree, though it was obvious this is not what he thought.

The friendship sunk as his reputation rose. In 1925, *In Our Time* became a very talked about book, an impressive accomplishment in a year when modernism was at its height with new *Cantos* by Pound, T.S. Eliot's "The Hollow Men," Virginia Woolf's *Mrs. Dalloway*, and Sherwood Anderson's *Dark Laughter*. But Gertrude Stein, whose books were mostly self-published and not widely read, was not ready to pay tribute to her young friend. She infuriated him by refusing to review the new book, saying that she wanted to see more before passing judgment and expressed the same sentiment about him to T.S. Eliot.

The Stein salon was not appealing to everyone. Writers, artists, and musicians, many more successful than this self-appointed sage, would attend her evenings to sit at her feet and be told how to write, how to paint, what music to perform. She was convinced that she was a genius on most any subject. Wives were of little value, including her own—Hadley never enjoyed visiting her because, like all the wives, she was relegated to talking to Alice in a corner. Not that there was anything wrong with talking to Alice, but it was clearly implied that they were not worthy of speaking with Gertrude. Some writers and artists did not want to participate in Gertrude's court. Jamaican Poet and novelist Claude McKay said, "I never went because of my aversion to cults and disciples."

Then came a great irony. After years of writing books that few would read or publish, in 1933 she decided to write a tell-all, and by writing more conventional language and furiously name-dropping, it became a bestseller. *The Autobiography of Alice B. Toklas* was written by Gertrude and pretended to be Alice's voice, thereby cancelling out her partner as

an actual person with her own thoughts. The narrator constantly talks of what a "genius" Gertrude Stein is, how brilliant her books are. A light touch of dirt on everyone else tries to keep it interesting. Her name-dropping gave few insights on any of the people.

The Hemingway segment was typical—brief, unexplained, and too ambiguous to refute, deny, or even discuss. She writes a few pages about who he liked or didn't and tells us almost nothing. She said that he was "90 percent Rotarian." She said he "looks like a modern and he smells of the museums." And she adds:

> But what a story, that of the real Hem, and one he should tell himself but alas he never will. After all, as he himself once murmured, there is the career, the career.

What does this mean other than the obvious that she was jealous of the career? Some have suggested that she was implying that he was gay, but it is most unlikely that a life so well-documented would have such a secret. The entire book was filled with these kinds of veiled reproaches. Occasionally a compliment would be thrown in, such as "Fitzgerald was the only one of the younger writers who wrote naturally in sentences"—odd praise from a writer known for convoluted sentences that no one understood.

Stein really wanted to talk about Gertrude Stein. For Hemingway the book was a betrayal and a real breaking point, and many of the other "characters" in the book, including Picasso and James Joyce, were also angry about it. She alienated many old friends but, at last, after years of saying she didn't care, she had learned how to be commercial.

Alice Toklas did not get to use her own voice until Gertrude was dead. Then she wrote an engaging and well-written cookbook, such artistry unfortunately rare in the genre.

• • •

Hem was making money but, more importantly, he had married money. Pauline was from one of the wealthiest families in Arkansas. Her Uncle

Gus was a pharmaceutical mogul whose niece was the closest he had to a child. Uncle Gus bought them a handsome house with big windows and wooden shutters by the water in Key West. It was not a lush area and had a water shortage, but it had date palms, palmettos, and big-rooted banyan trees. Gus financed a hunting safari to Africa and a trust fund for Hemingway's family, hard-pressed since the father's suicide. Hem could have a yacht made, a thirty-eight-foot black-hulled cruiser with a mahogany pilot house, that he would fish from for the rest of his life. It was a cabin cruiser, several feet short of the requisite length to be called a yacht. Hemingway chose the length and probably wanted to make sure his boat could *not* be called a yacht. Close though. He fished big fish with some literary friends and other rich people he knew off Bimini in the Bahamas and Cuba. Big game fishing, like big game hunting, is a rich man's game.

He was returning to Spain, working on his nonfiction book on bullfighting, which had been his dream project for a number of years. He would follow great matadors for a season or part of a season.

The most amusing Hemingway encounter I have found is in the autobiography of Sidney Franklin, a book which, unfortunately, is accused of many inaccuracies and complete fantasies. Franklin was a middle-class Jew from Brooklyn. He became taken with bullfighting and made the improbable decision to become a matador. He did well in Mexico and then moved to Spain where the critics said he would never be able to understand the meaning and culture of it. They changed their minds when they saw him, and Sidney became one of the most respected matadors in Spain in the late 1920s and 1930s.

He was known for his perfect kills. A good kill is the most important part of the ritual, the climax, since the entire affair is about the killing of the bull. In a perfect kill, known as an *estoconozo*, the bull is induced to charge directly at the matador. The matador stands tall and elegant with his sword held high but pointed downward. As the bull rushes toward him he inserts the sword between the shoulder blades and down into the heart so that the bull, just when he is about to hit the matador, collapses. It is hard to do well and is not always successful. Two or three attempts is awful to watch as the bull's thick neck is butchered. But Franklin did

it perfectly in one try.

In late 1929, Hemingway, working on his bullfighting book, requested through a mutual contact to meet Franklin. *A Farewell to Arms* had just come out and Hemingway, who was already a literary star, had become an international celebrity. The author showed up in his characteristic state of disrepair. Franklin recalled:

> This man hadn't shaved, and he needed a haircut. He wore a shabby suit that looked as though it had forgotten what a tailor's iron felt like. Battered bedroom slippers were on his feet. He approached very meekly and in a very small voice asked if I were Sidney Franklin the matador.

Franklin, who was a very big star in Spain and accustomed to fans, reached for some change in his pocket. But the man didn't want money. Unpretentiously he explained that he was Ernest Hemingway and he wanted to speak with him. Franklin, obviously not a reader, had never heard of Ernest Hemingway and didn't understand what he wanted. Ernest said he wanted to follow him on his tour and Sidney had to explain that it would be extremely expensive.

Ernest did not seem bothered by the cost, but then Sidney pointed out that when he came to town all the hotel rooms were taken, as were all the tickets to the *plaza de toros*. Franklin began to wonder if this were a wealthy person traveling incognito and asked him what he did. He explained that he was Ernest Hemingway, the author. Sidney asked him what kind of things he wrote and did he make a living at it. The author answered, "I manage to get along."

Franklin asked him if he was any good. Hemingway offered to send him some books, but Franklin said he wasn't interested. This did not seem to irritate Hemingway. He just moved on to talking about bullfighting. As they talked, Sidney started to like this Ernest Hemingway. It was a rare treat to meet a fellow American who seemed to understand something about bullfighting.

Eventually, Franklin offered to let him travel in his entourage and according to his recollection, Hemingway's eyes began to tear; he was so

moved by this generosity.

And so Ernie and Sidney, according to Franklin, went on the road together for about six weeks. Records show that it was really a shorter period. When Franklin got back to Madrid, there was great interest in the fact that he had been traveling with Ernest Hemingway. But the matador still had no idea who he was.

Years later, after being angered by an interview in which the matador talked about him, Hemingway told Robert Manning that it wasn't true, that he never traveled with Franklin's entourage. But they certainly did become very close, and there are many photos of them together in those years. Neither one was particularly wedded to facts.

• • •

Hemingway was in Spain following bullfighters at a pivotal moment in Spanish history. In 1931, King Alfonso XIII abdicated and Spain got its first elected democratic government known as the Second Republic. The first Republic from February 1873 to December 1874 fell so quickly between two monarchies that it was barely remembered. Now Spain—which except for that less-than-two-years, had always been ruled by a coalition of aristocracy, church, and wealthy landowners—was to become a democratic western European country. Huge changes immediately took place. Women got the right to vote, which further strengthened the democracy. The state no longer funded religious orders but did fund compulsory public education. The Basques got back their own government led by an elected Lehendakari, José Antonio Aguirre, a thirty-two-year-old mayor. The Catalans also establish an autonomous government.

The church and the landowners started fighting back. Guardia Civil started attacking striking workers. The Guardia Civil—whose uniform was distinguished by shiny black, patent-leather, three-cornered hats—was a military police founded in the nineteenth century. They often upheld the interests of wealthy landowners.

Pro-Republican mobs started attacking churches and clergy. Although the government soon put a stop to attacks on the church, it made a lasting impression on the Catholics of the world. At the same time, the

opposition turned to European fascists for support.

Hemingway saw the Republic as a very positive step. In October in a letter to Malcolm Lowry, he wrote, "Spain is in good shape—nice sensible little revolution so far." And when he came back a few weeks later, he wrote to his painter friend Waldo Pierce, "Spain was damn nice with the revolution. Had a fine time all spring and summer—hated like hell to leave the percebes and come back." Percebes, barnacles harvested in northern Spain and boiled in salt water, are one of the great Spanish delicacies. A native of Galicia, they are perfect with fruity Galician white wine. I always hated to leave them too, though I hated leaving angulas even more.

In 1932, the bullfighting tome, *Death in the Afternoon,* was published and not well-received. The longest book he ever published, it was not that it was bad work; it was simply much more about bullfighting than most people wanted to know. Max Eastman in a review titled "Bull in the Afternoon," said the book belonged to the "false hair on the chest school of writing." Famously this led to fisticuffs a few years later between the two in his editor Maxwell Perkins's office at Scribner's. When Hemingway fans, such as son Patrick or Herbert Matthews, complain that too much emphasis is placed on Hemingway's squabbles, this absurd and thoroughly reported incident is an example. But it is hard to ignore such ridiculous skirmishes between grown-ups.

• • •

In the beginning of 1934, Uncle Gus financed Hem's safari to East Africa, which led to *The Green Hills of Africa* later in the year. The book, like *Death in the Afternoon*, had obvious flaws. The locals are characterized disrespectfully, though this may be a way of portraying the white hunters.

Yet I do not think that *Green Hills of Africa* is without merit. He raises interesting issues, including why he comes to Africa just to kill animals and had no interest in the natives that live there. Characters keep coming up to him and asking him questions so that he can expound on all his pet theories And so, while hunting in Africa, he can lecture on a wide range of subjects, especially being a writer. And then, ironically, he

expounds on how tiresome conversations were that become interviews. People love to interview writers. It is one of the few curses of a writer's life. At all kinds of social gatherings, I hide from such conversations.

Hunting is where Hem and I part ways. I do not like to kill. I don't even like to kill the fish I catch. Whether a fish or a mammal or a human, at that moment of death a light goes out and this is a terrible moment. I love stalking. It is like fishing. You learn about the habitat and the ways of the animal. But then once I killed a deer. I don't like guns because they make my ears ring, and once fired, a rifle punches you in the shoulder.

It seems on unfair advantage, killing from a distance. It is like bait fishing instead of fly-fishing. So I tried hunting with bow and arrow in the Utah Rockies. I shot a buck and he ran. At this point, I knew the animal and I knew the terrain, so I ran to the stream I knew he was fleeing to by another trail. His legs faltered and he no longer had the strength to leap the stream. He looked up at me with those sweet dark eyes and I petted him on the head and said, "I'm sorry." The light faded out like on a dimmer. I knew then that I would never hunt again. I am not a hunter.

There is something important that has been missed in Hemingway nonfiction. It is not just on account of hunting. Hemingway, always an experimental writer, had the stated goal of writing nonfiction that read like fiction. He told stories with characters and dialogue. In the 1960s such writers as Norman Mailer, Truman Capote, and Tom Wolfe were credited for reinvented nonfiction, creating something called literary nonfiction. Hemingway had started exploring this idea thirty years earlier.

But the reading public and even Max Perkins at Scribner's didn't want nonfiction, literary or otherwise, from Hemingway. He had been writing good short stories, some of which were collected in a volume called *Winner Take Nothing*. Some of the stories from this period are among the best writing he ever did.

He started working on a novel about low-life in Key West and Cuba. It is about Cuban revolutionaries who hire a struggling Key West boat owner to transport money they robbed from a Key West Bank to revolutionaries in Cuba. Despite living in Key West for almost twelve years, this is the only book he ever wrote about the little island, and despite living in Cuba longer than anywhere else in his life, this was one of only two books

published in his lifetime he ever set there.

While working on the novel, he was periodically reminded that the lovely revolution in Spain was going badly. By 1936, a coalition of wealthy, church, and fascists were committed to a military overthrow of the Second Republic. At first the coup was given little chance of success, but then Hitler and Mussolini started contributing money, arms, soldiers, and pilots. The Soviet Union started contributing to the Republic but on a smaller scale. The Americans, British, and French did not help the Republic even though it was obvious that this was a dress rehearsal for a coming World War. But volunteers started coming in from all over the world, so this was turning into an international war.

Many of Hemingway's friends went to Spain, such as writers Archibald MacLeish and John Dos Passos. But Hemingway had to finish his novel. He also took time for fishing from his cabin cruiser and hunting at the L-Bar-T dude ranch in Wyoming where, in 1936, as the war was beginning in Spain, he bagged a grizzly.

His main concern when he heard that Madrid was being shelled was that the paintings in the Prado not be harmed. A priceless art collection that he regularly visited—he loved painting—was a real concern. He told Dos Passos in a letter that he was not concerned about the rest of Madrid because "everything looks better after being shelled." This could be seen as callousness but was really Hem's curiously sardonic sense of humor. He also said that if they were still shooting when he finished his novel, he would go to Spain.

Finally, in 1937, *To Have and Have Not* was published. It too was poorly received. This judgment may also have been hasty. It makes it clear that while Hemingway spent his time around the haves, his talent was depicting the have nots. Harry Morgan, the down-and-out boat owner, loves his family, his daughters. Neither Harry nor his wife are attractive, but they do have a burning physical passion for each other. Harry goes off on a bad deal in a boat with Cubans robbing a Key West Bank to bring money to a Cuban Revolution. What else can he do? He is desperate for money to support his family. Harry is shot and we don't really know what happens to him. The next scene is as fine a moment as Hemingway has ever written. A writer in Key West gets interested in the

story. He describes this grotesque fat woman and imagines the misery of the poor man married to this unsightly hag. He rushed home to write a story about the poor man with the hideous wife. It turns out its Harry's wife, and she looks wretched with red eyes because she has just received bad news about Harry.

The book should have ended there but goes on about the writer and his bad marriage. Hemingway was always very good about bad marriage and surprisingly open to the wife's point of view. But the problem is that we don't care about this writer. Hemingway didn't like writers and it shows.

The shortcomings of this book could have been fixed by a good editor. Harry's story was moving. How good was Max Perkins? Would Hemingway take editing? That wasn't the relationship. Perkins was a thin tweedy kind of man that Jack remembered as bookish and like a schoolteacher. He had no ego, which is an important trait for a great editor. Perkins did not rewrite nor urge rewriting. According to Hemingway, "He never asked me to change anything I wrote except to remove certain words, which were not then publishable." This was what Hemingway liked in an editor. Arnold Gingrich at *Esquire*, another favorite editor, was the same way. I've never felt that way. I think an editor is an alternative point of view that you can either accept or reject. I encourage editors to weigh in as much as possible with the understanding that I can reject their ideas. Good editors have helped me, and I think they could have helped Hemingway, but he did not want to hear it. Perkins, who did major work on some writers such as Thomas Wolfe, understood that about Hemingway.

In 1944, director Howard Hawks released his film version. He even had William Faulkner work on the screenplay. Aside from the lead character being named Harry Morgan, the film had almost nothing in common with the book. Instead of Cuba it takes place in Martinique because it was French and they tried to make the film look like the recent hit, *Casablanca*.

Ironically, in 1950 Michael Curtiz, the director of *Casablanca*, did his own version of *To Have and Have Not* called *The Breaking Point* with John Garfield and Patricia Neal. This version, a fine example of film noir, was much closer to Hemingway's novel. When Hemingway met Neal in Sun Valley, he told her that he thought it was the best film ever

made from his writing. His worst novel made his best film—except that, as Curtiz understood, it wasn't that bad a novel.

· · ·

The Spanish Civil War in Madrid became the classic example of what reporters call "a goat fuck." Because they do not get to use vulgar language in their work, journalists, especially back when we were reporters, use it whenever possible in their conversation. A goat fuck is a story so big that every journalist you ever met shows up for it. In the hotel, at the press conference, out on the story, even sometimes on the battlefield, colleagues flank you. You are lucky if you can get a one-on-one interview with someone, and if you do, they will be ushering out someone you know as you are entering. At night you are all having dinner together talking about *the story*. If it is in a war zone, there is something romantic about being all clustered in the same hotel while bombs and bullets are heard out in the darkness, sometimes getting close to the hotel. People are out there dying and some of you may die too. Often a love affair or two is spawned in the hotel. Everyone is much too close.

This allergy to goat fucks is one of the ways I was different than my fellow journalists. They didn't all love it either. But they love the stories that bring it on. I never did. Several times, while sitting at the bar or in a restaurant in a goatish situation, a non-journalist, curious about our subculture, would ask, "What is your idea of a great story?" Every journalist I ever heard had the identical answer: "To be a witness to a great moment in history."

That seems a perfectly commendable ambition, but it was never mine. My idea of a great story was to be the one witness to something that no one would have known happened if I hadn't been there. I once covered a civil war that no one else was covering—in Surinam, a country many had never heard of. Of course, if that could also be a "great event in history," that would be a very nice bonus. But often there were reasons why other journalist weren't there and to be honest, going my own way, I found small, important things but no great moments in history.

Of course, the newspaper sometimes required you to cover it. And

so, I was in the Intercontinental Hotel in Managua with everyone else during the war in Nicaragua, at the bar with the gang handing over huge piles of worthless currency for excellent rum. The Hotel Oloffson in Port-au-Prince, Haiti, turned into a goat fuck every time there was a coup d'état, which in the 1980s and '90s happened with regularity. This was unwelcome to me because I used to stay there in the days of Jean-Claude Duvalier when there was a murderous stability and no one covered it, and I was the only journalist at the Oloffson. The local newspaper ran an article about my coming there. No one had covered Haiti for years. Shouldn't someone go there and see what is happening? That was my argument for *The Chicago Tribune* sending me there. I had used the same argument to get to Spain. Murderous dictators such as Franco and Duvalier impose a morbid stability which does not lend itself to news coverage. Later when everything became a big news event, I liked to cover it from rural towns and not the capital just because everyone else was covering the capital. This often meant sleeping in very bad hotels. A goat fuck is often about finding the only decent hotel.

• • •

For Hitler, Spain was an opportunity to try out a new kind of airpower far deadlier than had ever been used before, against both military and civilian targets. Planes could level cities with bombs and strafe from the air with swift low-flying planes. In *For Whom The Bell Tolls*, Robert Jordan watches Italian and German warplanes overhead and says, "They move like no thing there has ever been. They move like mechanized doom." This was the most brutal warfare the world had ever seen.

There was a great deal of outrage about the fire-bombing of the Basque city of Gernika. But it soon became accepted. In World War II, the allies targeted every civilian city in Germany as well as Tokyo and, of course, Hiroshima and Nagasaki. And after that, who questioned bombing Hanoi and Huế? Today, the world notes with mostly indifference as cities of Iraq, Syria, and Afghanistan are bombed. It all started in Spain.

With Nazi support, the rebels captured large swaths of territory. But they could not take Bilbao, Barcelona, or Madrid. The Republic had been

good to the Basques and they fought tenaciously for their city of Bilbao, valuable for its steel mills and heavy industry. It had also been good to the Catalans, who would not yield Barcelona. The rebels thought they could take Madrid, but the Madrileños fought on with improbable strength and endurance, making Madrid the big story. As long as Madrid held, the Republic would not fall.

It is a fine thing to talk about compromise and open-mindedness, but there are moments like the Spanish Civil War when you are either on one side or the other, and there are no excuses. This was also true of the press. If you supported the rebellion and the fascists, you had to report from areas they held. To be an accredited journalist in Madrid, you had to support the Republic.

When Hemingway met Joris Ivens, a Dutch documentary filmmaker who was a committed communist and supporter of the Republican cause in Spain, at the Deux Magots café in Paris, the Dutchman asked him what he wanted to do in Spain. Hemingway said that he wanted to tell the truth about the horror of war. He was still on his anti-war mission. But when he got to Spain and came to see the fascists in action and the Republic they were trying to destroy, he grew angry and resolutely pro-Republic.

Herbert Matthews, *New York Times* correspondent in Madrid, later wrote,

> I always felt the falseness and hypocrisy of those who claimed to be unbiased, and the foolishness, if not rank stupidity of editors and readers who demanded 'objectivity' or "impartiality" of correspondents writing about the war.

Hungarian-born author Arthur Koestler wrote,

> Anyone who has lived through the hell of Madrid with his eyes, his nerves, his heart, his stomach—and then pretends to be objective, is a liar.

The *Times* had another correspondent, William P. Carney, a favorite of Catholic readers, who reported from the rebel side and did not disguise

his support of Franco's cause. The newspaper may have been trying to achieve a balanced point of view but in fact, they were confusing the readers. Carney's facts and those of Matthew were not in agreement, and readers did not know who or what to believe.

The war was complicated and confusing in any event. On one side were the Rebels ,so named because they had rebelled against the government. They were often called "the fascists," though they were not all fascists. Some were church people trying to hold on to their power, or wealthy people protecting their privilege. Franco himself had no ideology except Franco. On the other side were the Loyalists, those loyal to the Republic, for which they were also known as Republicans. In *For Whom the Bell Tolls*, Hemingway inserted a personal dark joke. The American told the guerillas with whom he was fighting, the Republicans, that his father was a lifelong Republican back in America. They were impressed and asked if he was still fighting with the Republicans. Robert Jordan said that he had shot himself and they asked if this was to avoid being tortured. Thinking of the depression that tormented Hemingway's father when the answer was "Yes, to avoid being tortured."

Some in the US saw the Republicans as Communists and some, especially among the American volunteers, were. The majority of Americans, according to regular Gallup polls, sided with the Republic. After all, we do have a tradition of supported democratically elected governments. In the 1950s, the US government in its fit of anti-communism started regarding well-known Republic supporters, including Hemingway, with suspicion. They labeled them "prematurely anti-fascist," but history had proven the US government to be belatedly anti-fascist.

With bombs and shells landing in the city every day, the foreign press crowded into their designated hotel in Madrid, the Hotel Florida. It had been one of Madrid's better hotels; all 200 rooms, they boasted, had their own bathrooms. The ornate façade was marble. The hotel was fairly new, having been completed in 1924. Antonio Palacio, a leading architect who gave Madrid its elegant look in the 1920s, designed it. It was well-located in the center just off of the Gran Via, a boulevard of fashionable shops, restaurants, and hotels. Now the Gran Via was torn up from bombs and some of the hotel windows were protected with piles of sandbags.

Hemingway, novel finished, put together his entourage for Spain. The exact opposite of me, he never liked to do anything alone. His trips to Pamplona, not just the one he wrote about, involved assembling his own crowd. He tried to talk Archibald MacLeish into hunting with him in East Africa, assuring him that Uncle Gus was buying. The poet reneged. Now he asked Sidney Franklin to help him cover the war. Sidney had by now understood who his friend Ernest Hemingway was. But he knew nothing about journalism and nothing about this war. He went through the entire arduous process of getting a visa and press credentials without any idea of which side they were covering. Hemingway would head in one direction and send Sidney in another and at night back at the Hotel Florida, Sidney would tell him what he saw. He was also a great scrounger who could talk people out of whatever they needed. Eventually the matador realized that they were supposed to be siding with the Republic; since he regarded the Republic as Communist, and he was anti-Communist, he left. He decided that his friend Ernie, who was passionate about saving the Republic and was working on a propaganda film to garner support for the Republic in the US, was just pretending to be Communist to gather material for a book.

But the more significant addition was Martha Gellhorn. Hemingway, though still an extraordinarily handsome man, was approaching the age of forty and exhibiting signs of that behavior that is often referred to in men as "midlife." He also had grown resentful of Pauline and Uncle Gus's money and didn't like feeling supported. Martha Gellhorn was tall and blonde and generally seen as extremely attractive. Neither of his first two wives had the kind of showy good looks that a crude man could brag about. Hemingway started telling friends and acquaintances that he was bringing to Spain a woman with incredibly long legs. She was a trophy, but she wanted to be seen as much more than that.

She was from an affluent St. Louis family and a friend of prominent people, including Eleanor Roosevelt. It cannot be a coincidence that all four of the women Hemingway married were Midwesterners. Though he left for good at a young age, Hem probably always saw himself as a

Midwesterner and he clearly was. He spoke with the soft accent of the Midwest that so often is associated with sounding "American."

Martha Gellhorn was flirtatious, a skill that she knew how to use. She met British author H.G. Wells when both were guests at the Roosevelt White House, and though he was in his seventies and she her twenties, he had a deep infatuation with her and helped promote her writing career. She started as a journalist and moved to Paris in 1930 where she had a four-year affair with Bertrand de Jouvenel, a well-connected journalist and stepson of Colette with whom he was rumored to have had an affair. Also, he was married. Martha's affair got her connected with leading figures in Paris, but after four years it was clear that he was never going to leave his wife, so she left him and Paris.

Back in the US, she took a job with the Federal Emergency Relief Administration, for which she traveled the country and became deeply upset by the degree of poverty she witnessed. She complained to her friend Eleanor, who passed it on to her husband Franklin.

In the meantime, she wrote a novel about the sex and disillusionment of college girls. It was poorly received. Her next book was fictional portraits of the down and out called *The Troubles I've Seen*. Now she used her connections. H.G. Wells got her a British publisher and after it was published in the US, Eleanor Roosevelt promoted it. Gellhorn became involved with another married man who was not going to leave his wife, a *TIME* magazine writer named Allen Grover. She tried for an assignment covering Europe for *TIME*. When she did not succeed, she moved into Wells's home in London. From there she wrote a story on the lynching of a Black sharecropper in Mississippi. She had supposedly witnessed this incident with de Jouvenel. It was sold in both Britain and the US and widely praised, but it later turned out that she had made up the incident and not witnessed it at all.

Hemingway, who collected scraps from everywhere for his novels like a junkyard fanatic who could never throw anything out because it might be useful later, had Robert Jordan recall a lynching in Ohio in *For Whom the Bell Tolls*.

By the time she met Hemingway in Key West, it would be easy to imagine that she was tired of married men, let alone one with three sons.

But Hem was charming, and he talked about her writing, and there may have never been anyone better on the craft of writing. Among other tips he told her about, the cure for writer's block (and this is absolutely *the* cure): "Get exercise and write whether it is possible or not."

Besides, she had hung his picture on the wall of her dormitory room at Bryn Mawr years before they had met, so she was already a Hemingway fan.

But there was something else. Pauline did not want Ernest to go to Spain. She was concerned about the physical danger, but she also did not like the Spanish Republic. She considered it anti-Catholic. Martha, on the other hand, was eager to go herself. Having some Jewish roots, she was deeply distressed by what she saw in Nazi Germany and even in France. Like Hemingway, she thought the survival of the Spanish Republic was essential.

Max Perkins also did not want his writer to cover the war and openly expressed admiration for General Franco. I was to learn about this many years later and it came as a blow. In my youthful fantasies of becoming a writer, I always imagined a Max Perkins type for my editor. But then I realized that I would never want an editor who admired Franco. Perkins was gone from the fantasy. But Hemingway did not seem concerned by his editor's attitude. He was more interested in getting Perkins interested in his new discovery: Gellhorn.

Hemingway was hired by the North American News Alliance (NANA), a large and growing newspaper syndicate. They offered him $500 for each 200-to-400-word dispatch and $1,000 for 1,200-word articles. This was excellent pay. One thousand dollars in 1936 had the spending power of almost $19,000 today. Initially, NANA was not happy with Hem's copy. His approach to newspaper writing had always been similar to his short story writing. He would find an interesting situation with good characters and tell the story. They were often insightful and great reading, but NANA complained that what they wanted was to know how the war was going.

Hemingway could get to the war better than most. Transportation was hard to find, and Hemingway was a celebrity who could easily make connections. While many correspondents could not get a car to use, Hemingway had two with gas allowances for both. He even had extra

gas in cans strapped to the car so that he could take long trips. His friend Midwestern novelist Josephine Herbst, who generally spoke well of him, admitted that she was one of many journalists irritated by Hemingway's two cars.

As with World War I, the amount of time that Hemingway spent in the Spanish Civil War became greatly exaggerated. He made four trips, the longest of which (the second one) was only four months, in the fall of 1937. But it could be argued that the intensity of these trips was such that he could not have lasted longer.

Hemingway had the advantage of being who he was, but he was also extremely skilled at handling people and, like any good reporter, attached great importance to having the inside line on everything. He spent a great deal of time at The Gaylord Hotel, irresistible to Hem because all of the top Communists were there and he could make valuable connections, but also because somehow, all during the siege, it had top-quality food and liquor. The Soviets kept it stocked with high-quality vodka and caviar. In *For Whom the Bell Tolls*, Robert Jordan, who also spent time there, said that it was "too good for a city under siege." From the outside it looked like a residence, which it eventually became. It had elegant marble hallways and luxurious rooms.

Hem told the Communist military chiefs that he was more of a writer than a journalist, less interested in fact and figures than in experiencing the war. They sent him out to Valencia province where they connected him with a band of guerilla fighters who blew up a bridge. The experience was the basis of *For Whom the Bell Tolls*. Hemingway had excellent relations with Stalin's secret service, the NKVD, forerunner of the KGB. The relationship was so good that according to military intelligence historian Nicolas Reynolds, who examined some of their files as they became available, the NKVD thought they could recruit him. They even gave him a code name, as they did with assets—Argo, after a ship in Greek mythology that sailed for adventure. But Hemingway was far too independent, as American intelligence would later discover, to be of much use other than occasionally imparting an interesting experience. He was cooperative but only on his own terms, not a man who followed instructions. He explained this in 1935, when the Soviets had already

become interested in the leftist leanings of the famous writer. In a letter to his Soviet translator Ivan Kashkin, he wrote, "A writer is like a Gypsy. He owes no allegiance to any government." Though a passionate supporter of the Spanish Republic, he was to demonstrate his gypsy-like ways.

He seemed better off than other correspondents and he took pride in that. He had two rooms in the Florida instead of everyone else's one, rooms 108 and 109 on the third floor. Martha was also there and there was little effort to conceal their affair. This did not stop a few journalists from flirting with her, and Martha seemed to encourage flirtations. But Sidney Franklin was there for his friend and he took to chaperoning Martha, glaring at frisky journalists. No one wanted to get in a fight with a matador.

Many, especially women, found Martha irritating—the way she was always smartly dressed and even spent considerable time shopping for luxury clothes, which could be found at bargain prices in the bombed-out city. It was not clear how Hemingway felt about this. He seemed completely under her spell. But in the play he wrote in the Hotel Florida, *The Fifth Column*, the lead character has a girlfriend who is tall and blonde and vain and a little bit bitchy. The lead character decides not to run off with her in part because he is annoyed with her habit of shopping in the middle of the war.

Herbst later wrote, "Martha Gellhorn sailed in and out in beautiful Saks Fifth Avenue pants with a green chiffon scarf wound around her head." Martha made disparaging remarks about Josephine Herbst's dowdy clothes, as though there were standards of dress for a city under bombardment. Besides, it is interesting that Josephine, a feminist who did not like done-up flirtatious women, could identify the stores where Martha's wardrobe originated.

Often the other correspondents joked about how Gellhorn had trouble finding Hemingway. She was often looking for him and he was off on some story.

Hemingway's rooms were packed with canned food and wine and liquor—surprising since he only stayed for weeks at a time. The journalists who had the habit of relaxing seated on the steps in the stairwells could hear Martha and Ernest popping corks. At times there was the seductive

smell of a roasting hare or partridge that he had managed to shoot and persuade a maid to cook.

Small groups of two or three worked together. A large group is too unwieldy, and it is too dangerous to work alone. Then these groups get together for dinner and compare notes. Josephine Herbst wrote, "Everyone talked learnedly during the evening meal on the Gran Via, about the number of shells that had come in, the number of people that had been killed."

Hemingway paired off with top journalists. He chiefly worked with Matthews of the *Times* and sometimes Henry Buckley of the London *Daily Telegraph*. Matthews's description of his colleague Hemingway is worth noting:

> Whatever the reasons, my picture of Ernest Hemingway would be of a warm, generous, brave and always friendly companion, hypersensitive and hot tempered, to be sure, and moody now and then. He was like an overgrown boy; it was as if he never grew up inside of him to match his big powerful body.

The hotel was filled with new rookies and famous old hands such as Dos Passos. There were many photographers and journalists from all over the world and a few volunteer combat pilots from Russia and France. The great war photographer Robert Capa was there with his protégée and lover, Gerda Taro. Taro, a small, coquettish woman with short-cut henna hair was a German Jew, and an anti-fascist political activist. She became his assistant and lover and quickly mastered the craft of photography. Capa, a Hungarian Jew whose real name was Friedmann, invented a fictitious Robert Capa. By the time they got to Spain, Friedmann was Capa and Gerda, whose real name was Gerta Pohorylle, became Gerda Taro, and both of them started sending out photographs under the name Robert Capa. Some of the famous Capa photos may have been by her.

David "Chim" Seymour, a Polish Jew, also became a distinguished photographer in the Civil War. Eventually all three would die in combat: Taro in Spain, Capa in Indochina, and Seymour in Egypt.

The Importance of Not Being Ernest

Of all the chapters in Hemingway's life, this is the easiest for me to imagine because I was there numerous times, in Port-au-Prince, Managua, and other places. Capa, Taro, and the other photographers went out to the fronts because there was no other way to get pictures. Some of the writers such as Hemingway, Matthews, and Gellhorn also did. Others hung around the hotel and the Gran Via. Some were desperately looking for transportation to get out to the war. Others were happy staying in and getting their stories from government briefings. Some had more fun than others. Bob Capa was up for a good party, throwing a dinner one night in El Botín, an old restaurant by the Plaza Mayor that specialized in suckling pig. It is still there and still does. The first time I took my daughter to Madrid, just one night on our way to Morocco, I took her to this restaurant to have a good Madrid evening not because Capa did or because it boasted of being a favorite Hemingway haunt in the 1950s, but as a way to make one night in Madrid magical. I didn't mention Hemingway. She wouldn't have cared.

At night they could compete over dinner at the Gran Via, which was often very poor fare but occasionally there was a lobster or a fish. Those bombers were German Heinkels. "Heinkel 111," someone said and then someone else added, "The new ones." But then someone identified a few old Junkers. And there were Italian planes. They competed for expertise. Everyone thought official casualties were too low, which always led to speculation on the real death toll.

Back in the hotel, the ideal was to get Hemingway to share some of his scotch. There was probably a lot of talk about Hemingway because he was the big star, although Dos Passos was also a very famous writer and a serious man worth knowing. And there was curiosity about Franklin. Hemingway actually brought a bullfighter. Franklin even managed a few appearances in the bullrings of Republican-held towns. That was also a curiosity to the journalists but not nearly as interesting as what they could learn from the flyers who stayed at the hotel. And of course, there was a lot of talk about this well-dressed Martha Gellhorn. Some journalists found Martha so engaging that they wondered if she was really committed to Hemingway. And what about the legendary Bob Capa and this Gerda who they said was "cute"? It was known she had rejected Capa's marriage

proposal, but this may have been more a rejection of marriage than a rejection of Capa. The Spanish called her *la pequeña rubia*, the little blonde, but she was utterly fearless, eager to get to the action.

There was romance at the Florida with Hemingway and Gellhorn, Capa and Taro, and possibly a few others. Maybe you saw too many mangled bodies or maybe a bomb fell a little too close and you didn't want to sleep alone with death all around. You would lie in bed at night listening to gunfire a few blocks away, trying to estimate how many blocks. Hemingway wrote in one dispatch to NANA in April 1937:

> The window of the hotel is open, and as you lie in bed, you hear the firing in the frontline seventeen blocks away…You lie and listen to it and it is a great thing to be with your feet stretched out gradually warming the cold foot of the bed and not out there in University City or Carabanchel.

They all built their temporary lives surrounded by the tragedy that was Spain. Sometimes the tragedy seeped in. So did the bombing, and people were killed near the hotel. During the war, according to the official count, the hotel was hit 156 times by enemy shells or stray pieces of shrapnel.

There were also assassinations and groundless executions on both sides. The press was reluctant to report on Republican misdeeds. It often had to do with infighting among Stalinist and anti-Stalinist communists. Exploring this subject could cause the press a great deal of trouble.

But then the Republicans executed someone the journalists knew. José Robles, a Communist officer, was a close friend of Dos Passos. He was arrested and accused of being a Fascist spy. Dos Passos did not believe this and tried to pressure the Republican government to release him, but Hemingway kept warning him not to pursue it because it would only create difficulties for all of them. It probably would have created difficulties for Hemingway who depended on his friendship with the Soviets and the NKVD for access. Eventually it became clear that Robles had been executed. This created a bitter rift between the two writers. The war formed and ended friendships.

Gerda Taro had a habit of ignoring caution and working alone. She went by herself to cover a battle near Madrid that the rebels had called a victory. Her photographs proved that it was actually a Republican victory. But she was accidentally run over by a tank backing up while she was shooting and died. In another version, she was shooting from a running board and was run over by a tank that clipped them.

Photographers who look at the world through a tiny viewfinder need a second pair of eyes. She had no colleague to warn her or push her away from the tank. It was a dangerous business. Even in the Florida amid bombardments, they were not safe. They were all making the best of living in horror, witnessing death everyday with or without chiffon scarves.

Hemingway tried to tell Americans that they either had to defeat fascism in Spain or later in a much bigger war. In a 1938 article for the leftist magazine *Ken*, a pet project of Arnold Gingrich, he wrote:

> It seems we are protected by the oceans, so we do not need to care what happens. But, brother, when a war starts, we will be put in it. And you'll hate those oceans, both the Atlantic and the Pacific, when you ride over them in the good old vomit-stink of transports. There is only one way to avoid or postpone that ride. That is to beat Italy, always beatable, and to beat her in Spain, and beat her now. Otherwise, you will have to fight tougher people than the Italians, and don't let anybody tell you that you won"t.

When the International Brigades were withdrawn, it meant that the cause was lost, and Hemingway broke down and wept. It was the only time Martha Gellhorn, who went through a great deal with him, ever saw him weep. Hemingway was always grateful to the Soviets for their support and angry with the British and Americans for not supporting them. He remained anti-British most of his life because of it.

As predicted, the war ended with the fall of Madrid, which was in March 1939. Barcelona had already fallen. A white flag in Madrid marked the end of the war and the beginning of Franco's rule. The witnesses and combatants who were not murdered by Franco went home or into hiding

or exile, with their hearts broken.

The war, like the one before and the one after, seemed to exhaust Hem emotionally. When he returned to Key West, he complained of terrible nightmares.

• • •

It is very hard to get a sense of the war. Matthews freely admitted that you couldn't get it from reading *The New York Times*. For all the journalists covering it, there is little giving a sense of the war or even making sense of the war. When I first started writing about Spain, realizing that nothing could be understood unless the war was, I read Hugh Thomas's thick history, *The Spanish Civil War*. As the title suggests, it is an attempted matter-of-fact presentation of the whole thing—helpful but not enough. The truth is that like Paris in the twenties, it comes down to a choice: Hemingway or Orwell. And as in the twenties Orwell had more grit, Hemingway more poetry.

While Hemingway went to Madrid as a celebrity journalist, Orwell went to Barcelona to fight for the Republic. Orwell's brutally honest account of the ensuing chaos, *Homage to Catalonia*, was published in Britain in 1938 but not in the US until 1952. It is such a scathing portrait of the disarray and madness behind Republican lines that many have thought of it as an anti-Republican book. That was most certainly not Orwell's intention. His struggle against Franco marked the beginning of a lifelong crusade against totalitarianism. But at the time he was ensnared not only in that fight but in the fight of the Stalinists against the Trotskyites and Stalin's push to make the Communists in Spain purely his communists.

The book gives as clear a picture as can be found of what will never be clear: fighting for the Republic. He describes "the smell of war" as being "a smell of excrement and decaying food." And there is his description of the louse with which they were all infected, and the cluster of cherries growing on a "bullet chipped tree." There is the most incredible description of firing a rifle from a ditch into a small break in a fascist wall. He would see khaki uniforms pass by and fire:

The Importance of Not Being Ernest

> I had several shots. I don't know if I hit anyone—it is most
> unlikely; I am a very poor shot with a rifle. But it was
> rather fun, the Fascists did not know where the shots were
> coming from, and I made sure I would get one of them
> sooner or later.

But instead, a sniper found him and shot him in the neck. Orwell, never without wit, was repeatedly explained while healing in a hospital that anyone who survives a shot in the neck is "the luckiest man alive." But he said, "I could not help thinking that it would be even luckier not to be hit at all."

• • •

The other alternative is Hemingway, who among other skills, was a great observer. The four short stories he wrote at the Hotel Florida are careful descriptions of the siege of Madrid. We learn about spying and betrayal, as well as the camaraderie of war. Nothing brings people so closely together as being shot at. We also learn that the restaurant everyone went to was in a basement and they served millet and water soup with yellow rice and horse meat, and that the Gran Via was just mud and rubble from all the bombing. The streets remained smoky and smelled of explosives. There was broken glass everywhere. Sometimes Hemingway ate with his Basque friend Paco Garay at a restaurant called Marichu. Garay, a Cuban Basque, was one of a number of Basques that Hemingway befriended during the war and remained close with in Cuba later.

In one story someone asked what Madrid was like before the war, and the answer was "...fine. Like now except lots to eat."

Though Hemingway was known as a hardcore supporter of the Republic, the novel presents as troubling a portrait as Orwell's. The good Republicans commit atrocities, in one memorable scene massacring captured Guardia Civil. Battles were brutal, horrific wounds described.

Robert Jordan in *For Whom the Bell Tolls* is a committed Communist who agonized over all the people he had killed. He thought that only a very few of them were actually fascist, just people who lined up on the other

side. Sifting through papers of one youth from northern Navarra that he killed, he wondered if he had run the bulls with him one year in Pamplona. But the tragedy of the wrong side winning was immediately apparent.

During the war, he wanted to avoid discussing the kind of murderous infighting that led to pointless killings such as that of José Robles. In his novel, Hemingway makes it clear that this too was part of the Republican command. He portrays the French communist leader André Marty, political commissar of the International Brigades, as a homicidal maniac, executing loyal soldiers for no reason. He wrote, "his face looked as though it was modeled from the waste material of his victims that you find under the claws of a very old lion."

In 1939, he explained to his Russian translator Ivan Kashkin:

> For your information, in stories about the war I try to show all the different sides of it taking it slowly and honestly and examining it many ways. So never think one story represents my viewpoint because it is much too complicated for that.

His non-leftist American readers were relieved by the fairness of the book, though some of his leftist friends regarded it as a sell-out. The Pulitzer Prize committee was inclined to give Hemingway his first Pulitzer but their chairman, a staunch conservative named Nicholas Murray Butler, blocked it because of what he saw as a leftist tone to the novel.

The Spanish only published a censored version, and this was also true in the Soviet Union. When you are censored by both sides, you have done something right.

Hemingway wanted to chronicle war more honestly than it ever had been. Josephine Herbst wrote:

> He had answered a definite call when he came to Spain. He wanted to be *the* war writer of his age, and he knew it and went toward it.

By the time of the Spanish Civil War, he had been thinking of war

as great material for many years. In 1925, before he had even written *A Farewell to Arms,* Hem told Fitzgerald, "The reason you are so sore you missed the war is because war is the best subject of all. It groups the maximum of material and speeds up the action and brings out all sorts of stuff that normally you have to wait a lifetime to get." I thought about this during the Vietnam War. I, who had decided to do everything to develop myself as a writer, was passing up an incredible opportunity. But should I kill people to gain great writing material? I suppose you could learn a lot of interesting things by murdering your next-door neighbor too. Reporting on war is one thing, participating another, and he was often not clear about the difference.

• • •

If Hemingway influenced my desire to go to Spain it was unconscious. When I was a child, you heard a great deal about Hemingway's exciting trips to Spain. You heard about it and saw pictures.

It was only years later when I knew Spain that I began to think how strange this was. At a time when he should have been encouraging a boycott, he was encouraging tourism. Much of the world refused to have relations with Franco's Spain. France did not have diplomatic relations with its neighbor. Many Spanish artists were boycotting Spain. Picasso said he would not let his famous painting of Guernica in until Spain was once again a republic. The great Catalan cellist Pau Casals lived in exile in Puerto Rico. In 1953 President Eisenhower signed a treaty of cooperation with Franco, opening up commercial relations in exchange for air bases. Franco had been trying to sell himself as a reliable anti-Communist. German Nazi criminals made the same claim. The supporters of the Republic were furious with Eisenhower. It appeared to confirm the suspicion that the US government was pro-fascist. Casals vowed to never perform in the US. (Jacqueline Kennedy got him to break his vow and perform in the Kennedy White House in 1961.) But the other thing that happened in 1953, the year of the hated treaty, was that while the others were all protesting, Ernest Hemingway—champion of the Republic, one of Franco's most well-known and vitriolic critics, avowed anti-fascist and

Franco hater—returned to Spain.

His Spanish trips of the 1950s were like human snowballs. He picked up more and more people at each stop until he was traveling with a huge entourage. Bands of friends, followers, and sycophants. It attracted a great deal of publicity, and while the Franco government hesitated to use his name in publicity until after he was dead, Hemingway was great advertising for Spanish tourism.

One of the people who joined Hem's entourage was Valerie Danby-Smith, an Irish woman who arrived to interview him, became his secretary, confidant, and one of his young unrequited romances. He would talk of love and liked to walk arm in arm. Valerie followed him to Cuba, New York, and Idaho, and later became one of the four unsuccessful marriages of his youngest son Gregory. Before meeting Hemingway, she had been married to the great Irish dissenter, one-time IRA activist, poet, novelist and playwright Brendan Behan. She told me that her husband had tried to go to Spain, but at the border the Guardia Civil asked him what he wanted to see in Spain, and he said, "Franco's funeral." He was not let in.

I would have liked to have heard a story like that about Hemingway. Hemingway's excuse was that all of the people he knew in Franco's prisons had been released within the past two years. But many had been killed and Franco still held thousands of political prisoners.

The Spanish government, starting with the Guardia Civil at the international bridge over the Bidasoa at Hendaye, were happy to see the famous writer return. The Hemingway group was taken to a room with the words "FRANCO FRANCO FRANCO" high on the wall. The official looked at his passport and asked if he was any relation. Then he looked again and stood up and shook his hand.

As his fourth wife Mary put it, "We moved now in a mob." Hemingway's moving crowd went to bullfights buying out huge blocks of seats, and to restaurants, and to more towns and more bullfights and more restaurants. They ate magnificently. "I wonder what the poor folk are eating," Hem liked to say, though that actually would have been a valid question. In Madrid, the Hotel Florida was still open and they stayed there.

Many years later, hearing Valerie's description of these trips, I realized, maybe for the first time, that I would not have enjoyed traveling with Hemingway. Too many people, too much noise, and too much alcohol and rich people acting badly.

. . .

When Virginia and I first arrived, it was exciting and disturbing to realize that we had entered the country Hemingway left in 1939. Traveling in Franco's Spain seemed like falling into a time warp. The Civil War ended and Hemingway, Orwell, and all the famous people had left. Franco had come to power, a 1939 fascist dictatorship with people acting the way they acted under Hitler and Mussolini. There were fascist rallies and fascist salutes. This wasn't a resurgence of fascism; it was the original fascism still there. More than thirty years later it seemed as though the Civil War had just ended. There were political prisoners, huge numbers of exiles, even a few who risked death to sneak back in and see their family. A great number of people had missing arms or legs that had been cut or blown off. And though it could not be talked about much, the bitterness and divide had not eased.

The image of Hemingway had changed in Spain since his death. The dictatorship and its profascist press, upon Papa's death, immediately claimed him as one of their own. A few years after Hemingway's death, a fascist travel journalist, a member of the Falangist movement, Rafael García Serrano believed that the Pamplona Festival was Spain's greatest chance to bring tourism back to the country and that Hemingway was the key. He asserted, "He liked Navarra better than any other part of Spain." Everyone wanted Hemingway's love, and wherever he spent time there was always this claim, especially after his death, that he loved this place best.

In Madrid elegant, bombed buildings were replaced with soulless new ones. There were once again shops and excellent restaurants, though it was not clear who they were for since there were few tourists and less businesspeople. Respectable businesses hesitated to get involved with Spain. You didn't really want to know who these people in suits dining

sumptuously in expensive restaurants were.

Many buildings in Spain had the name José Antonio Primo de Rivera written on them. He was the founder of a small fascist party in 1933, the Falange, financed by Italian dictator Benito Mussolini. He preached the violent overthrow of the elected Spanish Republic. Once that effort began in 1936, he was arrested and executed. Francisco Franco, the general who never commanded a single battle of the ensuing Civil War and yet through political skills became the dictator of Spain, paid tribute to the fascist movement of which he was never a part and celebrated the martyrdom of Primo de Rivera on public walls. It was usually written in red paint, which, I think intentionally, looked like blood.

There were many other signs of fascism. The national motto, trailed from planes during political rallies, was the Falangist slogan "¡Arriba España!" In Madrid, prominent citizens proudly displayed in their offices the iron crosses they had been awarded by Hitler's Third Reich for services rendered.

Chiefly through fear, the peace was kept by a number of organizations, especially the Guardia Civil. They had been divided during the Civil War and there was a large contingent of Guardia Civil loyal to the Republic. After Franco took control, such loyalist Guardia Civil were executed, imprisoned, or forced into exile and the organization became Franco's thugs. They patrolled in pairs, one taking the lead and the other standing behind. Famously, their black patent-leather hats were weird ornaments that made them look distinct and menacing, especially since the men perfected a certain glare and never smiled publicly.

One day, Virginia and I were wondering in the Aragon city of Zaragoza in our attempt to be tourists in fascistland. It had an Arab palace and a number of impressive churches. But it was known to be a very fascist town; Primo de Rivera's name was everywhere. The central Spanish military academy was there, as was the main training post for officers of the Guardia Civil. The patent-leather pairs were wandering everywhere with their little submachine guns.

One pair ordered us into an alley behind a building, one in the lead, one behind us, both pointing their weapons. It occurred to me that this shiny-hatted grim-faced pair could do whatever they wanted to us here in

Franco's Spain. They could shoot us on the spot or drag us to some prison. The one in front of us barked questions and jabbed his weapon at us while the one behind kept his weapon at the ready. The one with the questions started to poke Virginia with the barrel of the submachine gun. Her eyes started to tear. That was all they wanted. They rested their weapons and we were dismissed with a contemptuous flick of a hand. They had made her cry. This was what Spanish fascism was about.

· · ·

This was a story. It was time to purge the last monsters of the 1930s. I contacted every city paper I could think of in the US and promised them stories on the final push to rid Europe of fascism. Many of them signed on.

The problem was that I had completely misread the Spanish. The Spanish Civil War left Spaniards with a deep horror of war that has endured. From 1936 to 1939, almost 4 percent of Spaniards died in the war and another 7.5 percent were wounded. An estimated 365,000 died, some estimates are higher. Franco executed about 100,000 prisoners and another 35,000 died in his prisons after the war. Shunned and boycotted by much of the world, no one expected him to last. Many didn't think the allies would let him continue.

By the time I started reporting on Spain, most Spaniards felt that after going this long there was nothing to do but wait for him to die. But there was one exception, that one exception to everything Spanish: the Basques.

One of the reasons the Spanish were so casual about just letting the dictator die was that he had no successor. His choice, Admiral Carrero Blanco, had been lifted several feet into the air when the Basques planted 165 pounds of electrically detonated dynamite under his Dodge. The popular Spanish joke was, "*Un bache mas, un cabrón menos,*" which is even better in English—"One more pothole, one less asshole."

The assassination had been carried out by a group calling themselves Euskadi Ta Askatasuna, which in the ancient Basque language means Basqueland and Freedom. In the 1970s, this group that had begun by preserving the Basque language that Franco had outlawed was now

turning to violence. They were winning the public relations war. World leaders protested the execution of suspected ETA members, but there was little protest about ETA killings. Much of Spain cheered the killing of Carrero Blanco and there was no international protest. The violence lasted long after Franco until Spaniards and Basques regretted having given their support. But at this time, they were the heroes of the moment. They had not only destroyed Franco's plans for a successor, but they had destroyed the myth that Franco's security forces were invincible.

• • •

Then, and perhaps even more today, if I am in Southwestern France and I cross the Adour River, which runs through Bayonne, I sense having left France and entered a different country. People look different, the architecture, food, and culture are different. Though there are some regional differences within the seven provinces of Basque country, I feel that I am still in this same Basque country even when I cross into Spain. Finally in the Rioja, crossing the Ebro, it seems that I have left and entered Spain.

The Basque language, Euskera, is the oldest language in Europe and unrelated to any other surviving language. This has led to a great deal of speculation on where the Basque come from, but most of this inquiry comes from the French and Spanish who don't want to recognize that they come from exactly where they are and their language and culture were there long before Latin languages, culture, and people. There are a number of cultures and languages in Spain, but the Basques is the only ones who are not Latin-based.

I spent a number of years visiting Basque country without hearing the language. I wondered what it sounded like. That is because Franco outlawed it and a Basque could be arrested for speaking it. Franco understood that the language was the root of Basque identity. When Victor Hugo visited in 1843 he wrote, "the Basque language is a country, almost a religion." Under Franco, some spoke it at home, but they hesitated to teach their children fearing it would get them in trouble. Many households spoke it at home but spoke French and Spanish on the streets. On the French side, it became a secret code for Basques only. Basques could

plot in France and outsiders could not understand them.

When Hemingway first started going to Basque Country in the 1920s, he must have been hearing a lot of Basque, but he never mentions it. When Hemingway first went to Basque country there was a resurgence of Basque culture. The language was increasingly in use and Basque music was flourishing with huge traditional Basque choral societies in the cities, including Pamplona. A series of civil wars in the nineteenth century had resulted in an elimination of Basque rights. Before these wars, known as the Carlist Wars, the Basques for centuries had their own government and legal system They were outside of the Spanish customs zone, which gave them a huge advantage importing American products to Europe. It is why the Spanish, unlike other Europeans, ate corn, bean, chili peppers, and turkey, all known in Spain as Basque food. Starting with the voyages of Columbus and Magellan, the Basques always played a key role in the exploration and exploitation of the Americas.

At the end of the nineteenth century, a growing movement was demanding the return of Basque rights. A radical Basque Nationalist, Sabino Arana, invented a Basque flag and a name for the Basque nation, *Euskadi,* both of which are still in use today.

None of this seemed to register with Hemingway. At least he never wrote about it. As far as can be told from reading Hemingway, Basques were peasants who wore big berets and drank from wine skins. "These Basques are swell people," Bill told Jake in *The Sun Also Rises,* and that was about as astute an observation on the Basques as we get. In *For Whom the Bell Tolls* Hemingway makes a considerable point about the local mountain guide in the Guadarrama mountains, Anselmo, speaking a different dialect of Castilian. He illustrates it by having him speak in weird, contorted English such as "Art thou a brute." But in Basque country where a completely distinct unrelated language is spoken, there is no mention of it. Hemingway loved to include words and phrases of other languages—French, Italian, Spanish, even Swahili and other East African languages. But nowhere in his writing is there one word of Euskera. This is striking because the language, not berets or wine skins, is central to Basque identity.

I have only found two references to Hemingway and the Basque

language. Both were by people who did not speak Basque. One observer in Cuba said that he sang to his cat in Spanish and Basque, and one observer in Idaho said that he once started joking in Spanish and Basque with a Sun Valley official who spoke neither. Both references were to singing. No Basque speaker ever said that he spoke Basque, and speaking their language makes a big impression on Basques. He apparently knew one or two songs.

Hemingway's Basque country, and really Hemingway's Spain, has so little to do with the places and people I know that I would like to say Hemingway had no influence on me there. The problem is that while Hemingway's Spain was a product of his impressive imagination, he did it so well and wrote about it so powerfully that you cannot help but be influenced. It is as though you are looking at a horse but someone with great craft has described a giraffe. Doesn't that neck keep getting longer?

• • •

What was clear to me in those last years of Franco was that the only story was in Basque Country. Virginia and I already had the habit of vacationing in Saint-Jean-de-Luz, where you could see some of those peeks into that dark, forbidden, unhappy dictatorship. Spain was a slightly dangerous and intriguing place, and you could never forget that the fascist dictatorship was just over the mountains. Going a few miles to Hendaye, we could pass ourselves from Gendarmes to Guardia Civil, from one odd hat to another, a slow process crossing the international bridge over the mouth of the Bidasoa. No trains could pass from France to Spain. The Spanish had learned their lesson from Napoleon and made their rails a different gauge so the French could not roll in. Across the border we liked to spend time in San Sebastián, possibly the world's most beautiful city—a Basque city where Franquistas liked to play. I hate to admit it but that was exactly what Hemingway did: Hendaye to San Sebastián, with a little time in each.

Yet, despite all the time I spent in Basque country, I did not know what the Basque language sounded like. In Saint-Jean-de-Luz, we used to stay in a charming rustic hotel furnished in bulky antique Basque oak

furniture called the Euskaldun. The hotel was run by an elderly woman and her aging daughter, both of whom were usually in the bar on the ground floor ready to recommend scenic walks or restaurants. Saint-Jean-de-Luz was the kind of tourist town that always looked as though nothing would ever happen there, but the port had a long history of just the opposite. In the nineteenth century when the Spanish pursued Sabino Arana, he fled to Saint-Jean-de-Luz. So did refugees from the Spanish Civil war. My hosts, operating from their hotel, had been leaders of the anti-Nazi Basque resistance. They smuggled British and American flyers into Spain, from where they could escape to Portugal and back to Britain.

And there was something going on in the hotel now, though I could not find out what it was. We would walk into the bar and hear our hosts and several rugged looking men annunciating the odd phonemes of a strange language. But as soon as we appeared the language became either French or Spanish. This was the first time, and for a few years, the only place I ever heard the Basque language.

Sometimes, across the border, a statue would be defaced or there might be a killing or a shoot-out with police or Guardia Civil. But I was not getting any inside line on these events. And no one else was even trying. Saint-Jean-de-Luz, Hendaye, San Sebastián, the hallucinogenically beautiful countryside in between—these were all places Hemingway had known well. But one of the many attributes that makes Basques different is they were not afflicted with Hemingwayphilia. They really didn't seem to care where he slept or ate. I have never heard his name mentioned in any of these places, except for a few people who said or wrote, when my Basque book came out, that it had the virtue of "being nothing like Hemingway." It does seem my odd fate that though they never talked about Hemingway, they did feel the need for the comparison when my book came out, even a favorable comparison.

The one exception was Pamplona, which is so completely linked to Hemingway that there is a statue of him (by the Plaza de Toros, of course). Pamplona is culturally somewhat Basque. South of the city is the most assimilated Basque region. It seems like Spain. North of Pamplona is a traditional Basque region with small towns of typical Navarese Basque stone houses, Basque food, Basque everything.

In Pamplona, the first week of July every year, there was a little town festival called the Fiesta of San Fermín. Originally the only thing that separated it from other Basque festivals was the presence of bulls and bullfighting. This is not Basque but Spanish. The bulls to be killed by matadors that day are released into a street that has been blocked off with wooden barriers so that there is no way for the wild and furious animals to go but down the street until it opens out in the bull rings. A few locals with some understanding of bulls would run through the street with them. Of course, Hemingway did this too.

I am not sure how many Hemingway fans from Europe and America have been killed over the years running with the bulls. A few stumble, there is a pile up, the bulls charge through horns first. Those who survive have the ultimate Hemingway credential, having run with the bulls in Pamplona. Having been gored might be even better assuming you survived.

In 1924, Hemingway wrote to his mother from northern Navarra after the festival, "It is a purely Spanish fiesta high up in the capital of Navarra and there are practically no foreigners although people come from all over Spain for it."

This statement reveals some important facts. First it confirms that non-Basques from other parts of Spain came for the bulls. It also confirms that the festival was radically changed by Hemingway from a Basque folk festival to an international Hemingway festival. The number of foreigners was high enough in the 1970s but today it is estimated that one million tourists come to, what is for them, the Hemingway festival in Pamplona.

I got a note from a reader telling me that he had been to San Fermín seventeen times and stays in the auberge that Hemingway stayed in on the Irati. Seventeen times. I don't know that Hemingway would have wanted to go seventeen times. Out Hemingway-ing Hemingway. I wanted to tell him that Navarra is a beautiful place, and he ought to forget about Hemingway and get to know it. But I suspect he would not have understood, so I said nothing.

The hotel rooms were all reserved years in advance, even in Franco times when tourists were reluctant to go to Spain. The bars that Hemingway wrote about, such as the Txoko, were most popular. Txoko, which just

means a cozy little joint, is about the most common bar name in Basque country, but it drifts off the tongue of every tourist in Pamplona who has read *The Sun Also Rises*. Most tourists and locals have read it. Those who haven't would probably say they had. Those who haven't read enough Hemingway are probably the ones gored on Calle Estafeta. Hemingway probably ran with the bulls without twelve drunken Englishmen falling in front of him.

If you wanted a place to sleep, you had to book in advance in one of the small towns outside of Pamplona that had bus service into town. Actually, Hemingway and Hadley had to do this one year too because they had not booked in advance. Many of the younger set just wandered the streets all night drinking, often out of wine skins. Local people did not use wine skins very much anymore, but they could sell them to the foreigners who read it in Hemingway.

This was clearly Hemingway's town now and in case there was any doubt, a few years earlier, in 1968, the mayor had commissioned a bronze likeness of the writer. How strange that in Franco's Spain a statue to a dedicated Republican was erected. But only the censored version of *For Whom the Bell Tolls* was available in Spanish, and they were more interested in *Fiesta,* the Spanish version of *The Sun Also Rises*. Franco was never very concerned with what was written in English. Not long before his death, *TIME* magazine did what I was trying to do and ran an unflattering cover story on Franco. It was available in any news kiosk in Madrid. Spaniards weren't going to buy it.

One night during the festival I found myself wandering the streets with two young Basques who insisted they were in ETA. They kept punctuating ETA with a guttural staccato that was supposed to sound like machine gun fire. It seemed unlikely that they were really members of this clandestine organization with whom I had failed to make any contact. But reporting teaches you to look behind every door because you never know where there is a real passageway. Just claiming to be ETA was an unusual, bold, and dangerous act. So I spent most of the night talking to them. The only atrocity that I could clearly pin to them is that they took *vino del año,* a first-year fresh Basque red wine, kind of a Basque *Beaujolais nouveau*, and drank it mixed with Coca-Cola. In Basque the

drink is called *Kalimotxo.*

Virginia and I also realized something important about bullfighting. It is a bit like Walt Whitman said about poetry: For it to be great there must be a great audience. The best bullfight we ever saw was in Zafra, an old Arab town in the tough southern region of Extremadura. The stadium was rugged and unadorned, and so were the beefy men with loud gurgling voices who filled the stadium. The bull is usually a reliable co-star. He is a wild animal that enters the ring with such speed, strength, and unabated fury that even in the stands you do not feel completely safe. He is like descriptions of the wild aurochsen from whom cattle were bred—large, furious, unrestrainable beasts that became extinct in the early seventeenth century. These furious descendants want something to hook their horns into—a man, a horse, a wooden wall, a shadow, anything. But it is the perfect performance by a matador that is hard to come by. In Zafra, they shouted approval or disproval for everything and got it—six perfectly played bulls. You could never see this in Pamplona, at the San Fermín festival anyway. The stadium was full of drunk or hungover foreigners who only knew what they had read in *Death in the Afternoon*, if they read it.

Once after the festival, we took a bus north to the beautiful red and white villages along the Irati. We had brought fly-fishing tackle and tried but could not figure out the right fly to use. Virginia caught a par, a beautifully speckled underaged three-inch trout. I caught nothing. We hiked into the Pyrenees toward France. On the way we were greeted in French by an affable Basque with a beret who looked about forty. With a smile, he said in French, "You are Americans. You have just come from the festival in Pamplona, and then you fished the Irati, and now you are hiking to France. Am I right?"

Of course, he was. He had read his Hemingway.

• • •

On October 1, 1975, I was told that Franco would appear in the Plaza de Oriente, an oval-shaped plaza with many small streets leading into it. A crowd gathered with a kind of energy that seemed to suck in everyone

The Importance of Not Being Ernest

from the surrounding streets, like water pulled into a drain. Over head a small plane was putt-putting, trailing a yellow and red banner that said *¡arriba españa!* And the crowd snapped their arms at forty-five-degree angles, repeatedly thrusting out the fascist salute while shouting "Franco! Franco! Franco!"

A wizened, shaky little figure, balding to almost hairlessness, gingerly stepped out on the balcony. Hitler would have looked like this too, had he lived this long. It was the portrait of Dorian Grey at last revealing all the sins, all the evil, on this decrepit face.

His voice was so weak that I could not hear what he said above the shouting. He acknowledged the crowd, and I am not sure if he said anything. I wanted to ask someone but everyone around me was so consumed with their straight arm zieg heil-like ecstasy, shouting "Franco, Franco," that I couldn't talk to anyone. With an aide's help he staggered back behind a curtain and was never seen again. At last Spain had ended its 1930s.

Finally, could have been a real news story. But I had no way of knowing that this was his last appearance. He still didn't die for another month and two thirds. It was just another piece of fascist color.

Just like Hemingway said always happens, Franco did finally die. He was only eighty-two and the dying process had taken so long, some were beginning to doubt it would happen.

Now my elusive but wonderful story wasn't mine anymore. Foreign press poured in. Of course, I too now had a lot more to write about. Things happening is always a better story than waiting for something to happen. All those fascists with stiff-arm salutes were still there while Spain strived for modern democracy. For the first time in thirty-six years, Spain once again became a goat fuck. Should I try to find the Florida?

Figures from the 1930s returned, leading to the impression that it was picking up from where it had left off thirty-six years before. Santiago Carrillo, accused of the worst Republican massacre, returned. During the siege of Madrid, soldiers and civilians, men, women, and children who had been taken prisoners by the Republicans, were massacred and dumped in a common grave. He always denied his responsibility. He had been a Stalinist and even met with Stalin. A staunch supporter of the Soviet Union, he changed after the Soviet invasion of Czechoslovakia in

1968. Now he returned to Spain forming, along with French and Italian communists, a movement called Eurocommunism that was independent of the Soviet Union.

Dolores Ibárruri, the legendary Basque communist whose oratorical skill had earned her the name *La Pasionaria,* returned from the Soviet Union at age eighty-two. In the siege of Madrid, she had famously issued the battle cry *"¡No pasaron!"* At her Madrid press conference she said, "I said they shall not pass, and they didn't," which is only true if you deny the past thirty-six years ever happened.

But there was also a younger generation of leaders emerging from the underground, most notably Felipe González, born after the civil war, in 1942. The young socialist labor leader had considerable charisma, especially competing in a rather geriatric field. He wore leather jackets and made speeches to workers from the backs of trucks.

• • •

There were many things to consider in this reborn country. Would the culture of the old Spain endure?

I decided to write about flamenco. The origin of flamenco is not known. The name suggests that it was brought by Flemish, but some have suggested the music has roots in the Rajasthan region of India. Many associate it with gypsies. The distinct vocals, guitar, and dancing were developed in southern Spain, principally Andalucía, as spontaneous improvisations in night sessions, like the old-time blues, usually in caves. In the 1920s it started to be commercialized, performed in a less raw style in fashionable Madrid cafés, but of course southern cities like Seville, Cadiz, and Granada were still known for it. Then even more commercialized, it appeared in concert halls. A few authentic flamenco performers were still working, such as *Terremoto de Jerez*, whose real name was Fernando Fernández Monje, an illiterate singer from Jerez de La Frontera, Andalucía. His records had some popularity and he even appeared in two films.

But now, in the post-Franco era, Spain had a young population eager to join the world. Spain, which had always been apart, was eager to

be European, and the land of bullfighting and flamenco was certain to become a land of soccer and rock-and-roll. Flamenco did not disappear, but it changed. Flamenco-rock took over with groups like the Gypsy Kings, which started in France with the children of Civil War refugees. This music became an international success at a time when Spain had few and this seemed to be where everyone wanted to go, except a few purists saddened by the destruction of a great tradition. Numerous flamenco rock groups emerged from Andalucía playing Flamenco guitar, classic guitar, electric guitar, bass, keyboard, and drums. Such groups, like Mezquita, became hugely popular in Spain and abroad. There may still be a few real flamenco artists jamming together in obscure corners of Andalucía, but the chances of finding them are about like the chances of finding an authentic blues jam in the American deep south. A pale, less raw imitation was popular with tourists in Madrid bars. I was sorry to see what had happened, but moving on and modernizing seemed like a very healthy thing for Spain at the time.

• • •

I still had that Hemingway idea that if you are covering Spain, you needed to do something about bullfighting. But I didn't know what. To be honest, I never liked Hemingway's writing about bullfighting. I didn't like his bullfighters. They all seemed to me to be narcissistic wealthy prima donnas. They did not seem to think or talk about anything but bullfighting and their Latifundista land holdings.

But there was another side to look at. On Sundays, the Plaza de Toros in Madrid sometimes had *novilleros* presenting young matadors with smaller bulls. I went to several before choosing mine. He was a young torero named Paco Villalta. Villalta is a famous name—Nicanor Villalta was a celebrated matador in the 1920s who continued into the 1950s. Hemingway named his first son, John Hadley Nicanor Hemingway, after him. I don't think Paco was any relation to Nicanor Villalta, at least he never mentioned it. He often talked of the accomplishments of his own older brother who was a matador *clasificado*. Paco had the grace of a ballet dancer and seemed longing to show his courage. I went down to the

bottom of the Plaza, found him and told him I was an American journalist and I wanted to write about him. This idea seemed well-received and he asked me to meet him the next day in the Plaza Mayor, Madrid's big central square.

I went the next day. By then the Madrid writers had already come out with praise for the debut of young Villalta. There he was settled under an arch with his cousin, Ramón. They had bullfight posters, which always feature three matadors. But on these the middle one was missing and for a small fee they had a manual printing kit and would place a tourists name in the spot for the second matador. It was a popular tourist item.

He was from La Mancha, which was like the Spanish Midwest. In a nation of subcultures—Basque, Catalan, Gallego, Andaluz—La Mancha was considered one of the most Spanish parts of Spain. His family ran a small bakery. He had a mean scar on one arm, which might have been thought to have been caused by a bull but was from when his arm was caught in a machine in the family bakery. Like a Midwesterner, Paco's hope was to get out of La Mancha, become a famous matador, and earn a great deal of money, or (he always dramatically tagged on the end of everything) to die.

This young matador, Paco, talked constantly of death. It was part of the bullfighting culture. His cousin Ramón, who had no matador ambitions and never wanted to face a bull, didn't talk of death. It is easy to see why this death cult appealed to Hemingway. In *Death in the Afternoon*, he wrote, "All stories if continued far enough end in death...if two people love each other there can be no happy end too." Or one of the forty-seven different endings he tried out for *A Farewell to Arms* was, "That is all there is to the story. Catherine died and you will die, and I will die and that is all I can promise you." Wisely he didn't go with that ending. Paco had never read Hemingway, but he talked like this. Ramón who did not plan to die young or become famous would joke to me that Paco was *un poco loco*.

As Paco faced more bulls, his name was sometimes on the posters, one of the two names. Ramón would point out to the tourist that this really was that same Paco Villalta, but they never believed him.

Most of his appearances were not in Madrid and he and the *ban-*

derilleros and picadors had to cram into an old small car, pack in the uniforms, and drive off to face death on the cheap in dusty little towns. From that money he had to pay everyone and buy and maintain all those bright and sparkling uniforms. The best money he made was on the posters. Spain was a poor country with few opportunities and bullfighting was his one chance.

· · ·

In the new Spain, exciting and full of hope, there were many things about which you could worry. There was no attempt to purge fascists. The people with the stiff-armed salutes weren't saluting anymore, but they were still there, and no one took down their iron crosses displayed in their offices. There was always a clear, though unstated threat that if the new government went too far, if there were punitive moves against the fascists who had committed outrageous human rights crimes, if they were too socialist, if they granted too much freedom to Basques and Catalans, the fascist could always rebel again and take it back.

It was Franco who had appointed the king, Juan Carlos. Juan Carlos was not in line for the throne. The Republic had unseated his grandfather, and his father would have been next in line, but Franco favored Juan Carlos, believing he would be more receptive to a Franquista approach to government. He had always been seen as a lightweight who enjoyed sports and would not make trouble. After the death of Franco, Spain was declared a constitutional monarchy with Juan Carlos, not a legitimate heir, as king.

The fascists did not seem ready to give up and there were constant threats of a coup d'état. I was still living in Paris but taking frequent reporting trips to Spain for a variety of newspapers. I remember that the *Miami Herald* would illustrate my articles with a postage stamp-sized photo of Franco as though they did not believe that he was really gone.

In the winter of 1981, I became convinced that a coup d'état was in the works but could not convince anyone to send me there. The European editor of *Newsweek* laughed and said I was another of these coup d'état theorists. "Why? Who else is?" I asked.

"Our Spanish correspondent."

When the coup came on February 23, it posed the threat that Spain could go back. The plotters, not surprisingly, were my old friends, the Guardia Civil, hats and all. A dissident faction of the Guardia Civil held the Spanish legislature, with 200 troops standing by to back them up. The legislature was held at gun point until the King talked the rebels down, becoming a national hero. But there were disturbing questions. The coup had been done in the King's name and it seemed clear that they believed they had his backing. Why did they believe that? Did he change his mind? In an interview with a German diplomat many years later, according to the London *Daily Telegraph*, Juan Carlos said that the coup was the fault of the government for failing to establish good relations with the military. If the Spanish wanted a democracy, they had to be careful not to upset the right wing.

The coup seemed to do the trick. "Forgetting the past" became an established principle, the left became extremely moderate, there was little sympathy for the aspirations of Basques and Catalans. The Socialists would not be too socialist. And the Communists wanted to join the European Community (later EU). The Spanish government would do nothing to upset the extreme right.

The Spanish constitution had features never before seen in Spanish law. For one thing, it declared Spanish, the language of Castile, the official language of Spain. Since the fifteenth century when Ferdinand of Aragon and Isabella of Castile united all the kingdoms and entities of Iberia (except Portugal), it had always been accepted that everyone had their own language. Now Spanish was for the first time the official language, declaring all the other languages second tier.

The constitution also made it illegal to organize a movement or even a referendum to separate from Spain. Such referendums were legally sanctioned in Czechoslovakia, Britain, even in Canada where dissident Québec represents a third of the country. But not in Spain. These were troubling signs for the future.

Another thing that troubled me was my last interview with Felipe González. I asked him a question about the Basques and suddenly the charm, the warmth, the smile was a mask that was removed, and I had

in front of me an angry man railing against Basques. I was surprised because I always thought this was a left or right issue and never expected this leftist to be anti-Basque. But Spain is more complicated. Felipe was from Andalucía, one of the poorest regions, and its workers found jobs in the factories of the Basque provinces, one of the richest areas in Spain. Felipe apparently did not have good feelings about Basques.

But the story seemed pretty much over. You could see where it was going. Spain would become a democracy, just another European country, and the Basques, no longer persecuted, would become assimilated Spaniards. Having summed everything up incorrectly, I left Spain.

Europe didn't seem to have any more good stories and Virginia was always up for leaving. To a lot of Americans, including some of the less experienced journalists who replaced me, being a European correspondent was exciting. But in truth, it was a job for someone at the end of the career who only wanted to live and eat well and occasionally go to a press conference.

We were off to Latin America, a region full of wars and economic collapse. We moved to Mexico City, passing through California, stopping in LA to see Hank who had also given up on Paris and moved to the Los Angeles port of San Pedro. It was like when we first talked to him about Spain in Paris. Hank had spent much time in Mexico. He gave us tips on favorite places and accompanied us as far as Tijuana where we caught a bus to Mexico City, a long and frightening trip through rough country. For the sendoff, we went to his favorite bar in Tijuana where his favorite waitress, Josefina, served up the drinks. As she was approaching with a tray of drinks, Virginia asked Hank what the best sight in Mexico was. Without hesitation he said, "Josefina bringing margaritas."

It was the last time we ever saw Hank.

• • •

After more than ten spectacular years covering a few wars, coups, aborted elections, hurricanes, and the rich, sad cultures of the Caribbean, I returned to Europe, no longer a journalist and no longer married.

I had been based in Mexico and then saw an opportunity to cover the

Caribbean for the *Chicago Tribune*, which was an expanding newspaper with extensive foreign bureaus and competitive coverage. It was a great paper to be with at the time and I journeyed from island to island, most especially Haiti, Dominican Republic, Cuba, Jamaica, and Trinidad, but also checking in regularly in the small islands. There were always moving stories from these intriguing cultures, nations with violent and sorrowful history. In ten years of doing this, I who love the beach and the ocean, only once managed a swim. In Haiti on a very hot day, exhausted from covering a week of violence and mayhem, I took my wallet and notebook from my pockets and plunged into the healing warm Caribbean.

My divorce had a lot to do with the fact that I was almost never home, which was Miami. Virginia, who loved being married to a writer, did not like being married to a reporter. It was a sad, not angry, split, and I had this thought that astounded me. In the middle of guilt and depression I caught myself thinking, *I don't want to be Hemingway.* Hemingway was married four times. There was never time between wives. He would find someone new and divorce and remarry. He once said that he had this bad habit of thinking that every time he met a woman he liked, he should marry her. There probably would have been a number five if he had lasted longer. He believed a new wife was a great stimulus for a new book. The books were what he cared about. Certainly, there were a few auditions for number five. This was not my model. I did not want to learn about marriage or relations with women from Hem.

But what was disturbing to me was that at such a deeply personal time, I found myself thinking of Hemingway. It made me realize that Hem had gotten into my mind, my way of thinking, far more than I ever realized or intended—too much time around his ghost. But by the chances of fate, that was not about to end.

• • •

That time had come to move on from newspapers. My first book, *A Continent of Islands*, was about the Caribbean. When you are a newspaper correspondent you have to be back in your hotel writing by five in the afternoon. This meant that most of the time you had to start the day on a

story you could finish the same day. This was possible because you were only given a limited number of words in which to tell it. Now, in my book I could explore the depth of all those things that I had been forced to pass over lightly. It was a great feeling. I am proud that this book, a little dated now, has remained that rare book that truly explores Caribbean society for general readers. A different kind of beach read.

My second book, *A Chosen Few*, was about European Jews who returned to their homes after World War II. It was a story that could be done then. Now there is almost no one left. I moved back to Paris and used it as a base for Amsterdam, Antwerp, Berlin, Dusseldorf, Prague, Budapest, and several Polish cities.

The space that had been the Les Halles Market now had a shopping mall and much of the city was moving in this direction. The French government, or perhaps the Parisian government, had started putting plaques up to mark Hemingway sites. It seemed that Hemingway was moving into a new phase in history, less real but more documented.

And I had to check and see how my friends, the Basques, were doing. I was astounded.

The Basque language was flourishing. Soon after Franco died I covered a Basque environmental movement opposing a proposed nuclear power plant and was surprised that some of these young environmentalists spoke Basque. Aside from the ETA slogan on walls "*Gora Euskadi,*" *Long live Basqueland*, the first phrase in Basque I ever understood was "*Nuklearrik? Ez eskerrik asko,*" *Nuclear? No Thank you.*

But now, in the 1980s, Euskera, the Basque language, had become the lingua franca. The new Basque government conducted its business in Euskera, The elected president, the Lehendakari, was required to be or become fluent in Euskera. Signs were bilingual. It was the language of school children, the language in the classrooms and the language heard in school yards. Bars and cafés were full of people speaking Basque. The old people who grew up before 1936 were speaking it, and it was the language of the people born after 1975. In small towns, people who only spoke it in their homes discovered that many of the people they knew also spoke it. A new Basque literature movement was flowering led by Bernardo Atxaga, a natural storyteller who became the first widely translated literary star

to write in Basque. There were Basque operas and Basque theater and Basque language television.

Underground music from the sixties and seventies was out in the open. There was a movement in Spain and Latin America called *Nueva Canción*. These were soft sweet ballads calling for social change, often influenced by the music of Joan Baez. In Cuba, Silvio Rodríguez and Pablo Milanés became international stars singing of the virtues of the Revolution. But in much of Latin America and in Franco's Spain, it was music of resistance, and the musician's life was at risk if he sung publicly. There were singers in Catalan and singers in Basque. The most famous in Basque was Benito Lertxundi, with such songs as *"Gure Bide Galduak,"* "Our Lost Path." Now the Basques had built a railroad to unite Euskadi from Hendaye to Bilboa and climbing through the green, soft, cloudy Basque mountains listening to the sweet voice of the once forbidden Lertxundi piped in, you could feel that you were in a revived Euskadi.

There were Basque languages newspapers. *Gara*, the Bilbao paper, commissioned me to write and illustrate a children's book in both Basque and English so that Basque children could begin learning English. There was a growing tendency to make English, rather than Spanish, their second language, though most people still spoke Spanish and French. I wrote *The Girl Who Swam To Euskadi,* the story of an American girl in Gloucester, Massachusetts, who swam too far with her kickboard and ended up in a strange land with a strange language, strange sports and food—everything different. She swam back home and was taken to nearby Harvard where it was established that no such place existed. The little girl insisted. My daughter, Talia, was my model for the watercolors of the little girl, and she knows very well that it exists because she has been going there regularly all her life.

At last, this was the great story I had been looking for during twenty years. I would write what I called *The Basque History of the World*, which is a kind of inside joke because the Basque tend to think they are the world, which is why there are Basques everywhere. If I give a talk, almost anywhere, it is unusual for there not to be at least one Basque who comes up to say hello.

Once I realized that Marian was my great love with whom I wanted to share the rest of my life, it was clear that to know me, she had to know Basque country. This meant not only towns like Saint-Jean-de-Luz, Hendaye, San Sebastián, and Bilbao, but all the steep and winding back roads I loved over the green, green mountains of Vizcaya, the little fishing ports where Basques had been landing tuna, squid and sardines through all of time, the sweet white and red villages of the Nivelle valley with the mountain slopes looking like green velvet. Spain had joined what was becoming the European Union and there was no more border The international bridge by Hendaye, where the Gendarmes and Guardia Civil stared you down, was completely unwatched and had become largely a truck rest stop.

Through the mountains you could slide from France to Spain, from the medieval center of Saint-Jean-Pied-de-Port where good fresh trout was served up into the sloping forested farmland of the Aldudes to a small village, Arnéguy, never quiet with its swift running river, capped with a church sitting low in front of the giant face of the Pyrenees. Off to the left is a steep dirt road that twists up a mountain to a farm that makes sheep cheese. All the Basque cheese is the same sheep cheese, but it is different depending on what the sheep eat. Also, some use the authentic black-faced Basque sheep and some use French sheep that are easier to get along with, but with less flavorful milk (or so the Basques say). The French use these supposedly mild sheep to make Roquefort, which is big and fierce tasting. In the high country, like this farm above Arnéguy, the cheese has a more pungent flavor though some prefer the milder cheese of the valleys. I had to take Marian to meet my favorite cheese makers.

Then down to Arnéguy and the road into the Pyrenees. This is the most famous Basque pass. In the eleventh century, the oldest known piece of French literature, "*La Chanson de Roland*," was set here. The poem is a sad and beautiful tale of the treacherous Muslims destroying Charlemagne's rear guard as the brave Roland struggled to take the soldiers through the pass at Roncevaux. The Muslims vowed to destroy the Christians in the pass:

J' irai me batter avec Roland á Roncevaux,
personne ne pourra le preserver de la mort.

"I will fight with Roland at Roncevaux, no one can spare him from death," vowed the treacherous Muslim. Of course, this was all a lie. Charlemagne had not been fighting the Muslims in Iberia for seven years as is stated at the end of the poem. It reminds me of a Hemingway war myth. Charlemagne was there for only a few months in 778, scoring some easy wins because a Muslim feuding with the Emir of Córdoba over control of the Ebro valley had arranged for these towns to fall. Charlemagne could then have triumphantly slipped through the pass at Roncevaux but on the way he decided to sack Pamplona. Furious, the Basques, not the Muslims, waited for them in the pine forest and when the French had marched into the steep narrow part of the pass attacked and destroyed the rear guard. It was the Basques, nothing to do with Muslims, but the poem was written at the time of the first crusade.

From the Arnéguy side, the higher you climb in the thick forest, the more breathtaking it is. You can see past the treetops to rocky purple peaks. At its highest, it is only a mile high, but the mountains are so rugged that it feels far higher, lost in the clouds, almost dizzying. And it was at this place with the rocky roofs above the forest that I asked Marian to marry me. What could she say at such a spot?

• • •

When I was writing my Basque book, I rented a house in Hendaye. The true Hemingwayphile would say that I did this because this is the town where Hemingway wrote *The Sun Also Rises*, as he said, "like a fever that roared through my head" after he left Pamplona. But in truth, I would have preferred the graceful city of San Sebastián with a bathing beach in the center of town and always sunnier than any place else, or a fishing town like Saint-Jean-de-Luz, or Bermeo, or the cozy little castle town of Hondarribia. But I happened to know someone with a good price on a house in Hendaye. The owner had moved out to a nearby place, but her dog wanted to stay with me. He was a big cuddly old black dog named

Beltza, which is Basque for Blackie. Beltza always stayed with me when I was home and waited for me on the stoop when I wasn't. It is a Basque cliché to always have a dog at your side.

There were two parts to Hendaye: the old town by the border where I lived and the beach resort down the road, which was where Hemingway always stayed. He said that he took a room in an inexpensive hotel on "the big, long lovely beach and I worked very well there." Ugly high rises had been built since Hemingway's time. If you drove a little farther you were in a real town, crowded with red-trimmed Basque buildings. This was the downtown part where I lived.

In the downtown part, Hemingway didn't come up. You could live there and never know there was a Hemingway connection. People had other things on their mind. There were a few dark bars and restaurants where simple and good Basque food was served, and Basque was usually spoken. There was a small shop only open in the winter season that sold nothing but the ever-diminishing catch of angulas from the nearby rivers. Spain, if there really was such a place, was in plain view out the windows of my house. From my window I saw Hondarribia, which was in Spain. There had always been people in Hendaye who were wanted in Spain. They no longer had to climb through the mountain trails that only the Basques knew. The border was not enforced, and you could just walk across the bridge into France. There was a lot of whispering in the bars, though, since they were speaking Basque, they really didn't need to whisper.

When I left Europe, I had imagined that when I next saw Basque country two things would be gone: ETA and the Guardia Civil. But when I came back they were both still there, feeding off of each other. Although the Basque Provinces now had their own police force, the Spanish still flooded the provinces with National Police and Guardia Civil, ostensibly looking for ETA assassins.

After Franco died many people, both Basque and Spanish, changed their mind about ETA. Most of their members left. There was no reason for the violence. ETA was labeled a "terrorist" organization, though it was mostly not true. Governments love to call their adversaries terrorists, though they themselves can kill thousands of civilians and never call

it terrorism. ETArists were in fact murderers, killing more than 800 people, mostly civilians. But very rarely did ETA commit random attacks to spread fear, which is the definition of terrorism. Instead they did targeted assassinations, mostly against Spaniards but sometimes against Basques. They had been taken over by a young generation with little or no experience with Franco who had adopted a pseudo Marxist/Maoist point of view that almost no one understood.

There were ever fewer ETA commandos. At the time I was writing my book, the Spanish estimated that there were only fifty ETA commandos left. Yet the Spanish were holding hundreds of Basques in prisons. Amnesty international wrote regular reports on the Spanish abuse of Basques. González, who remained President for fourteen years and could have been credited with building Spanish democracy, was tainted by the discovery that his government had financed a hit squad that operated mostly in French Basque country, kidnaping and killing ETA activists. They killed at least twenty-seven people and many of their victims had no clear tie to ETA.

Many of the people arrested as ETA members had unclear ties to ETA. They could be arrested for "apology for terrorism" or "insulting the King." So while most Basques disapproved of ETA, they could not side with the Spanish either. There was a writer I wanted to meet, Joseba Sarrionandia. He wrote a book called *Ni ez naiz hemengoa*, *I am not from here*. There were now more authors in the Basque language than there had ever been before in history. He was one of the more interesting. He wrote,

> In people's lives and in social history there is always a first mistake, a little mistake, which happens almost imperceptibly a momentary slip-up, but this first mistake creates others, and these mistakes follow each other accumulating little by little, one on top of another. Eventually this creates a growing and fateful error.

After more than a quarter century of writing about all this, I thought this was an interesting way of seeing things. Both the Spanish and the

Basques had made little first mistakes and built on them. But I couldn't meet with Sarrionandia. He was arrested in 1980 as an ETA member and sentenced to twenty-two years. I could not speak to him in prison because in 1985, ETA activist helped him to escape from prison inside a loudspeaker during a prison rock concert. Then he went to France. And then he disappeared.

• • •

I wanted to take the mountain drive into Gipuzkoa to the town of Tolosa, a traditional town famous for its bean dish. Also there was a restaurant that only served a special grilled Basque steak with grilled peppers. Peppers, beans, all these Basque foods that came from the Americas. It was rainy and I put on my txapel, the Basque wool beret that is the best rain hat ever invented. Americans tend to wear them either like a beatnik painter or tilted to the side like a British commando. During the civil war, Hemingway wore one tight and small, like a Castilian peasant. I wore mine like a Basque, big and puffy.

Apparently, I did it right because only a few miles out of San Sebastián we were pulled over by the Guardia Civil. They ordered me out of the car. Same patent-leather hats. One in front one behind. But when I showed my American passport they backed down and acted as though they were about to salute. Later, I told my friend Ramón Lebayen about the incident. Ramón, a member of the Basque National Party and former Mayor of San Sebastián said, "You see! Now you know what it is like to be Basque."

• • •

The Spanish tend to turn their back on their history, and so it does not go away. In 2018, the few ETA activists left disbanded. The tension is still there between the Spanish and the Basques. The first historian of the Basque people, Esteban de Garibay, told the Spanish crown *"Garean gareana legez,"* "Let us be what we are." The Basque often in a soft voice, sometimes angrily, are still saying that to the Spanish. Spanish often say

to me that the Basques have to learn to be Spanish. They can live with Spain, even admire its culture, but they don't want to be Spanish.

In 2017 and again 2019, the Catalonian government held referendums in which a majority of voters (although less than 50 percent voted) voted for independence. The Spanish governments response was to arrest the organizers and sentence nine of them to prison terms for sedition. This is why the issue never dies.

In 2007, the ruling Socialist Party passed the "Historical Memory Law." The law, for the first time since Franco's 1975 death, condemns the Franco regime and denounces its atrocities. It pays homage to its victims and grants citizenship to surviving members of the International Brigades. It bars political demonstrations at the "Valley of the Fallen," the huge monument to Franco and Francoism built by forced labor of political prisoners. Franco's body has been removed from the site. Perhaps Spain will face its history and move on. It has taken some time. Some Catalans and Basques say that it still has not gone far enough.

Euskadi has changed a great deal and so has Spain. Spain used to seem like a non-European continent. Nutrition was low and people were small, and I was more than a head taller than most everyone. Now they are my height and Madrid seems every bit like a European city. The Guardia Civil are popular in the Spanish-speaking parts of the country. They are sent on foreign missions, such as to Iraq to support America.

In Madrid, the Hotel Florida had been replaced by a department store, and an apartment building stands where the Gaylord used to be. But Hemingway is still remembered in Madrid, his spots often pointed out. It is often said that he was a regular at El Botín, but being the oldest, most classically Spanish, and most famous restaurant in Madrid, this is not surprising. Of course, the author was said to be a good friend of the chef, but Hemingway always befriended the key people. Hemingway plaques abound. One is on the Tryp Gran Via, which Hemingway regularly went to during the Civil War when it was the Hotel Gran Via, though he did not write kindly about it. One grumpy restaurateur near the center of town posted a sign, "*aquí nunca comió* Hemingway," "Hemingway never ate here!"

A friend with whom I had covered Haiti for years asked me a question

one day. We had covered ten years of coup d'état and murderous mayhem and profiled the brave and the treacherous. You could not be the same after covering all that. She asked, "Isn't Haiti the greatest story you have ever had?" But I had to say the truth. "No, Spain was."

CHAPTER FIVE

Cuba and the Unspeakable Feast

A collective tobacco farm in the Viñales,
Pinar del Rio, a province west of Havana, Cuba

"La Mar violeta añora el nacimiento de los dioses,
ya que nacer es aqui una fiesta innombrable,
un redouble de cortejos y tritons reinando."

—José Lezama Lima, *Noche insular: Jardines invisibles*

("The violet sea longs for the birth of Gods,
for to be born here is an unspeakable feast,
a drum roll of commanding retinues and tritons.")

—José Lezama Lima, *Insular Night: Invisible Gardens*

Even if you were not born in Cuba, its tropical embrace, its furious story, its rough-hewn grace, made it a place that, once you spent time there, would never leave you.

All that was true when Hemingway was there and when I was there too. But if the Paris I knew was not the one Hemingway knew, the differences in our Cubas were even greater. Hemingway knew Cuba for three decades, lived there for two, with more of his life spent in Cuba than anywhere else, half his adult life. While for me Cuba was an isolated forbidden fruit, Hemingway knew it almost as an extension of the US. It was easy to get to in his time; many Americans went, the stores were filled with American products, and the US government had a lot to say about what went on there. Americans that he knew and even ones that he didn't were continually dropping by. Cuba invented Caribbean tourism and dominated it until the revolution. Aside from Jamaica, a Caribbean vacation almost always meant a trip to Cuba. The truth is that Cuba never in its history had been a sovereign nation until Fidel Castro's revolution, shortly before Hemingway left. This was one of the reasons for the revolution.

He went there because it was part of a life he had created for himself on his cabin cruiser fishing the Gulf Stream. He fished Key West to the Bahamas and then down to Cuba. It is often called the Straits of Bahama or the Florida Straits. In time, he realized that Key West and Bimini, a

small Bahamian island, were the backwater, and the real capital of his fishing grounds was the great city of Havana—coarse and elegant, tough and crumbling—implausible grandeur parked right on the Gulf Stream. The Gulf Stream, which has a deeper-colored water, is clearly visible from downtown Havana, just beyond the harbor entrance. The stream, like a wide river in the sea, is a deep blue, clearly demarcated from more muted water around it. Sometimes it seemed purple, according to Hemingway, because of a rich presence of red plankton swimming in the blue. Giant fish lived in this deep purple stream.

Technically Hemingway didn't fish the Gulf Stream but something known as the Florida Current, but this was part of a more extensive system known as the Gulf Stream because it took the warm tropical water from the Gulf of Mexico, rushing it between Cuba and the Bahamas on one side and Florida on the other, up North America and across the Atlantic to Europe, which is why Europe is far warmer than North America. Cornwall, where it arrives in Europe, is the warmest part of the British Isles and has subtropical plants including a Cornish palm tree. Another current on the Eastern side rushes cooler water back down. It is a circular cooling system.

The Gulf Stream has long been known for its distinct blue, which makes it visible as a unique body of water. Spanish commerce and pirates used the fast current to move their ships quickly from Mexico to Cuba. It was also a swift way for whaling ships to get home to New England from the tropics. Benjamin Franklin was the first to chart its course. Although it is a current set in the ocean, it operates like a river with a northern direction defined as downstream.

The western or left bank is the continental shelf of North America, and the right or eastern bank, the Sargasso Sea, a mysterious center of the Atlantic where eels deposit eggs that drift into Basque rivers as young angulas so I, and lucky Basques, can eat them in garlic and olive oil. The Sargasso Sea has intense pressure in its center pushing water out to the edges. The edge is as much as six feet higher than the adjacent Gulf Stream so that the Gulf Stream is also demarcated on its eastern bank by a lower level.

Sea water is mostly clear, if you were to look at it in a clear vase. Nor

does the color of the seabed account for the water's hue. It is reflected light. The depth of water absorbs the light, with yellows going first because they are very low energy rays. The sea is green until a depth where it too is absorbed, and then it is blue. If light makes it to a blue bottom, it will reflect back up. And this is the strange thing. Such blue waters, rich-looking to us, are not nearly as productive in sea life as murky green waters or, even better, brownish yellow or, as James Joyce described Dublin waters in *Ulysses*, "snot green." Anyone shopping for local fish in Boston and then Miami sees that snot green water holds more fish than blue. When I first moved to Florida and the Caribbean, I was surprised to see that there was not nearly the variety of seafood I had been used to in New England.

But the Gulf Stream is an exception. It is so rich in marine life that some of the many bird species that hunt there either learn how to land on water or spend their life, sleep time included, in the air so that they don't have to waste time going back to land. A drifting, unanchored variety of brown algae, sargassum (sometimes locally called Gulf weed) becomes home to many small fish, eggs, crustaceans, and turtles—dozens of species in any stretch of seaweed. Several varieties of frogfish, some called Sargassum fish, can swallow fish that are larger than they are. Flying fish, sometimes a few at a time, sometimes huge silver fleets of them, skip fifteen feet above the water's surface. Larger fish including many tuna varieties, some swimming fifty miles per hour, and even larger marlin find sufficient food in the stream.

Hemingway not only learned a great deal about the giant fish he was chasing but his writings on the stream, particularly *Old Man and the Sea* and *Islands in the Stream*, reveal accurate studies of birds and other Stream life. In *The Old Man and the Sea*, he describes with sound biology how turtles feed on Portuguese man of wars, interesting because why would anyone want to eat a purple bubble with poisonous hairs below it?

If you enter the Stream from Havana or Cojimar where Hemingway eventually docked his boat, you catch a fast ride on a swift current as soon as you enter the blue, carrying you toward Florida or the Bahamas. But if you enter from the Bahamas or the Florida Keys, as Hem originally did, you are fighting the stream to Cuba. So Cuba is the better entry point.

His one-time close friend, John Dos Passos, brought Hemingway to this violet corner of the sea. With a different way of seeing than Hemingway, Dos Passos was a more cerebral nature lover than a dedicated sportsman. Each in their own way loved many of the same things. In 1924, Dos Passos hiked down the Keys, which would be a beautiful experience in itself. But he was particularly struck by the last island, Key West, and he wrote Hemingway. Hemingway was in Paris but when he finally had a chance to look, taking a ship from La Rochelle to Havana and then a ferry to Key West where Uncle Gus had a new Model A Ford waiting for them, he too was charmed by the little undeveloped island.

Hem and Pauline first saw Havana when his ship from La Rochelle skipped past the ancient Spanish castle that guards the harbor entrance, the Morro. The port was in the bay and there they got their ferry to Key West.

Key West, where he originally settled, was a quiet place where nothing had happened in the two decades since 1898 when it was a supply depot for the Spanish-American War. Hemingway settled with Pauline in 1930. The following year, Uncle Gus bought them a house. It was a gem of tropical grace with a wraparound porch, wrought-iron grills, and huge windows that could be shuttered from storms or offer a view of the sea.

There he could sail his almost-yacht and fish the Gulf Stream between there and Bimini and Cuba. Key West went completely broke in the depression, unable to take in enough taxes to run the town, and Roosevelt's New Deal took it over. This was one reason why Hemingway, a democrat-leaning lefty who believed in social programs, was never a great fan of FDR or the New Deal. It ruined Key West for him, though it saved it for many others.

One of the ways the government tried to build up the Key West economy was tourism. This was annoying to the Hemingways because he had become famous and the Hemingway house was on the tourist itinerary. According to an article he wrote for *Esquire* in 1925, a list of "48 things to see in Key West" had his home listed as #19.

Hemingway first became familiar with Cuba in the 1920s, fishing with a local adventurer named Joe Russel. Before he had his own boat, Joe brought him to Cuba for fishing. Joe also brought him into a

rum-smuggling enterprise that kept Joe's bar in Key West open through Prohibition. Hem claimed to also be a partner in Russell's gambling operation for which they had to regularly pay off the local police. Hemingway loved these kinds of stories so it is not certain how much of this is true. But it was the material for *To Have and Have Not* and the book makes it clear that at the time he knew the seamy side of Key West much better than he knew Cuba.

The bar was called the Silver Slipper and, according to legend, it was Hemingway who convinced Joe to rename it Sloppy Joe's after the bar they frequented in Havana. Hem met Martha Gellhorn in Key West when his marriage started to become shaky. Then there was the Spanish Civil War. It wasn't until after the war that he divorced Pauline and in 1940 moved to Cuba with Gellhorn and his cabin cruiser to start a new life fishing the same waters.

Hemingway, like almost all the Americans, arrived by ship, though the first Pan Am flight from Key West had landed only months before. The ships docked in the port which was in Habana Vieja. The first thing everyone did was walk through the old quartier and find a hotel. So most of the Americans, like Hemingway, stayed in Habana Vieja.

Habana Vieja, where the port was located, was the original walled city of Havana—Old Havana, settled in the sixteenth century. In earlier centuries, the city was under constant attacks from pirates and the British. By the mid nineteenth century, the safety of the wall was no longer needed and wealthy people started abandoning their inner-city mansions for large homes beyond the walls. In 1863 they began tearing down the wall. Only a token remnant of it remains.

Habana Vieja, where commercial ships landed and departed with sugar and other good, as well as tourist ships full of Americans, became the tourist center of the city, filled with bars, restaurants, shops, and hotels. Also prostitutes, famously offered in all colors and preferences. It is not known if Hemingway partook, but he did once say that the main attractions of Havana were "fishing and fucking."

The first time Hemingway stayed at the Ambos Mundos, the hotel on the corner of Calle Obispo and Mercedes in 1928, it was a three-year-old hotel, one of the new ones in the Habana Vieja neighborhood. A little bit

Art Deco, it was a fashionable place with a sprawling lobby, an interior fountain, a long, polished, and inviting bar, and a cage elevator to the four floors above. The hotel, like much of Havana, was packed with Americans.

He would eat at the hotel or at a restaurant called El Templete, where he could dine outdoors with a view of the ships leaving the port, or one of the better restaurants, La Zargozana opened in 1830 by the wall.

Or he went to El Pacifico, in nearby Chinatown. El Pacifico was on the top floor of a five-floor building. You rode an elevator up. According to son Gregory, the second floor had an orchestra, the third floor a whore-house where the women would wave at the elevator passengers as they rode up, and the fourth floor was a hazy opium den. Papa's favorite dish at El Pacifico was the shark fin soup, which he and many others claimed was an effective male aphrodisiac.

Another favorite restaurant was the Centro Vasco, the Basque center. The Catalans, Gallegos, and Andalusians all had their centers, but Papa dined with the Basque. It was a prime location on the ocean front where the Prado, the old elegant boulevard beyond the wall, met the sea front avenue, the Malecón. The bar customers sang Basque songs into the night and Hemingway may have picked up a song or two in Basque there.

There were constant attempts in Havana to assassinate President Gerardo Machado, a hero from the war of independence who was popular when he came to power in 1925 but became detested in 1928 when his term ended and he refused to step down. He responded to the opposition with extreme repression.

At the Ambos Mundo, Hemingway always requested room 511 on the fifth floor because it was a corner room with good breezes and a view over the rooftops to the harbor. Hemingway always had favorite hotels everywhere. In those hotels, he identified what he thought was the best room—the sprawling corner suite on the Grand Canal at the Gritti in Venice with his favorite pistachio velvet stuffed chair and venetian glass chandelier, the rare suite with a balcony at the Sun Valley Lodge. At the Ambos Mundos, it was nothing so grand. Room 511 was a small room with 172 square feet. He brought in an adjustable table that rose to standing height to write on. Hemingway loved being there alone writing. In later years with his elegant Finca Vigía home in the hills, he would

The Importance of Not Being Ernest

still insist that the Ambos Mundos was a great place for writing and even suggested that it had an advantage over the Finca in that people did not constantly drop by.

The Hotel also had location. Calle Obispo was named because it was where, in the eighteenth century, Bishop Pedro Morell de Santa Cruz used to like to take his walks. It was still a pleasant stroll for Hemingway. The streets were beginning to stop up with Americans in Model T Fords, though historic accounts show that it wasn't much better earlier when jammed with galloping horse-drawn carriages. In fact, the carriages may have been more dangerous.

He walked past all the elegant shops with American luxury products to his favorite bar, El Floridita. It is a long and narrow establishment with huge doors for breezes running along one side and big ceiling fans thumping rhythmically over the bar. On a busy night, the crowd bubbled out onto the street. It was always famous for daiquiris, which were originally rum, sugar, and lime juice, a drink from eastern Cuba where there is a town called Daiquiri. It is believed that the inventor—there are several candidates—was an American. At least it was an American who added ice. Ice was an American signature and was imported from America.

The Floridita, which opened in 1817, had a Catalan bartender who arrived in 1914, Constantino Ribalaigua Vert, who became owner in 1918 and who of course was friendly with Hemingway. Hem seemed to know all important bartenders. Constante, as he was known, is credited with inventing the frozen daiquiri, although iced drinks were already a trademark of Havana. In the nineteenth century, Havana and New Orleans popularized iced cocktails, the two great customers for ice shipped from New England.

The Floridita had been called *La Piña de Plata*, The Silver Pineapple, but after Independence when Havana became engulfed with Americans, the bar became an American hangout and they insisted on calling it El Florida, which became more affectionately known as el Floridita.

Constante's daiquiri with crushed ice also added maraschino cherry liqueur. Hemingway always had his without sugar, which seemed very odd to the locals in a country built on sugar. It is often supposed that he must have been diabetic. At the very end of his life he was, but there is no mention of it earlier and Hemingway loved to talk about his illnesses.

His brother Leicester said that he was diagnosed with it in Key West in 1928 and always ignored the diagnosis. In any event his blood sugar was high, and he was advised to avoid sugar. Or perhaps, inconceivable to Cubans, he just didn't like sugar. In a long 1951 letter to his publisher, Charles Scribner, he said that his doctor had informed him that he gets a great deal of sugar from alcohol and doesn't need any more. If it came down to it, he would rather have alcohol than sugar.

His father had been diabetic and, though deeply depressed about finances and suffering a profound paranoia, as Hemingway was at the end of his life, it was diabetes that drove the father to suicide. One foot became painful and, as a doctor, he concluded it was from the diabetes and would gangrene and have to be amputated; this conclusion led to him putting the pistol to his head. This could be reason enough for his son to avoid sugar.

Hemingway did not mind El Floridita being an American bar. He did not want to live in America, but he enjoyed opportunities to talk to Americans. In the 1950s, as it became known as the hangout of the famous author, it started to lose its rough edge and become more of an upscale bar and restaurant. You could end your hot Havana day with a frozen daiquiri. It was the ice and the rum and the fruity tang of lime. You didn't need sugar. And if you could afford it, and most Americans could, a lobster dinner was available in the adjacent dining room.

Hemingway inadvertently changed the Floridita just as he did Pamplona. The Floridita became the place where Americans could go to see Hemingway, even possibly meet him or have a drink with him. When he wasn't trying to write, Hemingway was very open to people, always interested in them and had a way of looking at someone in a conversation as though fascinated by every word, which most people found extremely seductive.

• • •

Gellhorn found Hemingway's fifth floor room too cramped and moved them to the Sevilla Biltmore. He kept his room in the Ambos Mundos for writing and changed his address to the Sevilla Baltimore. That way

it was known that he lived in the Biltmore, but he could hide and write in the Ambos Mundos without visitors. The Sevilla Biltmore was built in 1908 off the Prado. Built along the outside of the city wall, the Prado was the first paved street in Havana. With a Moorish style, it was the first fashionable street outside of the walled city.

Near the Sevilla Baltimore was Sloppy Joe's, where Hem also drank. José Abeal, a Spaniard, opened the bar when the US passed prohibition in 1920 and Havana became a place where Americans could go to drink. The Sloppy Joe's motto was "Where the wet begins." It had an exceedingly long bar, even longer than the Floridita, where the Americans could line up.

Gellhorn, for whom living well and dressing well were essential, found a farmhouse on fifteen acres of land with a swimming pool and tennis courts only about fifteen miles east of Havana.

Mango trees led up the driveway to a giant Ceiba tree in front of the house. This large variety, with an intricate pattern of roots at the base and branches above that create a thick green cover, is a sacred symbol in Yoruba religion and by extension a sacred symbol of Cuba where many Yoruba had been shipped as slaves. To the right, a path lined by tall straight royal palms, another symbol of Cuba, led to a large swimming pool.

When Hemingway went to look at the property, there was a group of boys trapping a wounded vulture and he made them leave the bird alone. He gave each of the boys a dollar and they all treated him as a hero, a fuss that seemed to embarrass him according to one of the boys, a ten-year-old named Rene Villarreal, who recalled, "Perhaps he didn't realize that this was extraordinary for us sons of strong, hard-working men who didn't earn a dollar for a good day's labor." When the man who spoke Spanish with an American accent realized they were all there playing baseball with makeshift bats, balls, and bases, he told them that he might move into the gated property and they could play there if they played with his two young sons. He bought them equipment, even uniforms, organizing the games known as "Gigi's All Stars" or *Las Estrellas de Gigi*, after his youngest son Gregory who was called Gigi. He established rules including a Coca-Cola for anyone who hit a homerun. Villarreal grew up to become the head butler, manager, or *majordomo*, of the Finca.

All of Hemingway's houses were acquired by his wives. Hem was happy in a small room with a good view.

Cuba suited Papa in his early middle age. There were not many rules in Cuba, and he did not like rules. A guayabera shirt was about as dressy as he ever had to be. It didn't even have to be pressed or clean, and this with rumpled and soiled shorts and sandals were his standard attire. He could tie up his boat in the nearby little port of Cojimar and fish the Gulf Stream whenever he wanted. Despite a dissipating lifestyle, hauling in thousand-pound fish could keep him in shape. He could go to Cojimar and spend his time with uneducated fishermen when he was in the mood enjoying afternoon drinks and sharing fishing stories, or he could go to the shooting club with the aristocracy.

In 1959 a reporter asked him why he liked living in Cuba and he said, "…I can live on top of a hill and be fifteen minutes from the Gulf Stream and have my own fruit and vegetables year-round and raise and fight game chickens without breaking the law…"

Hemingway befriended many Basque jai alai players. The same way he gained expertise in bullfighting, boxing, and guerilla warfare, he became an expert in jai alai with no particular background or training. When he was interested, he learned. He would drink with the players at the Floridita and discuss fine points of the game. Julian Ibarlucci and his brother Patxi were two of Hemingway's favorite jai alai players.

Basque history in Cuba went back to the early Spanish exploration. In the nineteenth century, independence leader José Martí had a number of close Basque associates in his struggle against Spanish rule. The independence movement was reaching its height in the late nineteenth century when the Basque Nationalist movement was also at a high point. The Basques saw the Cubans as brothers, struggling together for independence from Spain. Basque Nationalist leader Sabino Arano wrote a letter to President Theodore Roosevelt, praising him for helping Cuba gain its independence from Spain. The Spanish arrested the Basque leader and he died from an illness contracted in prison.

After Cuba gained its independence in 1898, there was a large immigration of Spaniards to Cuba, many of whom renounced their Spanish citizenship to become Cuban. In 1899 alone, 2,453 Spanish Basques

immigrated. Many were businessmen, but also farmers and tradesmen came and settled throughout the island. Also, during this time and into the twentieth century, there was a large immigration of professional jai alai players.

The sport became enormously popular in Havana and Cienfuegos. Of the many Basque sports played with the pelota ball, jai alai, which means in Basque "happy game," was never the dominant game in Basque country, But it became extremely popular in Latin America in the late nineteenth century when Melchor Guruceaga, a Buenos Aires Basque, invented a new basket that was much longer. Whipping the ball up this straw shoot with the added centrifugal force of the longer basket made it possible to shoot the ball out at far higher speeds. It became a much faster game. A major fronton, a stadium for jai alai, was built in Havana in 1898.

Cuba had actually failed to achieve independence and was now being run by the Americans instead of the Spaniards. The Americans would not approve of jai alai even though it was also beginning to catch on in some American cities. But then the American military governor, Leonard Wood, gave his approval and in 1901 the fronton was opened with a ceremony including the Americans, the Cuban officials, and a blessing from the bishop.

Much of the popularity of jai alai was from the rapid gambling. Bets were placed in hallowed balls and tossed down from the stands. There was constant betting throughout the game.

The sport became one of the celebrated activities of Havana, and top jai alai players became sports celebrities on par with leading baseball players. In 1921 Babe Ruth came to Havana and tried his hand at the sport. It was said that he was not very good, a bit like Michael Jordan playing baseball, but he could hurl the ball with frightening speed.

Hemingway had many other Basque friends because they were among the Republicans who had fled Spain. The Civil War had been the most formative experience of his life, and this was true of most people who had experienced it. Herbert Mathews wrote, "Today wherever in the world I meet a man or woman who fought for Spanish liberty, I meet a kindred soul."

Among Hemingway's close Basque friends was Andres Untzain from

the coastal Viscayan town of Mundaca. He was a Basque legend. During the war he joined a machine gun battalion that was said to have the most firepower of any outfit in the Basque army, fighting on the bitterly defended "Basque Front." According to unsubstantiated legend, he was in the Basque capital of Gernika when the Germans firebombed it and was one of the surviving witnesses that got the story out that shocked the world. A priest, after the war he settled into a parish near Havana. Hemingway who loved nicknames called him Dom Black, and he was a frequent dinner guest at the Finca. Mary described him as "a sweet, devout, and innocent Basque who was also devoted to wine and food." He was probably more complicated and less innocent than he appeared. Another guest was Juan Duñabieta, a sea captain who served the Republic and then captained commercial ships in the Caribbean. The Hemingways liked to call him Sinbad the sailor, which eventually became just Sinsky.

There is a Basque legend of a secret affair between Gellhorn and a Basque named Felix Areitio. It is perfectly possible, but such Basque legends are dangerously unreliable.

Another Basque, Paco Garay, with whom Hemingway used to dine during the siege of Madrid, worked in Cuban customs. Garay could fix any government red tape, whether transporting hunting rifles, visas for friends, whatever they needed. Call Paco.

• • •

Hemingway and Gellhorn were sitting in the beautiful island in the Gulf Stream but out of the mainstream, wondering what to do. Gellhorn was itching to travel. In 1941 she managed to get an assignment in China where there was an internal struggle with Chinese Communists while facing an invasion from Japan. She urged Hemingway to come with her. According to military intelligence historian Nicholas Reynolds, the Soviets, the NKVD, and US secretary of the Treasury Henry Morgenthau asked him to pass on information. It is not clear how much he passed on to either. It turned out to be a better trip for him than for Martha because bad food and seedy accommodations were dispiriting for her. But did not seem to trouble him.

As in Spain, good Communist ties gave him inside connections. Joris Ivens, the Dutch Communist with whom Hemingway had worked on the pro-Republican propaganda film, *The Spanish Earth*, had left Spain even before the Republican defeat to work with the Communist Party in China. Now he had contacts for his old writer friend and Hemingway became one of the first Western journalists to interview the then-shadowy leader of the Chinese communists, Zhou Enlai. Zhou went on to be the head of government in the communist People's Republic of China from its founding in 1949 until his death in 1976.

Back in beautiful Cuba in their tropically gardened estate, they were both restless but with different impulses pushing them. Martha was a journalist, longing to get to Europe where World War II, the biggest story of their lifetime, was exploding. Hemingway's urges were those of a political activist. He had never recovered from the fascist defeat of the Republic and he was looking for ways to resume his fight against fascism, now more important than ever.

Cuba was full of fascists, many but not all Spanish—wealthy, well-connected supporters of the regimes that the US was finally fighting. According to Gellhorn, there was a Cuban fascist organization with 770 Germans and 30,000 Spaniards. The source of these numbers is not clear. The US Embassy in Havana took note of the author's militant and aggressive antifascism. The US government was finally anti-fascist too.

Hemingway told them he wanted to establish a counterintelligence operation where he and his friends would report on what fascists were saying and doing. He organized his Basque priests and jai alai players and even some aristocratic Spanish loyalists into what was called "The Crook Factory." They had a budget that may have been as high as $5,000 a month and twenty-five full and part time informants. When they had something to report, they would sit with Hem in his comfortable living room and drink copious amounts of alcohol, while formulating a report. The ambassador liked getting these reports, but the FBI said they were useless. Hemingway was always outspoken about his dislike for the FBI, which he believed was pro-Franco, and they were not fond of him either. J. Edgar Hoover regarded the writer as an undependable amateur.

Hemingway only pursued the Crook Factory for a few months before

he settled on what he thought was a better idea, probably because it involved physical action. Cuba was not completely removed from the war. There were German submarines in the Caribbean. In the spring of 1942, about fifteen freighters out of Havana were sunk every month. His son Patrick told me that living with his mother in Key West he could see from the roof ships in flames that had been attacked by U-boats. Hemingway started seeing survivors at the Ambos Mundos reeking of dark fuel oil and glopped with molasses which was a principle Cuban cargo. Cuba was at the center of trade between North American and South American ports.

He would take the Pilar to war. Hemingway started referring to his cabin cruiser, too small to be a yacht, as a "ship." It did have some features that were good for this new project. Its low black hull made it difficult to spot; it was moderate in fuel consumption, which would allow longer voyages. It could accelerate in seconds, though its top speed, sixteen knots, was not impressive for military action. Its ability to navigate shallow water, needing only three-and-a-half feet of depth, a feature originally designed for tarpon fishing, would be helpful and it slept five comfortably.

"Operation Friendless," named after one of his cats, was born. At the time he had eleven along with five dogs. Operation Friendless shows two things. One: that in wartime irrational ideas are easily seized on, and two: as was often observed by those who knew Hemingway well, a part of Papa always remained a boy. He was boyish all his life.

The US Navy remained skeptical, but the operation was financed by the US Embassy in Havana. It had the backing of a military official, Lt. Col. John W Thomason Jr., a decorated World War I marine veteran who befriended Hemingway. They agreed to do an anthology of war writing together in 1942, *Men At War*; Hemingway's introduction is one of his strongest denunciations of war.

The German U-boat, 250 ft. long, was larger and faster than the Pilar and had a gun on its deck that could obliterate the Pilar and crew with a single shot from almost any range they could sight it.

But there was a plan. The Pilar would go out with rods and lines and appear to be fishing. They would pull up to the unsuspecting submarine and offer to sell fish. Then with a spray of small arms fire, Basque jai alai champions, who could throw with speed and precision, would pitch hand

grenades into the submarine's hatch and blow up the ship.

Surprise was essential and only a very few people knew of this operation. I am not sure what the odds would be of the attack plan ever working but, in any event, they cruised from summer of 1942 into 1943 and only saw one submarine that quickly submerged out of sight.

. . .

It was beginning to look like the only way to be part of the anti-fascist struggle was to go to Europe. He got accredited as a war correspondent, flew to England, flew some missions with the RAF, and met an American war correspondent for *TIME* named Mary Welsh who gradually replaced his disintegrating marriage with fellow war correspondent, Martha Gellhorn.

In World War II as in the Spanish Civil War, he blurred the line between correspondent and combatant. He carried a weapon and possibly used it, he led soldiers and made strategic decisions, he participated in battles. He wrote little and filed few stories. But he told so many lies that it is not clear how much of this is true.

As the Allies were moving toward Paris, he met up with a group of irregulars, Communist underground fighters very similar to guerilla fighters he was with in Spain. He was a natural leader and they fell under the Hemingway spell. When Robert Capa ran across them, he said they were all imitating Hemingway's walk and way of speaking. Hem led them in what he claimed was the best route to Paris. Other correspondents started complaining about him. Had I been there, I would have been one of the complainers. News correspondents operate with the assumption that they are unarmed noncombatants and therefore should not be targeted. This doesn't always work, but it is the correspondent's first line of defense and backed up by international law. If there is an armed correspondent commanding troops and participating in the fighting, it puts the entire press corps at risk. They went to the military and Hemingway was questioned for possible expulsion. The charge was that he gathered a cache of weapons, commanded troops, and participated in the fighting to liberate Paris. Hemingway at various times made all of these claims. Photographs show

that he was carrying weapons and not wearing journalist insignias. But much of his fighting for the liberation seems like Hemingway exaggeration. For example, his famous story of "liberating" the Ritz Hotel is probably not true. Witnesses said that there were no Germans there when he arrived. He denied everything at his hearing, which pained him because he wanted to brag and tell stories. He said that he took off the jacket with his journalist insignia because he was hot. He advised the Resistance unit but did not command them and they only called him captain as a term of endearment. He was just storing weapons as a favor to the Underground. He only went out on missions to gather material to write.

No one ever could sort fact from fiction with Hemingway, and he slipped free of the charges and went on to fight illegally with an infantry division under Col Charles T. "Buck" Lanham in tough combat through Belgium and across Germany. Lanham became a lifelong friend. How much Hemingway participated in the combat depends on what you want to believe.

Before the end of the war, Hemingway became ill and exhausted. In March 1945, he managed to return to Cuba, showing his famous wide smile. No one had a bigger one. Patrick, who greeted him when he first came back, told me that he seemed tired, happy to be back, and his usual self except that, "He was pretty patriotic." He returned to Cuba with fantastic stories of all "the krauts" he had killed. But the claims seemed dubious. Villarreal said that he looked fit and "clearly happy to be home." But he wrote frequent letters complaining of depression, which he called "the black ass." He wrote regularly to Buck Lanham telling him how much he missed him and that he was "absolutely homesick for the regiment." He wrote him about how combat was the definitive experience. "It is wicked to say," he wrote Lanham, "But that is the thing I love best."

Oddly in 1947, the US Army, in a ceremony in Havana, awarded Hemingway the Bronze Star for his role in the liberation of Paris. Even Hemingway thought this was strange. There is a photo of him receiving the medal and looking very uncomfortable. Why were they now honoring him for that of which they once accused him? He thought he deserved a higher medal, the Distinguished Service Cross, and was disappointed in the Bronze Star.

He took to referring to himself as an old soldier, though he had never been a soldier, and presented himself as a veteran. When Spanish Civil War veterans talked to him about plans for a ten-year anniversary, they were frustrated that he kept insisting on talking about his World War II exploits instead.

He never wrote well about World War II, though the experience stayed with him and for years. He wore the thick army belt he claimed to have taken off a German soldier that said *Gott mit uns*—God with us—on the buckle; his only World War II novel is *Across River and into the Trees*. It is really a post-World War II novel.

Hemingway always claimed that he had to fall in love with someone to write a novel. He came back from World War II out of love with Marty and in love with Mary Welsh, the American correspondent he had met in Europe. But he didn't write a Mary novel.

He had also become infatuated with an eighteen-year-old Italian aristocrat named Adriana Ivancich. He showered her with attention, and she was flattered but was not going to have an affair with him. To Adriana's embarrassment, few missed the fact that his new novel was his Adriana fantasy in which he was a tough old warrior, an old soldier having an affair with a beautiful young Italian aristocrat, Renata. In reality he was neither a warrior nor Adriana's lover.

The novel about this fifty-something infantry colonel infatuated with an eighteen-year-old might have been a *Lolita* story. The old soldier is lecherous and ridiculous and tells the girl she is beautiful and he loves her every five minutes. At one point he describes a wine—"Its body was as full and as lovely as that of Renata." But in this story, the Lolita is completely receptive and does not tire of the old letch. And the author sees nothing wrong with this Humbert Humbert and asks the readers to believe this is a beautiful love story. In the novel's rare moment of realism Renata says, "But how would you like to be a nineteen-year-old in love with a man over fifty years old that you knew was going to die?" Hem made Renata a year older than Adriana who was only eighteen when Papa's passion began. The fact that the old colonel was going to die novelistically was the only way out.

When he finished the novel, he was convinced this was his greatest

work, but no one has ever agreed with this assessment. It is generally thought to be his worst.

As he grew more obsessed with Adriana, he became more abusive of Mary, and she decided to leave him. But for unknown reasons, she never did.

Even his worst novel was a bestseller. Adriana lived long after Papa and lived a sad life. Finally at fifty, she wrote her tell-all book, which did not have much to tell. It was titled *The White Tower* after the tower on the Finca that Papa turned over to her as an art studio (she was passionate about art and designed the cover for *Across the River and Into the Trees*). Mary had built the tower as a writing spot for him, but he seldom used it. Instead, Adriana remembered it as her place. At age fifty-three, in 1983, Adriana hanged herself.

• • •

Hemingway had taken to presenting himself like the Colonel, an old warrior frequently exaggerating or outright lying about his war experiences. But he was not a cold warrior. He believed the US needed to learn how to coexist in peace with the Soviet Union. He thought cold warriors, Winston Churchill in particular, were the great threat to world peace.

He settled down to write, getting up before daybreak and writing standing up. In his fifties, the Austrian schrapnel still in his leg was starting to hurt again. He wrote longhand by pencil with a clear deliberate script that looked like he was writing slowly. Eventually when the manuscript was ready, he switched to his typewriter for a more final version. Morning was his writing time. It took me many years to realize that dawn and not the middle of the night was the best time for writing. This is particularly true in New York because the middle of the night isn't quiet. He got up at six and walked very softly to not disturb anyone. He boasted that no one could hear him walking around in the morning because, like all good hunters, he had developed a silent step.

Morning in Cuba, in the Caribbean in general, is the one time of day never to be missed. The night is black and electric lighting is never certain, haunted by invisible sounds such as plaintive groans from tree

frogs that can never be seen. It is a desolate feeling, the long Caribbean night. The Barbados poet Edward Kamau Brathwaite wrote:

> A man may have marched with armies
> He may have crossed the Jordan and the red sea
> He may have stoned down the walls of Jericho
> here where the frogs creak where there is only the croak
> of starlight
> he is reduced
> he is reduced
> he is reduced...

Hemingway may be the world's greatest writer, but here in the tree frog night, he is reduced. He never slept well, and the frogs probably woke him. But finally, the morning would come, soft pastel light looking fairy-like in a hard world of true colors. The flowers that fold up at night unfurl and displayed their voluptuous organs to be pollinated by tiny iridescent hummingbirds—so beautiful you would have thought they were too vain to work this hard. It was this shameless opening that made the offering of a hibiscus to a woman in Caribbean culture a sexual proposition.

Hemingway would get up and look out his window at the tropical hilltops. He would start writing to quails cooing about the coming sunrise and then with the first blushing sideways rays of sunlight, tropical birds would begin singing and then came the Caribbean morning—roosters shouting for no reason and goats softly bleating and the smell of small charcoal fires coming in the window where he was standing. A dog or cat or two would keep the writer company, stretched out on the cool tile floor. They all loved him and there was some competition for who got the best morning spots in the bedroom.

The perfect morning was only about six hours long, until the light became so bright it hurt to see and the birdsong was replaced by buzzing insects and the whole world was broiling in wilting heat, daring everything to survive.

The bedroom was a large room, the white walls and yellow tile floor brightened by the first sunlight of the morning. His stand-up desk was

chest high in an alcove with chairs on each side and the top was cluttered with papers and books and five or six sharpened wooden pencils. He wore big floppy moccasins and stood on the pelt of what once was a kudu. There were dead animals all over the house, on the floors, the walls, draped over furniture. I suppose he could feel that he was still on safari. His father had been an amateur taxidermist and he had grown up with mounted dead animals on the walls. With a remarkable list of things at which he exceled, no one would say Hemingway had great taste in clothes or décor.

He did have great taste in art and his collection included the early Miró he had splurged on as a gift for Hadley in Paris. He also had a Klee, two by Juan Gris, a Braque (although this was stolen at some point), and five Andre Massons. He was a genuine lover of Modernism. He particularly loved the Spanish work, Juan Gris's *Guitar Player*, that hung over his bed and the Miró. Hadley logically took the Miró when they separated, but a few years later he asked to borrow it for five years and then never returned it.

And there were piles of books because he was a hungry reader. He read about three books a week and remembered everything. He read novels, history, art, music, politics, poetry, hunting, sports. George Plimpton said that the bedroom door was propped open with a huge volume on aircraft engines. Plimpton wrote "The room, however, for all the disorder sensed at first sight indicates on inspection an owner who is basically neat but cannot bear to throw anything away—especially if sentimental value is attached." And that was Hemingway, a notorious pack rat for which historians are grateful. It was not only physical things that he kept but every sight, thought, and experience was tucked away in an incredible memory. You never knew when you might be able to use something later. He rarely took notes but filed everything in his mind. "Just push the recall button and there it is," he once told Hotchner. This is a practice that, as any journalist with a good memory will tell you, can lead to slip-ups on details—the exact wording of a quotation for example. But accuracy was not one of his preoccupations.

Contrary to his popular image, Hem was usually a warm, gracious, and inviting man, full of charm and curiosity about strangers. By the late 1940s he was a well-known figure in Havana and wherever he went

people would wave to him. He usually waved back. Often, he knew these people but, with his bad eyesight, he could not recognize people from a distance. He waved back anyway. Although he hung a sign at the gate of the Finca: "No admission except by appointment," he was generally kind to gate crashers. A reporter for the *Toronto Star Weekly* magazine, Lloyd Lockhart, showed up uninvited in 1958 with the thin pretext that he wrote for Hemingway's old publication. Papa was quick to point out, "You've come to my house without permission. It's not right." But then he added, "but c'mon in," and asked if Lockhart wanted coffee or a drink. Lockhart found it hard to believe that Hem was only fifty-nine years old. "He looks twenty years older. Yet his huge brown eyes have glitter and when he grins—boom—he's a kid."

But he wasn't always *that Hemingway*. Patrick said to me, "I think he had a dark side. We all do. But that's not the type of personality he was. When you met him, you did not realize he had a dark side."

George Plimpton learned it early on. Despite his haughty mid-Atlantic accent that could give three syllables to his alma mater, Harvard (Where does that accent come from? He was raised in New York; Katherine Hepburn who also had it was raised ten minutes from me in Hartford), George was warm-hearted, enthusiastic, and good-natured. In 1958, he was in his late twenties and editor of the *Paris Review*; Hemingway invited him to the Finca and gave him the longest interview he ever did on the writing process.

But George told me that once when he was younger, he had the opportunity to go fishing with Hemingway off of Cuba. He struggled to contain himself the whole afternoon they were fishing.

He knew Papa famously did not like questions about writing; he said it was "fragile" and could break if you talked about it. The whole time they were fishing, George looked for an opening to talk about writing but couldn't find one.

But then they were carrying tackle back from the boat, the day was almost over, and he had to get in one question. "I've noticed," he casually began, "that whenever something is about to happen in your writing there is a description of birds. What is the significance of the birds?"

Papa turned to him, looking more massive than usual, threw the

tackle he was carrying to the ground and said, "I suppose you could do better!"

Young George was mortified.

But sometimes interviews could serve his purposes. He was pleased because in an interview with Robert Manning, Manning chose to include his plea to free his old friend Ezra. Here were the limits of anti-fascism. Pound was a fascist. He not only supported Italian Fascism but spent the war years in Italy broadcasting in their favor. He spewed vile Nazi propaganda, quoting from *Mein Kampf*, denouncing the "60 kikes who started this war." In 1945 he was arrested for treason. He was spared a treason conviction by the diagnosis that he was crazy. Pound was incarcerated in St. Elizabeth's Hospital, a psychiatric hospital in Washington, DC. He was either a traitor or mentally ill, and it was in Pound's interest for them to decide on the later. He languished there for twelve years while major writers came to see him. Most thought he wasn't crazy but hesitated to say so. Hemingway didn't visit, but he spoke up for him often, including when interviewed by *Life* magazine about winning the Nobel Prize, "This would be a good year to release poets," he said. In 1958 Pound was released. Hemingway sent him a check for $1,500 to help in his return to Italy where he lived a quiet life, writing poetry until he died at age eighty-seven in 1972. After his death it was found that rather than cash the check, he had it encased in lucite as a memento.

$$\bullet\ \bullet\ \bullet$$

Hemingway in his fifties was aging with unnatural speed. It almost seemed like he was in a hurry to get old. In 1950, depressed about the poor reception of *Across the River and Into the Trees*, he said to Mary, "I'm just a desperate old man."

That was how he felt even though Mary pointed out to him that he was not old. He was forty-nine.

He had always wanted to be older. During World War I, he wrote to one of his sisters with tremendous excitement that he was now "immensely older." He started calling himself Papa in his twenties, when he looked twenty years older than his actual age. His first marriage when

he was only twenty-two was to thirty-year-old Hadley.

Yet at the same time there was a part of him that always remained a boy.

In 1949, Mary had a tower built at the southwest corner of the house. It offered a splendid view over the tropical hilltops to Havana. Papa and oldest son Jack had a raucous time up there shooting buzzards. Jack did this to please Papa. He just wanted to fish.

Despite the ample desk, Hemingway did not like to write up there. He did not want to climb up there first thing in the morning, preferring to roll out of bed and go to work in his bedroom where his desk was about three feet from his bed.

He would write 400 words on a slow day, 800 on a better day, occasionally over 1,000. Then toward noon he would go to his large, tropically gardened pool and swim naked. Everyone swam naked at the Finca, as all Cubans now know. Hemingway grew up frequently swimming naked in the rivers and lakes of his Midwestern childhood. In his pool in Cuba, he would swim twenty laps, which he calculated to be a half mile.

Then drinking could begin. Watching expenses in 1957, Mary found that alcohol accounted for more than half the non-salary expenses of the Finca. He was a hard drinker for someone who grew up in a teetotaling household. By the time he got to Italy at seventeen, he was a serious drinker. But there are few accounts of his ever being drunk. Some have said that he was an alcoholic and his close friend and doctor José Luis Herrera frequently urged him to drink less, but can someone with the discipline to never touch a drop when writing be considered an alcoholic? It was true too. You cannot drink and write. If you drink you may feel very good about what you write, but the next day you will always be disappointed.

He had three cars for getting into town—a big red Chrysler with a white top, the yellow Plymouth convertible, nice for breezy cocktails on the way in, or a Buick station wagon. He was a noted celebrity around Havana, and people called him Papa or, if they wanted to be more respectful, Mr. Way. Cubans, like Hemingway, love nicknames.

• • •

He first started sketching out *The Old Man and the Sea* in 1936. Perhaps he was his most Cuban in Cojimar, that one story village along a bay where he kept his boat. The men were all fishermen working small skiffs with oars or a single sail. If he passed a fisherman coming home, he would give him a line and toe him in. If he had caught big fish, Gregorio, the first mate, would give a sign and the locals would help him take the big fish to the community scale, which hung from a wind-blown laurel and weigh it. Then everyone would go to the sprawling waterfront bar, La Terraza, where Papa would buy drinks and trade fishing stories with the locals.

But he really was doing more than chatting. He was gathering material—questioning them on every detail of their experiences. He became interested in the sad story of poor fishermen, how they caught the one they did, how they lost the other ones, the depth at which they fished and how the fish fought. He listened to the tale of Anselmo, the eldest of the fishermen, who had lost a prized marlin to sharks, not an unusual occurrence.

It is not certain how much of this was socializing and how much research, because he genuinely did enjoy talking to fishermen. It was originally material for *The Sea Book*, a part of a large trilogy on which he was working intermittingly, but a great deal ended up in *The Old Man and the Sea*.

The Old Man and the Sea is unique among Hemingway novels. It is the only one that is purely about Cuba. It is also the only one that is not about romantic love. Originally, he wrote it as an epilogue to the "sea trilogy" but it grew too long. It is really a novella, a long short story. He later talked about how he could have included more characters from the village and a more complicated plotline, but he felt that would be a kind of book that had already been done. He always wanted to "make it new."

In publishing, sometimes it is clear even before publication that all the stars are in alignment. It was clear when it ran in installments, in *Life* magazine. It won the 1953 Pulitzer Prize—at last Hem's first Pulitzer, even though the award said it was for a book reflecting on American life and there is no American in this book.

Just when everything seemed to be going better for Papa than it had in years, in his 1954 trip to Africa with Mary and eighty-seven pieces of luggage (they often traveled like that) after killing fifty-one animals, their small plane crashed. Then a second plane rescuing them also crashed. Hemingway never liked flying. "Got a feeling some plane's got my number on it," he would say. He was right. Surviving two plane crashes in the same trip is both incredibly good luck and incredibly bad. It caused a great deal of internal damage from which he would never completely recover.

The next year he won the Nobel Prize. The Nobel is for a body of work, not a specific book, but it was his latest book that pushed it over. He did not go to Sweden to accept it, saying that his health was too poor. He was probably in considerable pain.

When he received the prize, he gave it to the shrine of the Virgen de la Caridad del Cobre in Santiago. Many Cubans believe this figure saved three fishermen at sea in a storm and brought them safely to shore. The Virgin is connected to the Yoruba religion from present day Nigeria, known in Cuba as Santería.

Many of the slaves brought to Cuba were Yoruba and it became the dominant Afro-Cuban culture. Their religion was banned by the government, fearing it was a tool for organizing Black Cubans (it was), so the Black practitioners hid it within the Catholic religion with Yoruba Gods being represented by Catholic saints. The Virgen de la Caridad del Cobre appears to be a manifestation of the Virgin Mary but its double-arched crown shows a connection to the Virgin of Regla who is connected to the Yoruba spirit Yemaya, a goddess of the Sea, which is why she would rescue fishermen. Like the Ceiba that Cubans visit at El Templete, this figure is also mixed with Cuban Nationalism. So Hemingway's tribute to her does not necessarily show an interest in Afro-Cuban religion; he may have just been showing his Cubanness. Many Cuban recipients of prestigious awards, Olympic medals, for example, deposit them at the shrine to the Virgin in Santiago.

How connected Hemingway was to Santería, and several other African religions practiced in Cuba, is an open question. Although some white Cubans take an interest, especially before the revolution, it primarily

belonged to Black culture and it is not certain how much connection Hemingway had to Afro-Cuban culture or for that matter to Cuban culture in general. With the exception of the fishermen in Cojimar and a few prominent Cubans such as Herrerra, his doctor, the writer's circle was very international. He was friendly with Bola de Nieve, a celebrated Black singer and piano player, but he too was associated with international culture and not a Cuban folk artist. He also had a relationship, no one seems exactly certain the nature of it, with Leopoldina Rodriguez, a racially mixed Cuban woman who appears in *Islands in the Stream*, and may have been involved in Santería. She is thought to have educated Hemingway in Afro-Cuban culture.

He was also friendly with Nicolás Guillén, the Black poet whose lines imitated the rhythms of traditional Afro-Cuban music. A dedicated leftist, Guillén knew Hemingway from the Spanish Civil War. The poet had introduced Hemingway to the Cuban Communist Party in Spain, and they continued their contacts in Cuba. But after Hemingway's death, Guillén told Norberto Fuentes that Papa spoke Spanish poorly and did not know Cuba well. Or perhaps it was just that he did not know Guillén's Cuba, poor black Cuba, well.

In any event, after his death, the Santeros of Guanabacoa, an East Havana neighborhood famous for its Yoruba practices, created a special drumming to honor the deceased Papa.

How Cuban was Hemingway? In Cuba, as in every place he lived, it seemed he wanted to know everyone. He had some Cuban friends; the Spanish Civil War was one of his main ties to Spain, so many of his friends in Cuba were Spanish; many were American although he did not always embrace the American expat community. He did not get along with his neighbor the next estate over, Frank Steinhart Jr. who owned Havana Electrical Car Company. Papa would deliberately irritate him with pranks like throwing firecrackers on to his property. Yes, he was a boy.

• • •

Although Fidel Castro and Ernest Hemingway never met until after the revolution in 1960, Cuba was too small an island for two such large per-

sonalities not to have intersected. In 1947 the young dissident lawyer Fidel Castro (Papa loved dissidents) was involved in a coup to overthrow the brutal dictatorship of Rafael Trujillo in the neighboring Dominican Republic. The plot was led by Juan Bosch: unlike Fidel, he was a small man, but an outspoken leftist leader, an intellectual and author of a number of artful short stories and novels—a political force with his own style of charisma. Castro and Bosch became lifelong friends. There were said to be 15,000 involved—an interesting mixture of Cubans, Spanish Republicans from the Civil War, American World War II veterans, and Dominican exiles. Paco Garay was one of a number of Hemingway's Cuban friends who were involved. Hemingway offered advice and may have given money to the cause. American intelligence, which deeply disliked Bosch (in 1965 they invaded the Dominican Republic to prevent Bosch from lawfully resuming power), tipped off Trujillo and the intervention failed.

In a letter to Buck Lanham, Hemingway wrote that he regretted not doing more. It is not clear to what extent Hemingway was involved, but when the plot failed, Papa went to Florida for a few days to avoid being questioned by the Cuban government.

When Castro was leading a guerilla army in the Sierra Maestro mountains, Hemingway's old friend from Spain, Herbert Mathews, accomplished a major journalistic coup by meeting up with Castro and interviewing him at a time he was rumored to be dead. Mathews talked to him for more than three hours and the Cuban came off as intelligent and sympathetic, well-educated and well-read, and clearly a leftist. This was Hemingway's kind of man, but, to this day, Castro haters are furious with Mathews. It is a bit like Lillian Ross's 1950 profile of Hemingway in *The New Yorker*. Many were angry and said she was seduced by the writer's charm and failed to get at all that was wrong about him. Others say she made him look ridiculous. He insisted on speaking a kind of pidgin English and when Ross quoted him that way, she appeared to be mocking him or displaying something she should have been quiet about. But actually, Hemingway had been using this strangely curtailed, non-grammatical speech occasionally since the 1940s. On the other hand, punctuating every other sentence with the pronouncement to no one in particular "How do you like it now, gentlemen?" was new and odd

behavior. But that is what he did.

Even some of Hemingway's friends such as Hotchner thought it was harmful to Hemingway. There is a lot of argument over what Hemingway thought of it. He said he was fine with it. But did he really mean it? Ross argued that all she did was to spend time with him and record what it was like without any judgments. It came to be known as "the fly on the wall technique." Refusing to judge is unpardonable to readers who have already made judgments.

Mathews simply reported what Castro said and did when he was with him, and he was a highly intelligent and engaging young man. There is an accusation that Castro had fighters periodically interrupt them, the same men in different clothes to create the illusion that he had more men than he had, because it was believed he did not have enough to win. Mathews is said to have fallen for this ruse, but it is a moot point since obviously, however many fighters, later Matthews wrote, "he had, they were enough." Anti-Castro Cubans were infuriated by an assessment that was clearly true. Fidel Castro, whatever else might be thought, was remarkable. "This was quite a man...educated, dedicated, fanatic, a man of ideals, of courage, and of remarkable qualities of leadership."

It is likely that Hemingway shared his *New York Times* friend's assessment of Castro. Mathews wrote, of his author friend, "I was glad to find that his ideas on Fidel Castro and the Cuban Revolution are the same as mine."

Another connection to Castro was Papa's personal physician and close friend José Luis Herrera Sotolongo, a small bespeckled man with a hidden ferocity. A Cuban, he had served as a doctor in the International Brigades where Hemingway first met him during the Civil War. The doctor spent two years in a Franquista prison afterward, and Cuban family connections secured his release. In university days Herrera and Castro had lived in the same building in the then-emerging Havana Neighborhood of Vedado. A longstanding active member of the Cuban Communist Party, Herrera may have been one of the first communists Castro ever knew. They remained close. Herrera was Papa's leading source on Castro and his movement during the Revolution.

In any event Hemingway had never liked the vicious dictator, Batista, and his dislike was cemented when his men came to the Finca, were told

to leave and, on their departure, beat to death one of his dogs. Hemingway later said he believed that his dog was in heaven and, if not, heaven wasn't a place he wanted to be.

Time for Idaho, Papa and Mary thought when the Revolution was gaining steam, and while they were there the army collapsed and Castro took power. To Hemingway, Cuba now had a chance to regain what had been lost in Spain. In one American interview he said, "This is a real revolution. Something like we hoped for in Spain." He wrote, in near Marxist rhetoric, "I believe in the historical necessity for the Cuban Revolution, and I believe in its long range aims."

• • •

To Cubans, the Nobel Prize confirmed that the entire world revered their hero. A bronze bust of his likeness was installed on the wall above his favorite bar stool at the Floridita. When he and Mary returned to Cuba from Idaho after the Revolution, he had become almost a folk hero in Cuba, a status that has never paled. He had won the Prize and he had defended the Revolution. Returning from Idaho March 29, 1959, a crowd was waiting for him at the airport including journalists and an entire busload of people from San Francisco de Paula, the Finca's village. He had always been popular in his town because he contributed generously to infrastructure projects, fiestas, whatever project needed money, and always sent flowers to funerals. The crowd presented him with a Cuban flag, and he kissed it to wild applause. The photographers missed it and asked him to do it again, but he refused. "*Soy escritor, no actor. Señores, he besado esta bandera con sinceridad,*" he said in his correct but very American syntaxed Spanish.

Back in Cuba he tried to follow everything that was happening, reading every newspaper, listening to radio several times each day, attentively listening to the hours of extemporaneous speaking by Fidel. It was exciting. Revolutions are. When it was announced that Castro was going to the US, Papa sent word through Herrera to Fidel that he was available for coaching on the kinds of questions he would be facing from American politicians and journalists. Fidel did not take up the offer but

did send one associate, a journalist named Euclides Vazquez Candela. Papa graciously invited him in, served him wine along with his thoughts on how best to handle the Americans. Then he asked him to pass on to Fidel his support for the revolution. They still had not met.

Finally, in May 1960 they met—over fishing. Hemingway helped to organize an annual billfish tournament every May since 1950. In 1960 the new Instituto Nacional de la Industria Turistica sponsored the contest. Castro, who had fished but had little experience with big game fishing, managed to catch the biggest fish. It seemed written somewhere that Fidel would always land the largest everything. Hemingway was surprised that he did so well despite it being apparent to him that Fidel had limited skills. But he was, like Hemingway, an autodidact that could just do things when he wanted to. Papa presented Fidel with the trophy. Fidel, of course, looking much younger, but also larger. Fidel sent Papa photos of the meeting and Papa signed one "in friendship" and, according to Castro's autobiography, he framed it and always kept it in his office. He was a fan. Fidel loved *For Whom the Bell Tolls* and told Hemingway it helped him to understand guerilla warfare. That was the kind of flattery that would get to Papa.

But relations between the US and the Castro regime were steadily worsening. Hemingway was friendly with the US Ambassador Philip W. Bonsal who was not unsympathetic to Hemingway's position. But the US wanted Hemingway to live somewhere else and denounce Fidel. Hemingway did not want to do either of those things.

The American split with Cuba may have been inevitable, although a different President might have handled it less clumsily than Eisenhower. The Cuban Revolution was intrinsically anti-American, an attempt to wrestle free of the American domination that had been repressing Cuba since the Americans seized their war of independence. That and not communism was the central issue.

Bonsal made clear to Hemingway that he could not continue to be both a loyal American and a loyal Cuban. He threatened the author about the consequences of being seen as disloyal. Son Patrick told me that Bonsal had told his father "You cannot stay in Cuba and consider yourself an American." Patrick also believed he had been told that there

will be an invasion and he should leave but that it would be all right to return afterward.

Patrick thought that this idea of his father as pro-Communist was a mischaracterization of a man who tended to reject all ideology. Patrick recalled, "He used to say, 'water closets of the world unite, you have nothing to lose but your chains.' I don't think he liked isms."

On July 25, 1960, when Papa, Mary, and Valerie boarded the Havana ferry for Key West, he had still not decided what to do. He had every intention of coming back. He left behind his home, his boat, his paintings, his cats, his dogs, over 7,500 books—everything he loved. He left Villarreal a letter that began:

> René, *mi querido hijo Cubano,*
> Papa is running out of gas. I don't even have the will to read
> which is what I love above everything and writing is even
> more difficult

Villarreal knew that Papa would never be back.

• • •

When the news reached Cojimar that Mr. Way was dead, first told it was by accident and then by suicide, many of the fishermen concluded the entire story was false. He had been reported dead before and had returned. Many were confident that he would be back. It was almost unimaginable that he wouldn't. At times it seems some are still waiting for his return.

If he had, it is not certain what kind of relationship with the Cuban government would have been possible. Che Guevara proved bloodthirsty, executing large numbers of people every day and becoming much like André Marty, the French communist in the Civil War who Hemingway ended up regarding as a madman. And his old life in Cuba would have been impossible. There was no fuel for the Pilar and even if there had been, the government had stopped local fishermen from fishing on the north coast and in the straits of Florida. It is not likely that they would have allowed an American, no matter how prestigious, to freely cruise

around in the straits looking for fish. Nor would the Americans have accepted it. Each would have suspected he was working for the other, and they both might have been right. Papa loved to share information.

Even jai alai was fading away and the players moving to Miami because the new government banned gambling. But shutting down gambling would not have been entirely negative for Papa. In the 1950s, Hemingway complained that the plans for hotel construction were going to turn Havana into Miami Beach. That very well might have happened, or Havana may have suffered the fate of San Juan, Puerto Rico, which has one preserved Vieja neighborhood against a wall of white concrete high rise hotels. But Havana was spared just in time by the Revolution that halted construction.

. . .

The government took over the Finca to be a national museum but treated Mary with the utmost courtesy. She could remove papers, artwork, whatever she wanted to take. Fidel offered to set aside the guest cottage for her when she wanted to come and encouraged her to return, which she never did. She took the artwork and papers and personal items but made a gift to Castro of Papa's .256 Mannlicher-Schoenauer, considered one of the best hunting rifles ever made. Fidel thanked her but said that he would rather keep it as part of the museum. He was very serious about this. She gave the Pilar to Gregorio, but he gave that to the museum as well. He probably could not have gotten fuel or permission to operate it.

Fidel personally came to the Finca and asked Villareal to stay on as director of the museum. He walked in and Villarreal stared, and Fidel smiled and asked, "Do you know who I am?" and he assured the Comandante that he did. But Fidel was not involved in the daily running of the museum and the party people who were in charge grew increasingly distrustful of Villarreal because he did not join the party or any political movement. Good government jobs went to people who did. The relationship grew increasingly hostile until Villareal announced he wanted to leave the country. The government made him work as a sugar cane cutter for two years before he and his family were allowed to leave. Villarreal

settled into a Cuban community in Union City, New Jersey. He went back to Cuba in 1979 but was not allowed to visit the Finca. Finally in 1983 he was allowed to visit his former home.

. . .

When I first arrive in Cuba in 1983, as when I first arrived in Spain, it was much like the country that Hemingway had just left. Almost nothing new had been built. If you could have arrived on a ferry from Key West as Hemingway used to, Havana would not have looked much different because the historic buildings of Habana Vieja have been refurbished with United Nations funding. But that is not how you arrive anymore. It was very different in my time. You flew in over orderly agriculture and landed behind the city. It takes some time to clear officialdom in the hot airport. They use beautiful Spaniels to sniff out narcotics and claim that they are very effective. It is much harder to resist petting these beautiful bird dogs than the usual shepherd. But you need to resist because, like most Cuban cops, sexy in skin-tight uniforms and flirting with each other, they look cuddly but really aren't. Then a taxi takes you on Mister Toad's Wild Ride through the crumbling backside of the city looking like a bombed-out ruin until arriving at the center.

The problem is shortages and priorities on how to spend. Revolutionary policy defied the old approach of putting the needs of the capital first. Stairways are unsafe and missing banisters, live electrical wires are strewn everywhere, and the damage from flooding as hurricanes hurled the ocean across the Malecon does not get repaired. Caribbean cities bear the scars of hurricanes but most of Havana, not just flood zones, seems a wreck. If Hemingway were to suddenly return, he would be shocked by the difference—except for his house, of course. But he might like it. He said Madrid looked better with war damage.

Just as when Hem last left, Cuba and the US were not speaking. The US was embargoing Cuba. The Cuban revolution was ongoing, an experimental society financed by the Soviet Union—a "continuing revolution" as the Communists said. They had rewritten marriage vows for women to have more rights and men to assume more housekeeping responsibilities.

They were reinventing everything, trying to change the society and create "the new man."

Industry was learning to replace all the things they used to buy from the Americans. They were making shoes and soap and their own replacement Coca-Cola, which was very cheap and free on holidays. With American industrial ice cream not allowed in, they were making better Cuban ice cream to the satisfaction of Fidel, who loved ice cream. These were interesting and exciting times in Cuba; I could be one of the few Americans there and Cubans love Americans. After all, Papa was an American.

I first thought about Cuba before I thought about Hemingway. In the early 1950s when my parents went there on a vacation, I thought I might like to go there someday too. I always dreamed of travel. Friends of my parents brought us a small black wooden carving from Haiti and I wanted to go there someday too. I am not sure what Cuba meant to me. For a few years I kept a diary, and the only news event I ever mentioned was on January 3, 1961. I simply stated that the US had severed diplomatic relations with Cuba. Clearly this meant something to me though I am not sure what.

Going to Cuba for the first time, Hemingway was far from my thoughts. I was thinking about the Revolution, the isolation of Cuba, and about the CIA. I was a correspondent in Mexico and the Cuban government invited a group of us on a press tour of Havana. While we were in the US embassy waiting for a briefing on another subject, probably drugs because that was all the US wanted to talk about in Mexico those days, a man we didn't know came into the room and started telling us it was illegal to go to Cuba. We assumed that he was CIA, but he was also wrong because as accredited news people we could go to Cuba. Now it was even more fun. We were going against the wishes of the US government.

We were all put up in the Havana Libre. The hotel had opened in 1958 as the Havana Hilton, which was the last hotel before the Revolution ended the hotel building spree. It is proof of Hemingway's, belief that were it not for the revolution Havana would have ended up looking like Miami. This hotel was thirty stories high and, though without any visual charm, boasted being visible from anywhere in the city. It had a large swimming pool, a casino, and 630 rooms.

It was freezing. After the revolution, with Soviet-subsidized oil,

all government buildings had excessive air conditioning. Once, while shivering in the office of a government official who was talking about an environmental program to reduce energy consumption, I suggested turning down the air-conditioning. The official seemed more shocked than offended. The idea that someone would actually *want* less air-conditioning may have been the strangest idea to hit Cuba since Hemingway first told a bartender "no sugar."

The Havana Libre was where the government liked to put journalists. They apparently thought it made Havana look good to have such a hotel, so perhaps the government had spared Havana not out of taste or principle but just from a lack of funding. While prostitution had been supposedly banned, there were women available in the lobby, though it seemed like a trap that any smart journalist might want to avoid. Each reporter was assigned a government official and they waited in the lobby. They were gracious and tried to make helpful suggestions. Cuban officials often had this combination of charm and toughness, like "good cop, bad cop" all rolled into one.

When you came downstairs, they were ready to go. If you made an appointment on the telephone they knew where we were going because they listened to all phone conversations. One afternoon I came downstairs just to wander around looking for a story. There were stories everywhere and everyone wanted to talk to you because they hadn't spoken with an American in years. Or if nothing else, it would feel good just to get out into the heat.

But my keeper said, "Want to go to the Hemingway house?"

I had not been thinking about Hemingway, but now the name *Finca Vigía* and much that I had read about with Virginia in Carlos Baker started coming back to me.

The Cubans always wanted foreigners to partake in their most unrevolutionary showcases. They pushed hard to get you to the girly show at the Tropicana, even though such clubs were the very symbol of what they had overthrown, offensive to their ideology, and they were operating the only one they allowed to continue. Another favorite venue was the Hemingway house, and it seemed odd that these revolutionaries were so proud of a wealthy American's mansion that he had operated with nine

servants. Why did they push this more than the original Havana home of José Martí, Cuba's founding father, father of independence and in many ways the author of the ideology of the Revolution? But Martí didn't have as nice a house to show—just a simple piece of colonial architecture in Habana Vieja that the revolution restored soon after coming to power.

There was also a revolutionary significance to Mr. Way. After he died, Dr. Herrera Sotolongo told the Cuban magazine *Cuba Internacional* that the CIA had provoked the writer's suicide because they could not accept him living in Revolutionary Cuba. This is a difficult thesis to support. It was clear that the US did not want Hemingway to remain in Cuba and who can be certain what the CIA would or would not do in those day. They tried to slip Castro a poisoned cigar and really did try to poison a milkshake. But the causes of Hem's suicide are well-documented. However, as Cuban writer César Leante pointed out, even if not true, at a time with constant CIA plots against them, this accusation says much about how revolutionary Cuba viewed Hemingway—their hero, standing up for the revolution against the US government.

My guide called over a car, a 1957 Chrysler, which by chance was the first car I ever owned, though it was then ten years old and not in as good a condition as this one at age twenty-six. After the revolution, when bourgeoisie wanted to leave the country, they first had to turn over their cars to the Cuban government with a certificate of good condition from a mechanic. This is why Cuba has so many large, late 1950s, American cars.

You can wander through the Martí house and most museums that were homes to the famous, but, unless by special invitation, you cannot enter Hemingway's house. It is a sacred shrine. A one-story home with large windows, most of the house can be seen peering through the windows. When you wander through Martí's house, it is clear that he is dead. But sneaking around looking into the windows of the Finca, it was easy to imagine Hem coming up to me with his famous bear walk and asking me what I was doing.

I always thought I might envy Hem his house outside Havana. But it did not seem like a place where I would have wanted to live. To be fair, he had an extraordinary collection of modernist art. Had it remained, the Hemingway house would have been an important art museum instead

of just a relic for Hemingway fans. But the art was gone and there were just bullfighting posters and dead animals everywhere. To me, the house looked like a cross between a Spanish restaurant for tourists and the Idaho Fish and Game office in Boise.

But it was the way Hem liked it. Everything else is kept the way he left it so that it looks like a house that is lived in. His last round of mail and newspapers is still on his bed where he used to toss them. This house is only one of a number of indications that Havana is not ready to accept that Papa is dead.

The Ambos Mundos hotel keeps his room reserved, in case he might want it back. The lobby has changed. The walls are covered with Hemingway photos. Oddly most are not from Cuba, and none are from the hotel. They even blew up his signature and framed it and hung it on the wall, as though Hemingway had signed the Ambos Mundos itself. The original somewhat scary cage elevator is still operated by a staff elevator man.

Room 511 is never rented. A guide is waiting and for two pesos gives you the tour of a small room with a single bed in an alcove. The view that he loved is not as good as it used to be because Batista, who, had he stayed, would have ruined the city, tore down an ancient low-lying stone monastery and built a steel and glass three-story building, one of the ugliest in Habana Vieja, to block the view a little. Hemingway's adjustable table that rose to standing height for writing is still there. The other furnishings are a revolving display of things from the Finca so that it looks like Papa is still staying there.

The message seems to work. I took the tour with an Italian tourist couple. After the guide relayed substantial information about his life in the hotel and in Havana, the couple asked, "Where is he now?" Gravely the guide gave the news that he had died, and the Italians seemed genuinely upset to learn the news.

The key to the illusion at the Finca was, as you are constantly told, that everything is exactly the way it was left. Not everything. The big Ceiba tree in the front, thought to be more than a century old, was chopped down because branches were damaging the roof and roots were upending floor tiles. Hemingway had loved this ancient tree and never allowed it to be trimmed or pruned, which may have been part of the problem.

Actually, his gardens were always wilder than today because he did not believe in any kind of pruning and thought it was interference with nature. Hemingway loved vegetables, both for salads and Chinese food, and a wide variety were cultivated on his property.

As Papa and Mary found out, it is not easy to maintain a large country house in the tropics. Rot is always setting in somewhere. Leaks appear with little warning. There are hurricanes and tropical storms to survive.

Except for the art collection and Mary's jewelry, silver, linens, glass, and other possessions, the house is much the way they left it, with clothing, shoes, 500 records (classical and jazz), and up to 9,000 books, which is more than anyone thought when Hemingway was living there. Some pages in the books have a handwritten note in the margin.

The swimming pool was filled and well-maintained. This was not one of those sweet turquoise family pools in a sunbelt house. This was a grand pool, deep and broad and long and wedged into a leafy tropical Eden of mango trees and bright bougainvillea and seductively drooping orchids, where he could swim a half mile every day and have a Tom Collins. It was this pool, not his house or fame or Nobel Prize, that I envied.

Rabbits' feet, shell casings, many small totems that he kept for good luck are still there. Hemingway was a great believer in such things. He also thought it was bad luck to work on a Sunday and good luck to have the number 13, which was part of all his license plate numbers.

I noticed, though few others would care, that there appeared to be nothing Basque in the house. Years later when I was allowed to climb the tower to the top floor office Mary built for him that he rarely used, I found a large, polished desk, the kind of cleared and shining desk that looks like no one uses it. There was an old typewriter and a view over treetops to the sea and to Havana. On the desk I saw a dark tooled leather blotter case with pockets for stationary, very finely made with a seal on the top that says "Euzkadi," the Basque nationalist word for Basque country, and then shows the seals of the seven Basque provinces. At the bottom "Ernest Hemingway" is tooled. Which Basque friend gave him this, I wondered. The curators knew nothing about it.

Except for the dead animals on the walls and floors—Fidel first looked at them and wondered about the possibilities of domestication of wild

animals for meat production—it looked like the home of someone who wished he was in Spain. Hemingway often said he was mainly in Cuba for the proximity to the Gulf Stream. Everywhere there were momentos of Spain and with the exception of a multivolume complete works of José Martí and a black and red bracelet found in a drawer, there was almost nothing of Cuba in the Finca. The bracelet is a symbol of Elegua in Santeria, the spirit who controls paths and roads. It was also the clandestine symbol of Castro's movement. But it is not known how one ended up in Hemingway's drawer.

I wonder if this lack of Cubanness at the Finca is a problem for the people who maintain it and insist that Hemingway loved Cuba and knew it really well. Author Edmundo Desnoes was the first and one of the few to criticize the Finca's lack of Cubanness. Desnoes wrote in his novel:

> While the guide [Villareal] at the Finca Vigía after Hemingway's death went into details of Papa's boring house habits, I stood staring at a bald mangy spot on the tiger's head and I thought that Cuba never meant a fucking thing to Hemingway. Boots to hunt in Africa, American furniture, Spanish photographs, books and magazines in English, bullfighting posters. Nowhere in the whole house was there anything Cuban, not even an Afro-Cuban witchcraft conversation piece or a painting. Nothing. Cuba for Hemingway was just a place where he could take refuge, live quietly with his wife, receive his friends, write in English, fish in the Gulf Stream. Cubans, we meant very little to him.

Desnoes was strongly criticized for this, but on several visits, I have also been struck by how little Cubanness is in this home. It appears to be the home of a wealthy American living in Spain. It is surprising to me that the many Cuban visitors don't seem to notice this lack of Cubanness. This is strong evidence that people only see what they want to see.

It is difficult to explain the importance attached to this place. Ada Rosa Alfonso Rosales, the director of the museum, told me, "Here in Cuba the word 'Hemingway' is magical. If I need anything from anyone,

I say I am the director of the Museo Hemingway, and as soon as I say 'Hemingway,' the door is open." It is a major stop for tourists, but locals go there as well. Habaneros bring their children. Cubans, like most Caribbeans, feel that their homeland is passed over and ignored and not treated with much importance. But this was the place chosen by the great Ernest Hemingway and that is a source of pride. Fidel Castro said that he felt grateful for the pleasure he had gotten from reading his books and many people feel that way. Fidel often quoted Hemingway or referred to him, as do many Cubans.

Edmundo Desnoes's *Inconsolable Memories*, a remarkably outspoken book published in 1965 about a Revolutionary who feels lost because all his family and friends have moved to Miami, was one of the first post-revolutionary Cuban novels. The lonely central character wants to show the accomplishments of the Revolution to his uneducated girlfriend. One of those achievements was the newly established museum at the Finca Vigía. His girlfriend was particularly impressed with the size of a pair of shoes Hemingway had left behind. Authoritatively, he explained to her that all Yanquiis had huge feet, even, he continued, "the attractive women." This was a popular Cuban myth. Americans were called *patones*, which meant big feet. A century before Spaniards were the *patones*. Today Americans are frequently called "Yumas" though no one is certain why. Is it connected to the 1957 Delmer Davies Western, *3:10 to Yuma*, that was popular at the time of the Revolution?

Popular Havana mystery writer Leonardo Padura said that he had "a fierce love/hate relationship for years" with the author he had never met. What writer but Hemingway could provoke a love/hate relationship with someone that he never met? According to Padura, there was much to admire, especially the writing. But it was all too much. He said the Finca Vigía was "a stage-set devised in life to commemorate death." Padura's 2005 murder mystery, *Adios Hemingway*, was about a body found buried at the Finca. The central clue was the fact—all Havana swears this is true—that Ava Gardner went swimming naked in Papa's pool. This is probably true since he and his guests usually did. In the Padura mystery, the pivotal piece of evidence is a pair of lace panties that the actress tossed aside before the dive and for some reason never recovered. That's real

The Importance of Not Being Ernest

Habanero Hemingway fiction. Habaneros can tell you all kinds of things about Hemingway that others don't know, that he didn't wear underwear, that he had a habit of farting loudly, a list of women, both amateur and professional, with whom he made love, and more. Maybe the location of Ava Gardner's panties.

The Finca Vigía became a required part of the upbringing of Havana children and for some it was too much. Novelist Abelio Estévez said that as a child he was taken to the Finca several times a year and it had a funereal feel.

Desnoes, a passionate revolutionary, disliked the role of Villarreal, the obsequious brown-skinned servant. In the film based on the novel, René is called "a slave" by the central character. Desnoes, in an essay described Villareal's rather pathetic pride when he assures "I was the only one who could go into the room while he was writing." Sadly, he would declare that sometimes Hemingway would even eat with him. Desnoes described how Hemingway had taken René as a boy and "molded his personality to his own and to the needs of the house." Desnoes, understandably, found all this contrary to the ideals of the Revolution, but Castro thought he was the ideal personality to run the museum—indeed life commemorating death. It was the revolutionary Ministry of Culture that found him unsuitable.

• • •

Even on my first visit to Cuba, when there were no tourists, it was clear that Hemingway places were important. After the revolution, the government supplied Cubans with housing, health care, schooling, and food but with virtually no disposable income. This was bad for bars and restaurants, and it was a struggle to find places to eat. There was a restaurant in Chinatown—not the El Pacifico—with no prostitutes or opium and pineapple in their food. The Chinese don't cook with pineapple and, from Hawaii to the Caribbean, pineapple cuisine is a warning.

Many restaurants, even ones that Hemingway frequented like Sloppy Joe's, La Zaragozana, and El Templete, closed. There were new restaurants for the many Eastern Europeans and Russians including

one Bulgarian and one Russian but these were not appealing to me or the other newspaper correspondents with whom I had traveled. The two most dependable restaurants were El Floridita and La Bodeguita del Medio. They really were the best places for dinner, although El Floridita was no longer popular. It had become a quiet place. The huge doorways were glassed in so that air-conditioning, the Cuban government's idea of luxury, could provide arctic temperatures. You could still get lobster, which was a luxury for foreigners caught on the southern coast and generally not available to Cubans anymore. Few people ate in the curved dining room, but if they did they were still served by waiters in tuxedos, another unrevolutionary trapping lovingly preserved by the Revolution in the State-run establishment.

And there were still the famous daiquiris to sip while shivering in the air-conditioning.

Hemingway, but nobody else, called his daiquiri. "The wild daiquiri." The Floridita was still making them, calling them Papa Double—lime, maraschino and rum over crushed ice, still popular because it was Hemingway's drink.

In those days you could still get Hemingway's drink served by Hemingway's bartender Antonio Meilan. He had time to chat because there were not many customers. He remembered Hemingway as "a kind and affectionate man." Few in Havana spoke badly of Papa. Antonio reverently pointed out the stool at the end of the bar where Papa used to sit. No one was supposed to sit there. It was reserved for Papa as though he might come back.

By the 1980s the lively meeting place of foreigners was the Bodeguita del Medio. This was the rare place for good traditional Cuban food, which is mostly pork. There were no tuxedos here; it was a more casual place, more in keeping with Revolutionary Havana, though it too was attracting mostly foreigners. It was founded in 1942 by Angel Martinez who claimed, not always believed, to have invented the mojito. This was the place for mojitos. Groups performed traditional boleros and other Havana music by the bar. Miraculously, live music remains a strong tradition in Havana bars and restaurants. On the bar, an assembly line of glasses were stuffed with fresh spearmint sprigs, ready to be made into mojitos.

The walls are covered with decades of greetings scribbled by famous and unknown customers. The Bodeguita claimed to also be a Hemingway place. There is also a framed message in what purports to be Hem's handwriting:

My mojito in La Bodeguita
My daiquiri in El Floridita.

This is probably a fraud. For one thing Hemingway always made the mistake of saying "La Floridita." There is no record of him ever meeting with anyone at the Bodeguita. When I first went there it had become a state-owned establishment, but founder Angel Martínez, nearly blind, was still the host. Martínez was an authentic Hemingway fan, capable of quoting whole passages from *The Old Man and the Sea*, the favorite Hemingway in Cuba because it was set here. But he told me "I think he only came here three or four times. He came here, had a mojito, had a photo taken and went to the Floridita to have more pictures taken."

I know that Hem was not an habitué of the Bodeguita because if he had been he would have taught them a sugarless mojito. I love mojitos, and in fact the Cuban diplomat in Mexico who brought us over nick-named me "Mojito" or actually "Culanqui Mojito" which is how you say Kurlansky in Habanero. Havana is the only place to get a good mojito. In Miami and other places, mojitos, for some reason, don't cut it. It might be that their mint is not true spearmint. But I like a mojito with a double shot of rum and less cane syrup. Havana bartenders are always happy to give the extra shot of rum, but they resist reducing the sugar. I would like all Havana cocktails a little less sweet, but it is a sugar cane culture and the bartender protests, "it wouldn't taste good." What I like about daiquiris is that thanks to Hemingway that is the one cocktail you can get without sugar.

· · ·

The Cuban government, understandably, was not generous with press visas for American journalists. But they did like to herd them in for their

events such as an anniversary speech by Fidel in the Plaza in which we could see the thousands cheering that had been bused in from the provinces (free cola for everyone!). But you would be very controlled during the events with little time to explore other more interesting subjects.

Once *Audubon* magazine asked me to do an article on a new species of bird that had been discovered in Cuba. The affable press attaché would not give me a visa though I applied over and over again. Finally he said, "The Pope is coming for a visit. Why don't you come for that?"

I had some experience covering the Pope. Not much happens and you are expected to go everywhere in the event that someone attempts an assassination. It happened once. Besides the Cubans would have us corralled and there would be little chance for the bird story which was on the other end of the island. So I declined.

"Doesn't *Audubon* want you to cover the Pope?" he asked with disappointment in his voice.

I answered. "Only if he has feathers and knows how to fly."

Now, at that moment the Cuban government was pushing the Pope, but a true Cuban Communist could always appreciate a good swipe at the church and he burst into laughter.

I learned that another way to go to Cuba was with programs for visiting scholars on subjects that were of interest to me. I learned a great deal about Afro-Cuban culture traveling with serious anthropologists. I would learn from their program but also be free to explore on my own. So I went with a group of doctors and once even with a group of Hemingway scholars from whom I learned that there was no aspect of Hemingway that someone wasn't researching.

The only problem I had with such trips was the time I traveled with doctors. Healthcare was the pride of the Revolution, offering the best medicine in the Caribbean. Patients from other islands, even Puerto Rico, would travel to Cuba for medical problems. But, with a few exceptions, this was a strange group of doctors. They never asked questions and became noticeably irritated when I posed a relevant one. At one point they all stood up and announced that they were there to express their solidarity with the Cuban Revolution. I am not sure how Hemingway or Mathews would have felt at that moment but I was uncomfortable. I

did not want to oppose or support the revolution but just to observe and learn about it. Later a nurse, who as often happens was one of the smarter people in the group, warned me that the doctors had decided that I was a CIA operative. I got away from these doctors as fast as I could.

I moved out of the Habana Libre with five days left on my visa. I moved into a small hotel in Vedado with cramped rooms but no lobby for officials to wait in. I spent my days interviewing musicians. At night, Cuban TV offered the political channel and the cultural one. The cultural one offered brilliant Cuban movies, films the quality of the best of French and Spanish cinema. I looked forward to them every night. It was that or the Bodeguita—maybe both. One night, I decided to be a journalist and listen to Fidel's speech on the other channel. Fidel always offered words without end. It was not nonsense. There were even good points, and almost every line was the kind of statement that a journalist could quote. But it was just too much too absorb and it lasted too long. Fidel could always outlast you.

There was a pounding on the door and a voice announcing, "Ministry of Interior."

Yikes, the cops. My first thought was to wonder how they knew that I had fallen asleep on the Comandante? I went to the door and a man wearing a face like the old time Guardia Civil handed me a piece of paper ordering me in harsh language to report to the ministry the next morning.

Assuming the phones were tapped, I called the Reuters correspondent, the only Western journalist with a permanent Havana Bureau, and told him what had happened. We agreed to meet for lunch after I left the ministry.

The next morning a Guardia Civil face stared at me across a desk, but the instant I showed proof I was leaving the next day, the good cop took over his face. He was the charming Habanero, shook my hand, and wished me a good trip.

• • •

Once, *Gourmet* magazine asked me to write something on Cuba and I told them that people were hungry, and it was a very bad time to write about food. Like a great magazine, they said write about whatever you want.

And so, I went to Cuba to write about baseball, seeing one or two games everyday, traveling all over the island. Players always play for their home-town teams, and the fans support them by riding in the back of trucks to wherever they are so there is always a fan base for both teams. One of the pleasures of Cuban baseball is that the fans have a deep understanding of every subtle aspect of the game. It is like seeing a bullfight in Zafra. If you want to continue analyzing the game, men meet the next morning in the Parque Central in Havana, a spot they call the *esquina caliente*, the hot corner, which is what third base is also called. Here they argue furiously about yesterday's games and then hug each other and go home. It is difficult to remember that when Cubans start shouting at each other they are not really angry.

• • •

After the collapse of the Soviet Union, Cuba was desperate with shortages of oil, food, cash, even medical supplies, which had come from the now defunct East Germany. For the first time since the Revolution, there was real hunger. And the Americans, rather than sending aid, thought this was a good time to tighten the embargo.

Now that the Revolution could not provide for everyone's needs. The rules started to change to allow people to earn money. Their homes could be converted to restaurants. Cuba began to once again welcome tourism. Foreign companies could invest in Cuba though with never more than a 49 percent interest in anything. The Spanish in particular started providing skill and money to restaurants in Havana, and some old Hemingway haunts began to reopen. The Templete became a restaurant for excellent Spanish seafood cuisine. The Zaragozana reopened, though without the elegance of earlier times. Sloppy Joe's reopened with an exact reproduction with the very long bar and the high tables and stools so that if Hemingway were to walk in, he would find that nothing had changed.

The Floridita was once again crowded with foreigners and served them daiquiris and Papa Dobles. The Floridita's refusal to let Hemingway die is one of the weirder examples. At his end of the bar, on his favorite stool, there he is, permanently, so no one can take his spot. Hemingway

The Importance of Not Being Ernest

is bronze and slightly larger than life-size, which may be how he appeared in real life. He is wearing the kind of stupid, gee-im-so-happy-to-be-here smile that I've never seen him wearing in any of his many photos. A beguiling four-piece Cuban combo plays and sings son at that end of the bar, and there are young people dancing and smoking (not smoking does not catch on in Cuba no matter what Fidel said about smoking being unhealthy). Young women are dancing around Hem shaking their hips, sensual in the way for which Cuban women are famous and completely ignoring Hemingway; he is leaning against the bar looking at them with his silly smile—not a completely unbelievable scene.

In addition to the life-sized Hem at the bar, there is the first bronze, the bust on the wall and numerous photos of him are hung in the corner. It is a shrine to Hemingway in the style of the shrines to African spirits in Cuban homes. If you were going to build a shrine to Papa, it would make sense to put it in a bar.

. . .

In Havana too I became a flaneur. The only way to love a city is to wander it on foot. Those who do not understand this are just not city people. Hemingway had been a walker when he lived at the Ambos Mundos, but the estate in the suburbs changed him. He had three cars with drivers to bring him to town. Often visitors from other climates do not want to wander the streets of Havana because it is too hot. Sometimes they choose to come in January and February when the temperature is much milder. I think that is a mistake. Stumbling over pitted pavement to the beat of son with the weight of tropical heat slowing you down, like walking underwater, is the ultimate Havana experience. It forms the Habanero character, a graceful but slow-moving open window, out on the street kind of city dweller. What is the point of iced daiquiris if you are not hot? And there is the great Havana ice cream tradition, if you can eat it before it melts. Fidel loved ice cream and soon after coming to power he entrusted one of his close revolutionary insiders, Celia Sanchez, to build a great ice cream parlor. A ballet fan, Sanchez named it after her favorite, Coppelia. The ice cream was excellent and came in twenty-six flavors. It

was a traditional rite on a hot Havana afternoon to go with friends and stand in line for two hours for perhaps a scoop of crême de vie or guava. Chatting in the heat with Habaneros in the Coppelia line for a couple of hours was the city at its best. Now they are down to about three flavors and, because a separate currency has been created for foreigners, the visitor is no longer in line with the locals.

Habana Vieja is a peninsula with water on three sides. Certain streets line up well for sea breezes and on other streets it is hard to breathe. This is true throughout the city. The Malecon, which faces the sea, always has a good breeze, sometimes ocean spray and even a few splashing waves. The cooler streets have more people. I could go out any day and find an interesting conversation, sometimes even the beginning of a good story.

From when I first went to Cuba, it has always surprised me that Cubans express no hostility toward Americans. The US government has been trying and sometimes succeeding in starving them. But Cubans distinguish between the US government and the people. In some cases, this is more than we deserve. But Americans were always part of Havana culture and they like talking to them. Something opens up when you say you are American. Cubans are surprisingly well-informed about US politics. And they will talk about that or about Cuban politics or baseball or most anything else. The Spanish poet Garcia Lorca called Habaneros "Hablaneros" from the Spanish verb hablar, to talk. Of course, Fidel was the ultimate hablanero.

Sometimes there would be a good kids' baseball game with a bottle cap for a ball. Cubans have been playing baseball as long as Americans and even young boys seem to have deep understanding of the game.

Havana apartments have large windows and are always open because there is no air conditioning. This means that walking through the streets, you hear many conversations. And music. Every home has music, usually live. The bars and restaurants all have live music also—guajiros, danzón, conga, charanga, pachanga, jazz, Afro-jazz, rock, hip-hop. Sometimes it is played on the street, a rock band or Afro-Cuban group playing son. Sometimes there is a lone *tresero*, someone playing a *tres*, which is a small Cuban guitar with six strings strung in three groups of two. The two are usually tuned an octave apart for playing son, the old Afro-Cuban form that still dominates Havana. You can learn a lot about music, wandering in Havana.

African religion is everywhere, seen in colored flags, colored beads, and the drumming that can be heard from the street. If you get invited to a ceremony, they are generally spectacular for their drumming, chanting, and the sight of believers drifting into trances as African deities possess them. I was once taken to a farm within Havana where goats, chickens, and other animals were raised for gruesome sacrifices.

Shopping in Cuba is not like other cities. There are a few of the usual hat and T-shirt stores. But there are many little dusty stores that never seem to have customers. You don't need customers in the socialist state. There is very little of interest in these stores, but I have found many of the fascinating books of Cuban anthropologist Fernando Ortiz, a signed photograph from the revolution by its most famous photographer, Raul Corrales, some nicely drafted drawings of Havana in pencil or ink, and my favorite, the ultimate Havana souvenir, a sculpture of a mosquito made from auto parts.

The problem was that Cuba was on a cash basis. Because of the embargo, they cannot take American checks or credit cards, so I wandered with a sizeable wad of American and Cuban money.

In American cities if a neighborhood looks run down and has bad lighting, it is probably dangerous. In Havana all neighborhoods are run down with poor lighting, and they are almost never dangerous. Still, it is hard not to think about this drifting around in the dark usually in the middle of the street. Guillermo Cabrera Infante in *Three Trapped Tigers*, the funniest novel about Havana, claimed that Cubans anywhere could be identified by their habit of walking down the middle of the street. It is the only space in Havana. There is little traffic, and the sidewalks are often too narrow to negotiate.

One night either a look on my face or my body language gave me away and a tall, thin, young habanero whom I had never met walked up to me and said, "Don't worry. You are safe in Havana. There are two million people and one million of them are police."

• • •

One thing that Hemingway's Cuba and my Cuba had in common was the

presence of many Basques. Once Cuba opened to foreign investment, the Basques once again were a visible presence with an expanded commercial tie between the Basque government, which rules three Spanish Basque provinces, and Cuba. I would meet Basque friends in Havana at small Basque restaurants serving Basque food.

I met Basques in Cuba who were taking lessons from Havana for their tourist operations in Basque Country. Promoting Hemingway, outside of Pamplona, was not in the Basque tradition. Now, after visiting Havana, a woman owning a bed and breakfast in the Vizcaya seafront town of Mundaka emphasized the Hemingway connections to her town. He had been there while working on *The Dangerous Summer* toward the end of his life. And Andres Untzain, Hemingway's priest friend in Havana, is buried there.

A Basque friend cryptically invited me to lunch with "someone I think you would like to meet." Although now having a different name, it was Joseba Sarrionaindia, the Basque writer and accused ETA militant who I could not interview when working on my Basque book because he had escaped from prison in a loudspeaker and his whereabouts were unknown. This was his whereabouts. He was married to a Cuban and had children here.

A number of things have been named Hemingway, not as many as Martí but quite a few for a foreigner. The Barloventto Yacht Club where the marlin tournament was held is now called Marina Hemingway and in the earlier days of the Revolution, when houses of ill-repute were closed and soliciting was not allowed on the streets, the one place with that reputation was the Marina Hemingway. Technically prostitution was illegal, but some knew where to look. Historians argue about whether Hemingway is an appropriate name for a red-light marina. It was on the north coast where boating was not allowed, so you had to have something to do in the marina.

A dam built for electric power near the Finca is called the Hemingway Dam. There were other even less apparent recipients of the author's name. A ceramic high voltage insulator is called a Hemingway, named by the workers because it was strong and could resist extremely high voltage.

• • •

Anyone can see the dam or the marina or, I suppose, the electric fixture. But if you want to do Hemingway tourism, you cannot wander into it, you have to arrange it with the government which seems to feel that they own Hemingway. Pass under the bay in the tunnel and drive past the huge housing projects from the '70s in east Havana, past the groves of flamboyant trees all aflame; you can see the color change from the blue coastal water to the dark Gulf Stream not far out. Arrive in a slightly hilly coastal town of nice sized old houses, houses probably there long before Hemingway, not mansions but spacious, with ample front terraces facing the sea.

The sea was dark and calm; it was a well-sheltered harbor, not the bright blue of the Caribbean but the dark brown of the Atlantic. There was an empty concrete dock where the Pilar used to tie up fish.

Cojimar is an important Hemingway site. In fact, at this point that is really all it is. There is little sign of fishing, fisherman, or fishing boats. I remembered a speech Fidel once gave in which he said that a by-product of a good educational system is that no one wanted to be a farmer or a fisherman anymore. Still, there must be some people who want to be fishermen. Every time I asked about the absence of fishing, people got very uncomfortable. The Hemingway Museum explained that the fleet had moved into the river and was no longer visible from the port. But the fishing grounds were nearby and there should have been boats moving toward it, even fishing, or coming back. This northern coast is the Florida coast where boats can go to the US, and so it has been shut down. Most of the people here seem elderly. But tourists could still visit Hemingway's village of Cojimar.

In 1970 Fidel Castro was upset to discover that La Terraza was run down and mainly served beer in paper cups, and he ordered it to be restored to its Hemingway menu, bar, and glassware. Sometimes it is just great to be a dictator.

Refurbished, La Terraza is not really changed from Papa's day except for the many photos on the wall, especially from the filming of *The Old Man and the Sea*, and since cinema is more real than reality, many of

these are not even taken in Cuba because the fishing sequences were shot off of Peru where larger fish were to be found.

The town of Cojimar looks a little roughed up, as do all Cuban towns, but the one pristine spot is a concrete platform with stairs leading up it, a ring of pillars and in the middle a five foot stone block with a cheesy looking green bronze bust of Hemingway with the same silly grin he has in the Floridita. Supposedly the metal was all propellers and other scraps donated by the local fishermen and melted down for this dubious likeness.

The monument is vaguely reminiscent of the Templete, the Havana monument to the founding of the city, only with Hem instead of a Ceiba tree. There is a wreath of fresh roses and other flowers. No one could explain to me who provided the fresh flowers, but I am assured that fresh flowers are there most of the time.

Gregorio Fuentes, Hemingway's first mate on the Pilar lived off of the Hemingway myth. He drank at La Terraza and for a fee he would tell you all about Hemingway and imply that he was Santiago, the lead character in *The Old Man and the Sea*. He probably wasn't. Several other fishermen made the claim, and Hemingway said it was based on no one in particular. How would Gregorio know. He admitted that he never read the book. But people loved his stories and paid to take his picture.

It was something to do when in Cuba. You could go to Cojimar and talk to Gregorio. He may not have been the most reliable source, since his stories kept changing. He was a good example of why journalists are not supposed to pay for interviews. He died in 2002 of lung cancer and people would say, since he, like many Cubans, smoked many cigars, that this was the cause. But he died at the age of 104. How long would he have lived without cigars?

Enough foreign Hemingway fans turned up in Cuba that you could live off of having known him. But there are few people left with Hemingway memories. Even when not looking for money they get dragged out for visitors like an artifact. There really is such a thing in Cuba as Hemingway tourism.

An emaciated octogenarian with a raspy voice called Oba, Osvaldo Carnero, was presented to me. Oba, a fisherman, went with Hem to

Peru with the film crew to shoot *Old Man and the Sea* and caught a 1,539-pound marlin. The other remaining fisherman, not nearly as old, did not really know Hemingway but was dragged out anyway because he remembered when he was ten years old watching Hemingway in Cojimar at the shoot of *Old Man and the Sea.*

The Hemingway Museum introduced me to Oscar Blas Fernandez, an octogenarian who grew up in San Francisco de Paula. This small wiry man was one of the last of Gigi's All-Stars. Older than Gigi but younger than Patrick, he was one of the boys who played baseball with Gigi. Hemingway, who he always calls Papa with the greatest reverence, named him Cayuco Jonronero—Cayuco, the home run hitter. I asked if he hit a lot of homeruns and he smiled. "No, Only one!"

Talking to people who vaguely remembered Hemingway, from the Floridita to Cojimar, never yielded very much critical insight. It was like asking a nun for her insights on the Virgin Mary.

I was invited to a conference of Hemingway scholars in Havana sponsored by the Finca Vigía Museum. Among the Hemingway scholars, any of the men who were old enough to have grey or white hair wore khaki, grew beards, and wore wire rimmed glasses. Some were more subtle about it than others, but it occurred to me, worried me, that if you spent enough time thinking about Hemingway you might turn into one.

They presented papers on a variety of obscure aspects of the Hemingway life. Some were, of course, more interesting than others. One was trying to figure out a genetic reason why so many of the Hemingway family committed suicide, including his father, his uncle, his brother, one of his sisters, and one granddaughter. There must be something genetic going on. I always thought manic-depression was a good bet but this one scholar was testing out a theory that they suffered from hemochromatosis. This genetically transferable but difficult to diagnose illness causes an inability to metabolize iron, which leads to deep depression and mental disorder.

Listening to these scholars I couldn't help wondering if they are going to run out of material. For all his events and the different chapters of his life, the places, the wives, and lovers, it really was a short life. Sixty years is not a lot.

Strangest of all, at this conference there were two men who were consciously trying to look like Hemingway, though it was really about costume and hair style. The big one and the small one really didn't look much alike. One of them was an actor trying to promote his career, which was entirely portraying Hemingway wherever he could. Both were dressed in khaki safari suits, something Hemingway never wore in Cuba, but I suppose the imposters didn't want to wear a dirty guayabera and old shorts. One wore a large medal suspended from his neck by a ribbon. He had been last year's winner of the "Hemingway-look-alike" contest that was part of a festival in Key West called Hemingway Days. Jack, Patrick, and Gregory worked together to stop the festival, which they found distasteful and disrespectful. They also pointed out that the festival ignored any royalty payments to the Hemingway estate. For a time, they succeeded in closing it down but later it came back.

British author Julian Barnes once on the Greek island of Naos encountered a white bearded man in khakis who was imitating Hemingway, He wondered why this happened. After all, he reasoned, the British don't go around disguised as Shakespeare. The Germans don't produce fake Goethes, nor the Italians imitation Dantes. The French don't have, as Barnes put it, "faux Voltaires."

Key West has its own Hemingway strangeness. The Hemingway house is a museum open to the public. Unlike in Havana, you are free to wander amid the Hemingway furniture and possessions. A tour guide identifies items for you and tells you about the six-toed cats on the property, direct descendants of Papa's six toed cats. There used to be a white and orange porcelain cat, which was said to have been done by Picasso. They sold reproductions of it. But one day it disappeared without explanation and no one said anymore about it. How can a genuine Picasso disappear without comment?

Patrick, who grew up in the house, and even lived there for a year after his mother, Pauline's, death, said he recalled no such Picasso. He went to Key West once and took the tour without identifying himself. "The house and its furnishings are a complete travesty," Patrick said. None of the furniture is authentic according to Patrick. He said that he and his wife moved it all to California, to Berkeley where his wife and he were

living and in the 1960s it was all destroyed in a fire. He said the family only had two Persian cats with the normal number of toes. There was a neighbor with six-toed cats. The grounds have also been changed. There was a tremendous lack of water and the property was gardened with exotic drought resistant plants. Later a pipeline came in from Homestead and lush tropical vegetation was planted.

On the other hand, he credited the Finca Vigía with being authentic.

· · ·

There is a street theatre group from Matanzas that goes to other towns in Cuba and, with creative lightweight props, performs in the street so that the audience can follow on foot. In many towns they perform Don Quixote but, of course, in Cojimar, it has to be *The Old Man and the Sea*. There is a strange loud noise. After a minute, I realize it is coming from the loudspeakers at the monument; it takes me a few more minutes to realize that it is supposed to be the sound of the sea. The reason it took time for me to understand this is that I am standing by the sea and could hear it before the sound came on.

A man with a long bushy white beard says goodbye to another actor and shoves off on a boat built onto a bicycle and rolls down the street followed by large paper birdlike creatures held up on sticks.

Santiago put out a line and soon there is a fish larger than his boat and made of sticks and canvas. But then come other creatures with movable jaws and big clacking teeth. Children from the village who have come to watch spontaneously hit the sharks. But it is too late, the big fish is gone.

I really liked their performance, but I wonder what Hemingway would have thought. He hated Spencer Tracy in the film and said he looked like a fat rich actor. This Santiago, with his great beard and strong face, was neither fat nor rich.

When I went out to Cojimar with the Hemingway scholars, the Hemingway look-alike and the Hemingway actor took places above the steps of the Hemingway monument. The monument loudspeakers were playing Guantanamera, the popular Cuban song of the 1950s. In truth the look-alike was a little too large and the actor a little too small and neither

looked especially like Hemingway but neither did the Hemingway statue. The two were autographing and the Hemingway scholars were taking their programs up, one by one, to have them signed. I was relieved to note that they were signing their own names. I didn't really understand this, but being a writer, I know that people really like signatures.

Overhead huge live buzzards, *aura tiñosa*, were circling with their wide black wingspans, looking for dead meat to eat and it occurred to me that they might be the only ones that understood that Hemingway was dead. Poor Hem, he wanted to die and here in Cuba they just won't let him.

One June I was walking on the narrow streets of Habana Vieja and people, maybe one or two per block, would call out "Papa!" One of the reminders of how close the US and Cuba used to be is that the Cubans celebrate the American Father's Day holiday on the same date. I was feeling a little sad that I wasn't with my daughter for Father's Day. They just assumed I was probably a father and were wishing me well. Habaneros can be very kind.

Wait!

Suddenly I realized that I was misreading this. It was given away by a man in the shadowy doorway across the street (everyone in Havana stays in cooler shadows) who called out "Hemingway." It was that Papa. They were calling out to Papa as they always did in Havana when he was alive. He would smile and wave back. As long as there was a six-foot American with shoulders and a white beard, Hemingway was not gone. "Ola, Papa." They could still do it. But I didn't wave back because I do not want to play that role.

It was my fear coming true. If you spend too much time thinking about Hemingway you become a Hemingway clone.

A Black woman journalist was interviewing me and said, "Don't you know that you look like Hemingway?"

"I don't think so," I replied.

But she insisted, "You do."

Then I said to her, "Do all white people look alike to you."

She smiled and nodded in the affirmative.

Next time I go to Cuba, I am shaving off my beard first.

CHAPTER SIX

Idaho and the Last Escape

The Big Wood River from a hill on the last day of rainbow
trout season, Ketchum, March 31, 2010

"Each man believes in his heart he will die.
Many have written last thoughts and last letters.
None know if our deaths are now or forever:
None know if this wandering earth will be found."

—Archibald MacLeish, *New Found Land*

I remembered Idaho from my childhood as rugged green wooded mountains with thick forests of tall ponderosa pines that made a human feel miniscule. Parts of Idaho are like that. North from Boise along the Snake that forms the border with Oregon is a high mountain. Ponderosa forest on the Idaho side and across the steep wide gorge to Oregon as far as you could see. This was classic Rocky Mountain majesty. But Ketchum and Central Idaho are something different. The mountains have few trees and much sage brush, mostly concealed in snowy months except for a few skeletal branches. The rest of the year, the brush is a jade cover on the slopes with tough yellow or purple flowers in spring. Other inclines are almost pure rock, and some have the liquefaction of tall waving grass. Some of these steep rock-bound rises descend to the main street in Ketchum, blocking the town from any more expansion in those places. The steep mountains look too gnarly to climb and in winter are glistening white. The main towns of the Wood River Valley—Ketchum, Hailey, and Bellevue—are small and distinctly Western with wooden false fronts on the one- and two-story buildings and wooden planking for sidewalks to walk above the snow or the mud. The rivers rush and twist and are rich in illusive rainbow trout, a spectacularly colored, almost iridescent animal out of the water that is barely visible camouflaged in the river.

It is often said that Hemingway was drawn to this part of Idaho because it resembled Spain. In places it does, as the Basques chopped down their oak forests for their great shipbuilding industry, they replaced it with Rocky Mountain pine. And the balder regions of central and southern Spain resemble central Idaho. But Idaho has its own Rocky Mountain splendor, the grace of the White Cloud Mountains and the striking ferocity of the Sawtooths.

The Importance of Not Being Ernest

I don't think I ever went to Ketchum as a child, and as I went there now, on that splendid road across the cattle ranching plain and through the rough mountains dropping slowly down to the Wood Valley, the only time I could recall the name Ketchum was when I read Carlos Baker. Yes, this is Hemingway's Ketchum, but that was not remotely why I was going there.

My first trip to Ketchum, like Hem's first trip, was by invitation, though they were very different offers. Hemingway's was one of a series of bold moves to build a famous ski resort in the middle of a remote unvisited area. In 1935 an Eastern aristocrat, Averell Harriman, inherited a family fortune that included being chairman of the Union Pacific Railroad. The Union Pacific was part of Western legend, one of the rail companies that, starting in 1862, opened (or some might say, helped to steal) the American West. By the 1930s the Union Pacific owned much of the Western rail links and had a thriving cargo trade. But they had few passengers, especially on their Northwest line that ran through Idaho.

This was at a time when Alpine skiing was becoming popular in America. The 1936 Olympics included it for the first time. An estimated 10,000 Americans went skiing in Europe every winter. In 1936 nearly 12,000 skiers took trains from New York City to the Berkshires. This caught Harriman's attention and he decided to build a ski resort, a luxury lodge with first class European ski instructors. His model was Austria. It would have to be in a spot with good skiing that was close to the Union Pacific line.

Western passenger cars had become very run down. Carpeting, bucket seats, and many other improvements were made in an effort to make train travel pleasant.

He hired an Austrian count from a Viennese banking family, a haughty aristocrat whose family traced back to the Middle Ages, Count Felix Schaffgotsch, to search for the right mountain. Numerous places were rejected as too far from the rail line. Finally, they bought a huge cattle ranch just outside Ketchum and built the lodge in the spot where the cattle, mostly Texas longhorn, gathered, because cattle always retreat to the warmest spot on the range.

There were spectacular potential ski mountains near the mining town

of Ketchum, but Ketchum was a failed town. In May 1879 a prospector named Dave Ketchum found valuable silver and lead deposits near where the Warm Springs meets the Big Wood River. I know this spot well because, though I see no sign of metal deposits, it is a very good spot for catching rainbow trout. Ketchum built a log cabin there but only mined for one year, 1879–80, and then left. Some say he went farther north and others south. Not much is known about Dave Ketchum but he left behind his name.

Ketchum had enjoyed a silver boom in the late nineteenth century. The town had been bustling with silver miners, wealthy entrepreneurs invested in silver but always ready to move if there was a better strike somewhere else, and Chinese laborers who endured a great deal of discrimination but remained to lay tracks for the railroad that would transport the ore and bring in supplies for a growing population.

From 1880 to 1885 twelve million dollars' worth of silver and lead ore was hauled out of the valley, which, though not even the richest vein in Idaho, was significant enough to make the Union Pacific run a line to link them to its system. Many of the extension lines of the Union Pacific were to mining centers. Starting in 1883, ore moved out of the Wood River Valley by train.

But in the 1890s, with a severe national depression, the value of silver rapidly declined, and Ketchum began to disappear. The mines closed and the population left. If you wanted to stay you had a choice of abandoned homes into which to settle. The population of Ketchum dropped from 2000 in the 1880s to about 300 in 1900. Boom and bust is a common story in the American West.

As silver mining died, the sheep business outside of town grew. A sign on the side of a building urging people to eat more lamb can still be seen. The locals never have been lamb eaters. They are beef people. But Ketchum became an important center for shipping lamb east on the same railroad that used to ship silver. It was said to be the largest sheep shipping center in the world, or second only to Sidney, Australia, or at the very least an important lamb center. Harriman brought Hemingway, but sheep brought Kurlansky.

···

The Austrian count, Felix Schaffgotsch, was taken to the top of what is now Dollar Mountain, today a smaller mountain for beginning skiers. From there he had a view of the larger mountains and the graceful Wood River Valley. Yes, this could be the place. There was good powder snow on the mountain and he skied down.

By the time Harriman discovered Ketchum, it had a winter population of only about 150 people and no more than 300 in the summer when some returned from parts of the state with a less harsh winter.

There were other nearby attractions: deer and elk in the higher spots, even mountain lion and, a little further off, antelope and big horn sheep. There were a variety of ducks and other aquatic birds for shooting. It was a great hunters' spot, and the rivers were teaming with rainbow trout and the nearby Salmon River even had giant steelhead.

The Sun Valley Lodge opened with rooms for 250 guests in 1936. It was designed by Union Pacific architect Gilbert Stanley Underwood, who had already built for Union Pacific famous lodges in the Grand Canyon, Bryce Canyon, Zion Lodge, and Old Faithful Lodge at Yellowstone. The resort had been fully constructed in only seven months and, though mostly concrete, it was molded and painted to look like a log cabin construction. For skiers, they built the world's first chairlift.

Harriman decided that the way to give this unknown resort by a washed-out Western mining town the panache and air of sophistication of a prominent European ski resort was to bring in celebrities and then bring press to publicize their presence. They would invite people they wanted to the opening and would have no reservations available for those that didn't interest them. Their list came mostly from the New York Society register and from Hollywood. Producer David O. Selznick said he could bring stars if Harriman would provide a direct train. He was upset when he learned that the train would take thirty-six hours. He wrote to Harriman, "Could you not give instructions to Union Pacific to route car in some manner as to cut down time." The Snowball Express went to Shoshone. Ads said they would be taken by sleigh to Sun Valley. The "sleigh" turned out to be a bus, but a few choice guests were brought by

dogsled. Arriving at Sun Valley they were met by a band and had flowers in their rooms. The right guest would have champagne in their room. The opening was covered by *Life* magazine with photos by Alfred Eisenstaedt who was becoming the new magazine's star photographer.

Sun Valley did attract celebrities. Hollywood was a major target and they were able to get Gary Cooper, Claudette Colbert, Errol Flynn, Joan Bennet, Darryl Zanuck, and David O. Selznick. Other guests were just as famous for their wealth such as William Paley and Jock Whitney. Even more dubious celebrities such as the Shah of Iran showed up. And so, the press loved writing about Sun Valley because they loved the rich and famous.

In 1938 a young writer and hunting and fishing guide from Twin Falls, Gene Van Guilder, working in Montana, heard that Ernest Hemingway spent time every year hunting in Montana. He passed this on to friends at Sun Valley who told the New York office of Union Pacific. An agent was sent to Key West to meet with Hemingway and offered free food and lodging in Sun Valley for him and his guests for two seasons, provided he would agree to allow his visits to be publicized. He told them that he was too preoccupied with the Spanish Civil War but would consider it for later.

In September 1939, forty-year-old Hemingway decided to take the invitation not with his wife but with Martha Gellhorn.

Even today it is not easy to get to Ketchum, but in 1939 it was a journey. He had come from Yellowstone following the Snake to the magnificent Grand Tetons and past Henry's Fork, a popular fishing tributary, and into Idaho, across the desolate Arco plain into miles of black lava desert. He and Martha traveled on gravel roads and by the time they got to the lava fields, what is called the Craters of the Moon, he considered turning around and going back to Wyoming. He thought this Sun Valley that no one had heard of was just not worth it. Craters of the Moon is a forbidding place at night and Hemingway said, "It was like something out of Dante's *Inferno*." But he drove on.

In the nineteenth century when migrants traveled West on the Oregon trail, this was considered the toughest part. Along the entire trail, the stretch most likely for an Indian attack was the Snake River Plain

in Idaho. The Shoshone and the Bannock were furious about strangers intruding on the wild plants that were their food, as well as interfering with buffalo migration.

When finally his yellow convertible Buick, an impressive 1939 car, arrived covered in dust, they were warmly received. Lloyd Arnold, the official Sun Valley photographer, and his wife Tillie took charge of them. Arnold had received instructions from the New York office of Union Pacific to handle him carefully. "He spooks easy," said the instructions.

This was a common misunderstanding of Hem. He did not spook easily but was generally warm and gregarious. He liked people. He and Marty became close friends with Lloyd and Tillie, and Gene Van Guilder and a number of other locals. Hemingway was delighted when Van Guilder told him that there were many Basques in the area.

Bud Perdy, a small, fit, young rancher with a genial disposition who had a number of ranching properties, took Hem fishing and hunting at the request of Sun Valley. Silver Creek ran through Bud's property and, since years later he kindly let me fish it, I can attest that it was one of the extraordinary stretches of that most spectacular fishing creek. This marshy creek is fed by underground springs and is, as the British like to say, gin clear. Sapphire gin at that. You can see the rainbows in the blue clear water, and they can see you, so you literally have to sneak up on them to catch them, usually from the bank. The creek is rich in nutrients, so the rainbow eats well and is not desperate for a fly that looks less than delicious.

Historians frequently say that Hemingway did not fish in Idaho. But Bud Purdy distinctly remembered taking him fly fishing on the Silver Creek, and Lloyd Arnold shot a photo of him with two large rainbows and his famously broad smile, also on the Silver Creek. A fishing trip on the Big Wood on September 28, 1939, was organized by Gene Van Guilder and is well documented. But Hem was never a connoisseur. He used wet flies rather than dry. Wet flies that run through the water are a less refined technique than a dry fly that alights on the surface like a real fly.

Only a few years before he had enthusiastically taken his sons wet fly fishing for cutthroat on the Clarks Fork of the Yellowstone in Wyoming. Cutthroat are fun and lively but not nearly as challenging as Idaho's

powerful and wily rainbow trout. Hemingway's son, Patrick, told me that his father used tackle exclusively from the British tackle maker Hardy Brothers. In sporting equipment and hotels, Hem wanted top-of-the-line. He had a trunk with Hardy reels, rods, and flies. Somehow the trunk got lost and, according to Patrick, he never again showed interest in fly fishing. In Key West and Cuba, his passion became fishing for giant marlin. He was very different from his oldest son Jack who was a passionate fly fisherman—a dry fly fisherman. According to Patrick, Jack told Papa that he would rather have an hour fight with a trout than six hours with a marlin. When they grew up, it was Jack who became a Ketchum resident and earned a reputation as one of the world's great fly fishermen. He was also revered in Ketchum for his work on fish conservation, including promoting catch-and-release fishing and helping to establish a conservancy for the Silver Creek. Ketchum fishermen thank Jack Hemingway for there still being plentiful trout in the area. It is surprising that a man whose father was Ernest Hemingway, whose godparents were Gertrude Stein and Alice Toklas, and who was circumcised by the poet William Carlos Williams (it's okay, he was a pediatrician) never had any literary aspirations; he just wanted to fish.

Hem went to Idaho in the fall to shoot birds, mostly in the duck season and pheasant season. Despite his bad eyesight, he was a remarkably good wing shot, as bird shooters are called. Don Anderson who was in charge of sport for Sun Valley called up Bud and asked him to arrange a duck shoot for the author. Bud had a wealth of waterfowl on his ranch in the marshes around Silver Creek. Bud told me that Hem had no patience for waiting in a blind for ducks to fly by. He would wander fields and look for pheasants, sage hens, partridges, and other game birds to shoot. "He liked to walk along the ditches and the creeks," Bud recalled, "He was a hell of a shot."

After the first hunt they were friends and hunts were no longer arranged through Sun Valley. He would just call up Bud and set up a hunt with friends. He always liked to do things in groups. Lloyd Arnold was a regular as was Gene Van Guilder. Van Guilder was killed in a hunting accident and though Hemingway had only known him for six weeks he wrote a eulogy so beautiful that it has remained part of the literature of

Ketchum. "Gene loved this country. He saw it with the eyes of a painter, the trained mind of a writer, and the heart of a boy who had been brought up in the West. He loved the hills in the spring when the snow goes off and the first flowers come. He loved the warm sun of summer and the high mountain meadows, the trails through the timber and clear blue of the lakes. He loved the hills in the winter when the snow comes. Best of all he loved the fall..."

He personally delivered the eulogy, which, though they may not have realized this in Idaho, was extraordinary. Papa had a fear of public speaking and, with the exception of when he had to promote his Spanish film, almost never did it, which may have been the real reason he did not travel to Sweden for his Nobel Prize.

No one could have written this moving eulogy who didn't love the place himself, and Hemingway was becoming established as a true son of the Wood River Valley. People would insist, and still do, that this was his true home: the place he loved best, even more than Cuba, though this was probably not true. The Cubans, aside from Desnoes, make the same claim as do some in Spain.

There was something in Hem that drew him to shooting birds. It was not that he hated them; he just wanted to shoot them. Bud told me of how he found a wounded owl and kept it and got everyone to shoot black birds to feed his owl.

"Then there were the magpies," said Bud. Everyone hated magpies because they ate the eggs of ground nesting birds. The government paid five cents a head for dead magpies. They would build wire traps to catch them. "Then one day," according to Bud, "Hem said, 'Hey, why don't we shoot them?'" He would have the trapped birds thrown in the air for him, one at a time, and shoot them.

Hemingway had different experiences and different tastes than his shooting chums. In the world of game birds, there is a steep divide between European and American game eaters. The French in particular believe that game should be aged to bring out its strong flavor, making it very distinct from the taste of domestic meat. A wild pheasant should not taste remotely like a chicken, which often in America it does. Jean Anthelme Brillat-Savarin, the celebrated eighteenth and early nineteenth

century French food writer—also a lawyer, politician, and for a brief stint in exile, first violinist for the Park Theater in New York—recommended that pheasant be hung by the tail and kept there until the meat was so decomposed that the body fell off. Bud Purdy listing for me his friend Hem's endearing foibles said, "He liked to hang ducks until they were rotten and barely cook them and eat them bloody. I wouldn't touch them."

$$\bullet\ \bullet\ \bullet$$

Sun Valley gave him room 260, at the time the only large suite in the hotel. Hemingway, who had to have a nickname for everything, called the lodge "The Glamour House" and with intended irony called his room "the Harry Morgan room." Harry Morgan from *To Have and Have Not* was one of the poorest, down on his luck characters Hemingway ever created. The room had a balcony over the swimming pool. He would sometimes sit there at a desk writing. The hotel claims he wrote *For Whom the Bell Tolls* on that balcony, which may be partly true. He also wrote it in Cuba. A photo by Arnold of Hem seated at a desk in his Sun Valley room ran on the jacket of *For Whom the Bell Tolls*.

The pool was always heated to over ninety degrees so it was popular winter recreation. You could go for a swim in a snowfall. It was also therapeutic for skiers. My first time there, I went skiing for the first time in many years and after a long hot soaking had no sore muscles the next day. So the skiers could soak in the heat and, if they chose to, look up and see one of the great writers punching out a masterpiece on the balcony.

Bud said, "People didn't bother him. Ketchum used to be like that. Hemingway and Gary Cooper and all these celebrities could go to bars and restaurants and around town and no one would care. No one would bother them." It is still somewhat like that. There is a code here not to harass celebrities.

Sun Valley is about capitalism, so they were not going to leave the suite empty so tourists could see the Hemingway room the way they do in the Ambos Mundos in Cuba. They did have a Hemingway plaque, but many of the rooms were marked with the names of celebrities that had stayed there. The hotel was recently remodeled and now has many suites,

all completely redone so that the Hemingway experience at the Glamour House has not been preserved.

• • •

The January 6, 1941, issue of *Life* magazine ran an eight-page spread on Hem and Marty titled "The Hemingways in Sun Valley: The Novelist Takes a Wife." Their Civil War colleague Robert Capa, who had become a photojournalism star from that conflict, took the photos. They look very happy together. The article informs us that *For Whom the Bell Tolls* was written there.

The article also said "Today, in prime physical vigor, 210 lbs. in weight, a good boxer, a crack wing shot and an excellent soldier, he is an acknowledged master of his art." Well, he was a good wing shot. It is a clear demonstration of the strength of the myth that a man who had never had a professional bout or even an organized amateur contest could be termed "a good boxer" or that he could be an "excellent soldier" when in fact he had never been a soldier at all. It was the kind of image Hemingway had tried to give the world and one of the reasons Hemingway fans understood so little about him.

Even earlier, in 1934, *Vanity Fair* ran a series of paper dolls of celebrities, including Albert Einstein and J.P. Morgan. Hemingway's had the caption "Ernest Hemingway, America's own literary cave man, hard drinking, hard fighting, hard loving—all for art's sake." One costume, a leopard skin loin cloth with a club in one hand and a dead rabbit in the other, is labeled "Ernie the Neanderthal, man."

Hemingway had created a false image of himself that has endured. "Hemingway was an artist," Valerie told me. "People forget that. If you wanted the best of him, don't talk about war or bullfighting. Talk about literature or painting. He was wonderful when he talked about these things."

• • •

Among Hemingway's circle of hunting friends was actor Gary Cooper. Cooper, a native of Montana, was already a regular when Hemingway

started coming. Besides having both grown up hunting and both coming from professional families—Cooper's father was a State Supreme Court Justice—they seemed to have little in common. Cooper's conservative politics did not match Hemingway's leftist ideals. Hemingway did not always support Democrats. In 1920, his first Presidential election, he voted Socialist for Eugene V. Debs, a fact that probably would not have pleased Harriman since Debs was most famous for his union fight against Western railroads. Cooper was a committed Republican and had campaigned for Wendell Willkie against Franklin Roosevelt shortly before first meeting with Hemingway. And while Hemingway was an intellectual who read every day from a wide range of books, Cooper once boasted that he thought he had only read six books in his life.

Hemingway was a complicated man and there was a different Hemingway available in Idaho. The Idaho Hemingway was also truly him, the man who loved hunting and the outdoors and a good joke and laughing and camaraderie. When I asked Bud Purdy if Hemingway could be difficult, he said,

"I just liked him. He wasn't a glad hander but if he got to know you, he was a great friend. He was fun to be out with. He talked game or birds, not the heavy stuff. He never talked politics. He talked about his house in Cuba and fishing. He never showed a temper around us. He never talked about what he was writing."

He knew that Hem had a temper and recalled him getting into a fistfight once, "But if you were his friend he was a real friend. He gave signed copies of his books." He even gave them to his friends who didn't read books. He inscribed a copy of *For Whom the Bell Tolls* to Cooper and his wife Rocky, "To the Coopers to make something to supplement *The Idaho Statesman* as reading matter…"

• • •

Hemingway was more worldly than most of his Idaho crowd and was an observer of rare acumen. He seldom showed this side because he did not want to separate himself, but occasionally treated them with insights that were not common in Idaho. In the fall of 1941, he and Marty were

The Importance of Not Being Ernest

entertaining the gang with tales from their trip to China. Marty talked about how disgusting accommodations were and how glad she was to see the Golden Gate Bridge.

Then Papa became more serious, and he said that the US was going to enter the World War in the Pacific. He said that relations between Japan and the US had become extremely bad and that Roosevelt had frozen Japanese assets, which was threatening their oil supply. Japan, he was certain, would retaliate. "We'll probably get it for a Christmas present," Hem predicted, off only by three weeks.

Historians argue about whether Roosevelt was surprised by the Pearl Harbor attack. Hemingway briefed Army and Navy intelligence and Secretary of Treasury Morgenthau, who was a leading expert in the administration on Chinese relations. Was he believed? Was it passed on? Did others say the same thing or disagree? It seems unlikely that Hemingway would have known more than Roosevelt about what to expect in December.

· · ·

After the Nazis came to power, the general public in Idaho began to question Harriman's policy of staffing Sun Valley with "the best ski instructors" from Austria. Rumors spread that these Germanic men were Nazis. In most cases this was unfair, but Count Schaffgotsch, the man who chose the site for Sun Valley, took to praising Hitler as did a number of the Austrian ski instructors he selected. The count returned to Europe, joined the SS, and is believed to have been killed on the Eastern Front.

In 1942, Sun Valley was closed and for the rest of the war Union Pacific turned it over to a naval hospital. Hemingway did not return until 1946. Lloyd Arnold found them log cabins with several bedrooms just south of Ketchum on the road from Main Street Hailey to Main Street Ketchum, along the black cotton wood and white aspen valley of the Big Wood and the rugged sage brush and rock mountains. They rented one to live in and one for him to write in. He wrote in the morning and hunted in the afternoon.

His friends had enjoyed Marty and were disappointed to hear of the

divorce. But they also came to enjoy Mary, who easily fit in with the Idaho gang. Friends gave them rainbow trout caught that morning in the Big Wood, and Hemingway cooked them in butter, insisting that the lemon be added while frying, the way he always cooked trout, and, according to Mary, left the kitchen "a disaster."

But Hemingway started questioning the appeal of Ketchum, with, as Mary put it, "Too many new coming jerks among the returning old timers." The same thought is often expressed today, sometimes even by me, but he kept coming just the same and so do I.

They ate steaks at the Alpine, which I know today as Whiskey Jacques, where they were served sizzling on metal plates. There were dark long bars on either side. The block was popular with the sheepherders whose supply store was there. Across the street was a drug store, where ice cream sodas were ten cents and huge sundaes were fifteen cents. I miss those drugstores.

A black dog with some sporting blood started following Papa, wouldn't leave him, and eventually ended up part of the gang at the Finca back in Cuba. Hemingway whose modernist simplicity extended to animal names called him Blackie. Another stray brought home from the Floridita was named Negrita, which is Spanish for Blackie.

Hunting three days a week, fishing on occasion, writing most of the mornings, he drank huge quantities of alcohol in the evenings. He did not touch it in the morning when he was writing. For all the famous quantities, he was a disciplined drinker. Bud Purdy noted that he would never drink while hunting. "He had no problem with alcoholism, but he liked to break open a bottle after the hunt."

In 1959 the Hemingways found a house to buy on the north side of Ketchum. This was not the Finca Vigía. Mary called it "the block house" because it was made from four slabs of cement with a roof. "As strong as a prison and as charmless," said Valerie. Those two-story slabs had a familiar look. They were the same fake log sides as the Sun Valley Lodge construction. The house was new, having been built in 1952. The owner, Henry "Bob" Topping was one of those unconnected wealthy who drifted in and out of Ketchum. No one seemed to know why he came or why he left. He was by coincidence the brother-in-law to Sonja Henning, the

Olympic ice skating champion who had starred in the 1941 movie, *Sun Valley Serenade*, which had greatly publicized the resort.

Topping had decided to build a house after he was no longer welcome in the lodge because of a fistfight stemming from his failure to pay back bar bills. He somehow got hold of some of the wooden cement forms used for the lodge. But after a few years he decided that the Arizona desert would be better for his health and sold his cement house with seventeen acres of land for $50,000.

At the time the house stood alone on the bank of the Big Wood with a clear view up a scenic section of the Wood River Valley known as Adam's Gulch to the big rough Boulder Mountains and the white glaciers of the White Cloud Mountain behind them. The house had huge windows for the views. The best was the picture window in Mary's bedroom. As in Cuba, they had separate bedrooms and hers had what might be the best view in Ketchum. Hemingway liked to sit in a low, not very comfortable chair at the foot of the bed and gaze at the view.

They furnished the house in that streamlined not particularly comfortable furniture of the 1950s. Incongruously there were a few pieces of thick ornate Spanish style furniture from Cuba, tables with antique Spanish tiles of bullfighting. and a few bullfighting posters on the walls from the Dangerous Summer.

The kitchen was not attractive but efficient. It had a linoleum floor and Formica counters. The stove had electric burners which are not ideal for cooking, but did had two large ovens.

They had a separate one room heated cottage where the dogs lived.

A cable in the living room brought them television from Twin Falls. It was the first television in Ketchum as well as Hemingway's first television. Boxing used to be broadcast every Friday night and Hem invited friends over for the fights. As Bud put it, "He thought he was a boxer and would have us all over for food and drinks for the Friday night fights."

These were jovial, raucous events. They were out in the woods and could make all the noise they wanted. Some of the participants, including Bud Purdy, not very far in the future, would be his pallbearers.

How was it that the Idaho gang never saw Hem's dark side? I asked Bud if he ever saw this dark side that you always hear about. "Never," he

insisted but then he thought about one night at the house watching the fights. The phone rang and Mary answered. She told Hemingway that Leonard Bernstein was on the line. He was in Sun Valley and wanted to see him. Hemingway shouted, "Oh I don't want to talk to that son of a bitch." Bud had a perplexed expression on his face. All these years later he couldn't understand why Hem would talk that way about Bernstein. Bernstein did meet Hemingway in 1959 either before the call to the house or after and was deeply impressed by his "charm." It all depends on which Hemingway you meet.

• • •

In 1959 when Castro took control of Cuba, the press found Hemingway in Ketchum and wanted his comments. The author remained as supportive of the Revolution as he had been from Cuba. He said that it was a "real revolution" not just a change of leaders. Later he wrote his son Jack with great excitement, "This is the real revolution. Something like what we had hoped for in Spain."

He called Herrera to voice his support and called Villareal to tell him to give the revolutionaries all the ammunition and anything else in the house that they needed. Later Herrera claimed that Hemingway also wrote an article defending the Revolution for an Idaho newspaper; he did not identify which, and the paper refused to run it. Hem sent a copy to Fidel.

When *TIME*, Mary's former employer, called asking for a quote on the Revolution, Papa said he was "delighted." This worried Mary, who was not as enthusiastic. Mary persuaded him to call them back and change "delighted" to "hopeful." But he continued to make statements enthusiastically supporting the Revolution. He and Mary had different experiences. Mary, who had not been in Spain, was horrified by the executions being carried out by the new government. But Hemingway recalled that the Republic had to shoot people as well. He even supported the show trials that were going on, saying that they needed to show the world that they were serious. And as for the executions, "If the government didn't kill these people they would be killed anyway." He gave this defense of

on the road that keep changing, an Idaho trick, and though you seldom encounter other cars, a patrol car will give a ticket. The inside story is to watch out at lunchtime because he likes to get lunch in Hailey and drop one or two tickets on the way. In any event when you get to the Wood River Valley, especially in a snowy winter storm, you feel like you have made a journey.

· · ·

In the late nineteenth century when mining was failing and sheep ranching was taking over, there were not many people who knew how to live in the mountains and tend the flocks. There were not many people there at all. But in the great depression of the 1890s, they found Scottish shepherds, for whom life was not working in Scotland, to come to the American West and herd sheep. A generation later in the early twentieth century, their children either went back or became Americans working at more lucrative activities. But at this time, small farms were failing in the northern part of Basque country. Basque from the French side were recruited from the hard-pressed farms. These were not sheep ranches. They raised a few sheep for meat, wool, or cheese along with crops, pigs, and sometimes cows. None of them had ever handled thousands of sheep at a time. But they were persuaded that opportunity waited in American sheep. Immigration to the Americas was a long-standing tradition among Basques. They used to say that one of the definitions of a Basque was someone with an uncle in America.

They came by ship and when they arrived in New York, an agent from the Western sheep producers met them and took them to a boarding-house in Greenwich Village. They found them positions in Idaho, Nevada, Eastern California, Eastern Oregon, and Eastern Washington and these are the places where Basques are still found today.

A trailer was designed for these shepherds, small and easily trans-portable over the mountains, mostly wooden, just long enough for a bed with space for storage and a cooking grill. Many believed that these shepherds lived so remotely that they could not even speak, but in reality, they only spoke Basque and no one could understand them.

They were unprepared for their lonely life, the vastness of the West, or what it meant to be responsible for thousands of sheep. But they knew how to do it. The entire Basque country, which includes four provinces in Spain and three in France, is smaller than Idaho alone—closer to the size of New Hampshire. They had never seen such space. One old time Basque in Nevada told me that he saw that the next mountain was better for grazing and so he decided to herd his sheep over there. He was amazed when it took him more than a week to get there.

There marked their lonely presence by carving their names on trees, and there are still many trees in Idaho with Basque names carved in them, sometimes with a date, sometimes a rough portrait. They did not want their passing to be unrecorded.

Subsequent generations of Basques got out of the trailers. They were English speakers, and the ancient language was forgotten though they always remembered that they were Basques. Now their grandchildren are starting to learn their grandparent's language in keeping with the prediction of Sabino Arano that if you do not teach your children Basque their children will teach them. The University of Nevada Press republished my bilingual *The Girl Who Swam to Euskadi* to help these Basque Americans learn the Basque language. Some of the children of the shepherds acquired their own sheep ranches, and some moved to other endeavors. Peruvians were brought in seasonally to tend the sheep.

And so, the trailing of the sheep celebrates the Scots, the Basques, and the Peruvians. Three more different cultures are hard to imagine, but they do have sheep in common. The festival has competitions for the black and white border collies that herd sheep. There is also food, dance, and music. One year when very young, my daughter Talia danced down main street in costume with a local Basque dance troop. A dancer, she had learned the steps and acquired the dress from our trips to Basque country.

We were drawn to Ketchum and its Basques and its mountains and rivers. On years when they are featuring the Basques, they often invite me to speak. It is a relationship developed over many years. I seem to please the Basques and they make me feel very good—a people who can assimilate and remain who they are at the same time. And there is always that grand finale when you go out to Main Street and see everyone you

know and then the sheep come through. Sheep are sensitive animals. Some years they run through Main Street like someone is chasing them or they are trying to escape. Other years they meander. Sheep follow each other. If one sheep wanders, the sheep herder has to be very careful in how he turns it around or the entire flock could follow just running in a circle. Whatever happens, Main Street is a mess, but they have become remarkably efficient at cleaning it up so that the townspeople are not reminded of why they don't like sheep.

The first year they brought me, like Hemingway, they put me up at the Sun Valley Lodge and made life very nice for me, though I did not want to shoot any birds. Marian and Talia came with me and we liked it so much we resolved to come every year, not in the fall when the trailing of the sheep takes place but in the winter, when there is skiing. My skiing was over once I learned that fly-fishing on the Big Wood is open in the winter. Nature has few animals more beautiful than a Big Wood Rainbow Trout.

This and not Hemingway, was our life in Ketchum, but there is no escaping Hem in Ketchum. His photo is everywhere. There is even an electronic billboard for no particular reason with the famous Yousuf Karsh turtleneck sweater portrait. It is said to be Hemingway's favorite photo of himself, which surprises me because there are so many others where he is more natural looking.

There are a few Hemingway photos in the Sun Valley Lodge, mostly shooting birds, sometimes with Gary Cooper. He posed for some to earn his room and board. There are photos of him in his prime, looking more handsome than most of the movie stars seen on the same wall. There are pictures of him looking eighty but actually only in his fifties. There are photos of him in the library and in most restaurants. In The Sawtooth Grill is a rare and unflattering snapshot of him drinking with a passage from Hunter Thompson claiming Hem liked to blow off steam at this very bar. I thought I could escape Hem at the Ketchum Grill, a cozy, rugged nineteenth-century house with good food, until I used their men's room and there he was, hanging over the urinal fly fishing with a grin as big as an alligator's.

At the Pioneer Saloon, though I had said not a word about Hemingway, the owner proudly showed me a shotgun that had belonged to him.

Fortunately, it wasn't *the* shotgun. The suicide weapon had been chopped up and buried in an undisclosed location.

I bought a 1940 Royal typewriter at the Goodwill store. "Watch this," I said to Marian, as the saleswoman came over. "She is going to try to tell me this was Hemingway's."

"I think this typewriter belonged to Ernest Hemingway," she said.

Except that Hemingway used a Corona in some photos and an Underwood in others, but this was a Royal, a nice old Royal in good condition. Someone may have written something great on it, but it wasn't Hemingway.

South of Sun Valley, the opposite direction from Ketchum and his house, is a monument to Hemingway in a stand of aspen, a bust on a tall rough-hewn stone pillar. There are some of the words from his eulogy to Van Guilder, which have become a eulogy to him, only slightly misquoted. It is about how he most of all loved the autumn. It was Hemingway writing about his friend, not about himself, and the locals work hard to have him love the Wood River Valley perhaps more than he ever did. He complained of the "new jerks" moving in and stayed away for ten years. He came back after the Cuban Revolution when he was sick and did not know where to go. He spent his last days in Ketchum deeply depressed that he would never see Cuba again. And he often talked to his Idaho friends about Cuba and the Finca. Of course, back in the Finca it looked like he loved Spain far more than Cuba.

Mary continued to live in the Topping house, not changing it very much. When she died, she left it to the Nature Conservancy, which wanted to preserve it as Hemingway's home. It was not opened to the public, but scholars could get special permission to be taken through it.

The Big Wood had changed course and now, instead of running by the bottom of the hill that was his backyard, a flood plain had grown of black-trunked cottonwoods and the river was further behind it. There were a lot of rainbows and it was a good spot for fly-casting. The neighbors would complain. The irony is that Hemingway didn't have any neighbors. Affluent new people had built these homes after he was gone. Were these "the new jerks"? Hemingway probably would have left the house because of them. All the new houses were damaging the river

because construction destroys the brush and insect life on which a trout river depends.

There was not much to do in the house. It did not have the charm of the Finca Vigía. Hemingway did not have a strong presence as he did in the Cuban home. You might find a clay pigeon on the lawn. There are a few left. Hemingway used to like to challenge friends to trap shooting from the house balcony. He excelled at trap shooting and, according to Bud, no one could beat him.

Once inside, it was easy to imagine an unhappy man in a temporary transitional home. You could go to the basement where the gun rack was kept and up to the kitchen where the keys were stored and out to the vestibule where he did it. And it would show that it was not a sudden impulse. It took a little time and determination. But this left me sad and empty.

In 2017 the house was turned over to the Community Library. Now there are literary events there. A group of writers had a dinner. What a horror for Hem where he once hosted Bud and his other hunting buddies to watch Friday night fights; I began to see why the Cubans kept people out of his house.

But I can't criticize. I have given two or three writer workshops in Ezra Pound's house in Hailey, a simple white wooden house. There is nothing of Pound in the house where he was born in 1885. His father, who had the house built, was a mining assayer and as the mines were dying out they left for Philadelphia when Pound was only two years old. But the poet liked to call himself "the Idaho Kid," and sometimes faked a Western accent, sometimes even in some of his poems. He would try out most anything in his poems.

Bud Purdy was a sprite nonagenarian even though he walked with a cane, a man with a warmth and generosity and sense of humor that made it easy to see why Hemingway befriended him. At ninety-five he was still only the second oldest pilot in Idaho with a private pilot license. There was one flying at ninety-seven and Bud always joked that he was going to get him. Typical of his generous spirit, he let me fish his magical stretch of Silver Creek.

I'd say, "Hey Bud, I grabbed a couple of your rainbows this morning," and he would say "Just put them back where you found them."

In the winter the cemetery is buried in snow but once, when it wasn't, I went to see the grave—a flat polished marble slab next to Mary, near Jack and Gregory, not far from Van Guilder, maybe the very spot where he delivered the famous eulogy. Someone left flowers, some left empty liquor bottles. Someone left a ballpoint pen. Everybody has their own Hemingway.

Such a short life, really, but as the first century Roman philosopher Seneca, who committed suicide at age seventy, pointed out: "It is not that we have a short time to live, but that we waste a lot of it." Hemingway tried not to waste a second.

Unnatural New York

Looking west toward the Hudson from Fifth Avenue
in Manhattan in the 20s, June 1994

> "The terrible thing about having New York go stale on you is that there's nowhere else. It's the top of the world."

> –John Dos Passos, *Manhattan Transfer*

I have lived more of my life on the island of Manhattan than any other place in the world. I find it somewhat of a comfort that although he passed through from time to time, New York is not a Hemingway place. When I was young and stayed at the Hotel Earle because it was cheap and well located, no one and nothing indicated that Hemingway had stayed there before shipping out in the ambulance service for World War I. This was one of the most significant moments in his life. But no one here cares; New York is not a Hemingway town. No one cares which hotels he stayed in or his favorite restaurants such as Toots Shor's, now long gone, where he was not as famous a celebrity as Joe DiMaggio.

New York is famously a tough town. "It's murder," Hem told Lillian Ross. He said it was a town you only went to for a brief period of time." "It's a very unnatural place to live," he said. It took me years to realize that, because living in an apartment in the heart of a city was my idea of normal. Paris is also unnatural for the same reason. I sometimes entertain the urge to live in a more natural place—to live by the white foaming rock bound coast of New England, or by the blue Caribbean Sea, or cradled in the soft green Basque mountains, or even in a Cuban villa with a very large, well-gardened swimming pool and a view of the sea, or on a bank of the Big Wood River with rainbow trout swimming past your back yard. That, I suppose, would be more natural.

Hemingway made clear his distrust of New York writers in *The Green Hills of Africa:*

> Writers should work alone. They should see each other only after their work is done, and not too often then. Otherwise, they become like writers in New York. All angle worms in a bottle, trying to derive knowledge and nourishment from their own contact and from the bottle.

It could be true. I wouldn't know. I work alone in New York and only rarely have contact with other writers in the city. Other writers seem to know each other and drink together in Brooklyn. My chief contact is with fellow dog walkers on the Upper West Side. I know all the dogs by name, though only a few of the owners' names. Aside from the astounding New York Public Library, where I actually held in my hands (gloves on) Ezra Pound's handwritten revisions of T.S. Eliot, and the way on any day I can drop in at a museum and see a masterpiece that will inspire me, the biggest New York contribution to my writing is other peoples' conversations. I delight in overhearing strangers on the street, and there is no better place for this than New York.

I was happy with Hem's lack of relationship with my town. But then I had this long and very pleasant lunch with Valerie Danby-Smith Hemingway, and she told me something disturbing. She just mentioned it in passing. Papa had an apartment in New York.

Would it too be turned into a Hemingway museum, something to do in New York like the Metropolitan Museum, Rockefeller Center, or Yankee Stadium? Isn't that what happens?

In 1999, Gregory Hemingway spoke at the dedication of the Hemingway-Pfeiffer museum in Piggott, Arkansas, in what had been the Pfeiffer family home, the home of Hemingway's second group of in-laws. He remarked that his father "is quite fortunate in having just about every place he ever lived in immortalized." But did they all have to be immortalized?

The house where he was born in Oak Park has become the Ernest Hemingway Birthplace Museum. In 1968, the US government designated the Hemingway family cottage on Walloon Lake in Michigan, where Hem and Hadley spent their honeymoon, "A National Historic Landmark." Ernie's younger sister Madelaine "Sunny" accepted the plaque with the understanding that they would not have to display it and the cottage would not be open to the public.

The Hemingways, though they loved Ernie and tried to protect his good name, were not without humor about all this. Sarcasm is a Hemingway family trait. After the plaque had been presented to the Michigan cottage, a family friend put up a sign on the outhouse in the back that said, "Ernest Hemingway sat here." Ernie probably would have approved.

Like all the post-Hadley Hemingway homes, the New York apartment was chosen by his wife, who liked New York and enjoyed spending time there. 1 East 62 Street, at 62 Street and Fifth Avenue, is in one of Manhattan's most expensive neighborhoods, which makes it one of the most expensive in the world. The limestone mansion was originally built in 1903 by Horace Trumbauer, a leading architect of ostentatious mansions for robber barons in the Gilded Age. He was somewhat disparaged by colleagues, but today his homes are vaunted classics. This one was built for John R. Drexel and his wife Alice Troth Drexel, who paid Trumbauer $500,000, which is the equivalent of about $5 million today. The Drexels, famed for extravagance, filled the mansion with the most expensive antiques they could find, though with homes in Newport and Paris, they spent little time there.

By the standards of the neighborhood, the Hemingway apartment was not extravagant—just 900 square feet, which is a very large one-bedroom apartment, but nevertheless just a one-bedroom apartment. There was no room for Valerie when she was with them, and she stayed in the nearby Barbizon Hotel for Women. It was an elegant marble apartment with big windows and good light, but a small kitchen for Mary who loved to cook. She was very taken with the marble entryway and its curving staircase that was once the entrance to the fabulous home.

They were in the process of moving from Cuba to Ketchum and did not have much in the apartment. Mary wanted to be in New York in 1959 to work on the Kennedy campaign, but this was Papa's final tragic year and she spent most of her time trying to save him. She later wrote, "In the little flat in Sixty-second Street Ernest acted as though he were a stranger, courteous but unfamiliar with the rooms, quiet, inattentive to news issuing from the radio, preoccupied with problems he seemed not to wish to communicate."

Hemingway's favorite New York activity had been to go with sports writer Grantland Rice to the Bronx Zoo and look at the animals. But Rice died in 1954, before Hemingway had his New York apartment.

There were the museums where certain paintings were old friends.

He once said that if he couldn't be a writer, he would have liked to be a painter. He enjoyed going to the Metropolitan with Valerie and spent hours looking at Winslow Homer's paintings of fisherman.

The ghost of Ernest Hemingway is very different in each town. The Idaho Hemingway has little in common with the Cuban one, who is also completely different from the ones of Spain or Paris. In New York, Hemingway is largely about real estate value.

In his 1934 poem about New York, Claude McKay wrote, "The air is charged with selling." New York is a commercial town. It is all about money. And Hemingway was a commercial writer, and in death he became a money-making commercial property. He was more suited for New York than he ever knew.

As for the apartment, there will be no Hemingway museum at the heart of Fifth Avenue. Not with the value of that real estate in a building where apartments rent for more than $27,000 a month. But you could always use the Hemingway name to up the value, although at the moment the big hype is about the late comedian Joan Rivers who had the penthouse. You can rent an apartment in Joan Rivers's building. But the Hemingway name is still worth something. In 2012, a Sotheby's broker listing a two-bedroom apartment pointed out that it was Hemingway's building. He said, "Hemingway, during his many years in the mansion, wrote 'The Snows of Kilamanjaro (sic)'." I wonder why he chose that particular work in this completely erroneous statement, since that story had been written years earlier. Papa probably didn't write anything in his brief time there or if he did, it was work on "Dangerous Summer" or one of the other unfinished books.

In March 2020, a real estate listing for a two-bedroom duplex in the building for $27,500 per month stated simply that the building "has included Ernest Hemingway as one of its residents." How would Papa feel to know that his name was being used to promote over-priced Manhattan real estate?

• • •

You can know the ghost of Hemingway or at least one of them, but knowing Hemingway himself is impossible. There is never only one way to see

him. He was like fifteen people in one.

Almost any way friend or foe characterized him was not always true. He was a gentle and kind man of notable openness and generosity, except for every now and then when he became a bully. He was a champion of the underdog who had no tolerance for people being mistreated, but then sometimes he seemed to be a bigot. Or was that a kind of rough character he was playing? He loved the language of bigotry but never really did anything bigoted.

It is a mistake to confuse Hemingway with the characters in his books, even though he appears to be the prototype for some of them. Hemingway lived up to the Flaubert ideal of an author in his books being "present everywhere and visible nowhere." Papa did not try to change the world, only to describe it.

The problem with judging Hemingway from his writing is that his characters express all kinds of points of view, and it is never clear which (if any) express the thinking of the author. A lifelong devoted hunter, he has characters who denounce hunting. He thought different points of view were interesting. In *True at First Light,* which he never came close to finishing, there is a character named Ernest Hemingway who denounces not only hunting but the entire role of a white man in Africa, calling it "stupid to be a white man in Africa."

What gave Hemingway his lasting power was a singularly important idea. Yes, he was romantic and often engaged in questions of love, which was part of his appeal. But Hemingway in all his writing takes on the question that is seldom spoken but always preoccupies us, the question of questions, which is: Since death is a certainty that awaits us, how will we face it? This question is in everything he ever wrote. Maybe it began in that one week in the Italian trenches horrified by incoming mortars.

This is surely why he was drawn to bullfights. The bull enters the ring, wild and alone and ignorant. There is only one ending. He will die. But how well will he die? That is the essential question of bullfights. It is why my matador friend, Paco Villalta, always talked about death. Not because he was depressed or afraid, but because arranging good deaths was his trade. He was engaging in this question of "how to face death." How will the bull face his inevitable death? We all have this question,

whether we want to talk about it or not, whether we ask it or not. Life is an arena that you enter and in the end, you die there. The nature of his own death always weighed on him. He became upset when Scribner's started working on his *Death in the Afternoon* manuscript with the working title, "Hemingway's Death."

In *Death in the Afternoon*, Hem wrote, "All stories if continued far enough, end in death." That was certainly true of bullfights, but it was not the case with Hemingway. His story has gone on long after death.

To understand how Hemingway remained in my life even though he was dead, you have to understand what happened after he ended it. He didn't die. More than a million Hemingway books are sold each year. More Hemingway has sold since his death than in his lifetime. Few living writers get as many hits on the internet as Ernest Hemingway. The ongoing project to publish his letters in seventeen volumes, now working on number seven, has been an enormous success. "Since the Hemingway Letters Project was initiated in 2002 to produce this edition, I have learned that it is almost impossible to overestimate public interest in Hemingway and the broad appeal of his work," General Editor Sandra Spanier said. Even the FBI did not recognize his death and continued filing reports on him until 1974.

In addition to the many biographies and critical essays, at least nineteen reminisces by people who knew him—two sisters, a brother, two of his sons, and many friends and acquaintances—have been published. This includes A.E. Hotchner's final book, *Hemingway in Love* in 2015. I had called him in his Connecticut home. He was well into his nineties—would he still have the energy and the clarity for a good conversation? He told me that he could not talk to me now because he was trying to finish a book. The book was this one last attempt at the impossible: telling us who Hemingway was.

Algren had it right when he said of Hemingway, "He was a big man who had a big life; that had made those who had known him bigger."

When I was a boy, there was Hemingway and there was Lawrence Ferlinghetti, my two biggest literary heroes. Ferlinghetti came out with a good book at age 100 and died at 101. That's better than a writer dead at age sixty-two. But Hemingway outsells him.

Norman Mailer wrote, "What characterizes every book about Hemingway I have read is the way his character remains out of focus." It can't be nailed down. Shelves of books have been written about him. I have three shelves full and there are more. Every one of them presents a different Hemingway, and most of them have a few small errors but in general are true. The problem with Hemingway was that you could not capture a complete picture. It was only one or two of the Hemingways. Hadley had said, "Just so many sides to him you could hardly make a sketch of him in a geometry book." Even those who knew him felt they didn't really know him. In 1937, F. Scott Fitzgerald, a close friend for a dozen years, wrote that he wished he had spent more time with him because he didn't really know him. Robert Manning, who knew Hemingway only late in his life, said "It is possible that to have known him...makes it more rather than less difficult to understand him."

If I had known him, which was my dream when I was young, it would only have confused me. One of his contradictions was that while often talking of suicide, he also frequently talked of the importance of surviving. Typically, in a 1932 letter to Maxwell Perkins he wrote, "The first and final thing you have to do in this world is last in it..." I sometimes wonder if, in this frequent declaration, he was talking about lasting beyond death.

He was so large, and he intended to be; he left something of himself in the ether wherever he went. While the man has been gone more than sixty years, the presence he left behind still remains. It seems there is no escaping it. Most of the millions of Hemingway fans in France, Spain, Cuba, Idaho, and everywhere else do not have the confusion of having known him. The mythical Hemingway is so much easier to grasp—flowers, liquor, or pen?

BIBLIOGRAPHY

Algren, Nelson. *Notes from a Sea Diary: Hemingway All the Way*. New York: G. P. Putnam's Sons, 1963 (revised from 1959).

Arnold, Lloyd R. *Hemingway: High On The Wild*. New York: Grosset & Dunlap, 1977.

Arrozarena, Cecilia. *El roble y la ceiba: Historia de los Vascos en Cuba*. Tafalla, Navarra, Spain: Txalaparta, 2003.

Baker, Carlos. *Ernest Hemingway: A Life Story*. New York: Charles Scribner's Sons, 1969.

---ed. *Ernest Hemingway: Selected Letters 1917---1961*. New York: Charles Scribner's Sons, 1982.

Bellavance-Johnson, Marsha and Lee Bellavance. *Ernest Hemingway In Idaho*. Ketchum, ID: Computer Lab, 1989.

Brian, Denis. *The True Gen: An Intimate Portrait of Hemingway by Those Who Knew Him*. New York: Grove Press, 1987.

Bruccoli, Matthew J. *Fitzgerald and Hemingway: A Dangerous Friendship*. Columbia, SC: Bruccoli-Clark Layman, 1994.

Buckley, Peter. *Ernest*. New York: Dial Press, 1978.

Cirules, Enrique. *Hemingway: Ese desconocido*. Havana: Editorial Arte Y Literatura, 2015.

Cummings, E. E. *The Enormous Room*. New York: Boni & Liveright, Inc., 1922.

Dearborn, Mary V. *Ernest Hemingway: A Biography*. New York: Alfred A. Knopf, 2017.

Desnoes, Edmundo. *Memorias del Subdesarrollo*. Havana: Ediciones Union, 1965 (or *Inconsolable Memories: A Novel of Cuba Today*, London: Andre Deutsch, 1968).

Diliberto, Gioia. *Paris Without End: The True Story of Hemingway's First Wife*. New York: Harper Perennial, 2011.

Donaldson, Scott. *By Force of Will: The Life and Art of Ernest Hemingway*. New York: Viking, 1977.

Ernest Hemingway, The Last Interview and Other Conversations. Brooklyn: Melville House, 2015.

Farrington Jr., S. Kip. *Fishing with Hemingway and Glassell*. New York: David McKay Company, Inc., 1971.

Feldman, Andrew. *Ernesto: The Untold Story of Hemingway in Revolutionary Cuba*. Brooklyn: Melville House, 2019.

Franklin, Sidney. *Bullfighter from Brooklyn: The Amazing Autobiography of Sidney Franklin*. New York: Prentice-Hall, 1952.

Fuentes, Norberto. *Hemingway In Cuba*. Secaucus, NJ: Lyle Stuart, 1984.

Gerogiannis, Nicholas, ed. *Complete Poems: Ernest Hemingway*. Lincoln: University of Nebraska Press, 1992.

Hemingway, Ernest. *A Farewell To Arms*. New York: Charles Scribner's Sons, 1929.

---.*A Moveable Feast: Sketches of the Author's Life in Paris in the Twenties*. New York: Charles Scribner's Sons, 1964 (revised version Scribner, 2009).

---.*Collected Poems, originally published in Paris*. San Francisco: Pirated Edition by Brayton, 1960.

---.*Death in the Afternoon*. New York: Charles Scribner's Sons, 1955.

---.*Green Hills of Africa*. New York: Charles Scribner's Sons, 1935.

---.*Islands In The Stream*. New York: Charles Scribner's Sons, 1970.

---.*Men At War*. New York: Crown, 1942.

---*On Paris*. London: Hesperus Press, 2012.

---.*The Complete Short Stories of Ernest Hemingway*. New York: Scribner, 1987.

---.*The Fifth Column and Four Unpublished Stories of the Spanish Civil War*. New York, Charles Scribner's Sons, 1969.

---.*The Garden of Eden*. New York: Charles Scribner's Sons, 1986.

---.*The Nick Adams Stories*. New York: Charles Scribner's Sons, 1972.

---.*The Old Man and The Sea*. New York: Charles Scribner's Sons, 1952.

---.*The Sun Also Rises*. New York: Charles Scribner's Sons, 1926.

---.*To Have and Have Not*. New York: Charles Scribner's Sons, 1937.

---.*True At First Light,* edited by Patrick Hemingway. New York: Scribner's, 1999.

---.*Winner Take Nothing*. New York: Charles Scribner's Sons, 1933.

Hemingway, Gregory H. *Papa: A Personal Memoir*. Boston: Houghton Mifflin, 1976.

Hemingway, Jack. *Misadventures of a Fly Fisherman: My Life With and Without Papa*. Dallas: Taylor, 1986.

Hemingway, John. *Strange Tribe: A Family Memoir*. Guilford, Connecticut: Lyons Press, 2007.

Hemingway, Leicester. *My Brother, Ernest Hemingway*. Cleveland: The World Publishing Company, 1961.

Hemingway, Mary Welsh. *How It Was*. New York: Knopf, 1976.

Hemingway, Valerie. *Running With the Bulls: My Years With the Hemingways*. New York: Ballantine Books, 2004.

Hendrickson, Paul. *Hemingway's Boat: Everything He Loved in Life, and Lost*. New York: Alfred A. Knopf, 2011.

Herbst, Josephine. *The Starched Blue Sky of Spain and Other Memoirs*. New York: HarperCollins, 1991.

Heyman, Stephen. *The Planter of Modern Life: Louis Bromfield and the Seeds of a Food Revolution*. New York: W. W. Norton & Company, 2020.

Holland, Wendolyn Spence. *Sun Valley: An Extraordinary History*. Ketchum: The Idaho Press, 1998.

Hotchner, A. E. *Hemingway in Love: The Untold Story*. New York: Picador, 2015.

---.*Papa Hemingway*. New York: Random House, 1966.

---.*The Good Life According to Hemingway*. New York: Ecco, 2008.

Jiménez, Edorta. *San Fermingway: Otras historias de Ernest Hemingway*. Tafalla, Nafaroa, Spain: Txalaparta, 2005.

Kiley, Jed. *Hemingway, An Old Friend Remembers*. New York: Hawthorn Books, 1965.

Kurlansky, Mark. *Havana: A Subtropical Delirium*. New York: Bloomsbury Publishing, 2017.

---.*The Basque History of the World*. New York: Walker & Company, 1999.

Leante, César. *Hemingway y la revolución cubana*. Madrid: Editorial pliegos, 1992.

Lee, David S. *Gulf Stream Chronicles: A Naturalist Explores Life in an Ocean River*. Chapel Hill: University of North Carolina Press, 2015.

Manning, Frederic. *The Middle Parts of Fortune*. London: The Piazza

Press, 1929.

Matthews, Herbert L. *A World in Revolution: A Newspaperman's Memoir*. New York: Scribner, 1971.

McKay, Claude. *A Long Way from Home*. New Brunswick, NJ: Rutgers University Press 2007 (originally published in 1937).

Meriweather, James B. ed. *William Faulkner: Essays, Speeches and Public Letters*. New York: Random House, Inc., 1965.

Meyers, Jeffrey. *Hemingway: Life Into Art*. New York: Cooper Square Press, 2000.

Miller, Madelaine Hemingway. *Ernie: Hemingway's Sister "Sunny" Remembers*. New York: Crown Publishers, 1975.

Morris, Larry E. *Ernest Hemingway & Gary Cooper in Idaho: An Enduring Friendship*. Charleston, SC: The History Press, 2017.

Orwell, George. *Down and Out in Paris and London*. New York: Harcourt, 1961.

---.*Homage to Catalonia*. London: Secker and Warburg, 1938.

Padura Fuentes, Leonardo. *Adiós Hemingway*. Translated by John King. Edinburgh, UK: Canongate, 2005.

Raeburn, Ben, ed. *Treasury of the Free World,* introduction by Ernest Hemingway. New York: Arco, 1946.

Reynolds, Michael. *Hemingway: The Final Years*. New York: W.W. Norton & Company, 1999.

---.*Hemingway: The 1930s through the Final Years*. New York: W.W. Norton & Company, 2012.

Reynolds, Nicholas. *Writer, Sailor, Soldier, Spy: Ernest Hemingway's Secret Adventures, 1935---1961*. New York: William Morrow, 2017.

Ross, Lillian. *Portrait of Hemingway*. New York: Avon Books, 1961.

Sanderson, Rena, Sandra Spanier, Robert W. Trogdon, eds. *The Letters of Ernest Hemingway Vol. 3: 1926---1929*. Cambridge and New York: Cambridge University Press, 2015.

Sauter, Van Gordon. *The Sun Valley Story*. Hailey, Idaho: Mandala Media, 2011.

Spanier, Sandra, Miriam B. Mandel, eds. *The Letters of Ernest Hemingway, Vol. 4: 1929---1931*. Cambridge and New York: Cambridge University Press, 2018.

---.*The Letters of Ernest Hemingway, Vol. 5: 1932---1934*. Cambridge and New York: Cambridge University Press, 2020.

Spanier, Sandra, Albert J. Defazio III, Robert W. Trogdon, eds. *The Letters of Ernest Hemingway, Vol. 2: 1923---1925*. Cambridge and New York: Cambridge University Press, 2013.

Spanier, Sandra, Robert W. Trogdon, eds. *The Letters of Ernest Hemingway, Vol. 1: 1907---1922*. Cambridge and New York: Cambridge University Press, 2011.

Swift, Daniel. *The Bughouse: The Poetry, Politics, and Madness of Ezra Pound*. New York: Farrar, Straus and Giroux, 2017.

Vaill, Amanda. *Hotel Florida: Truth, Love, and Death in the Spanish Civil War*. New York: Farrar, Straus and Giroux, 2014.

Villarreal, René and Raúl Villarreal. *Hemingway's Cuban Son: Reflections on the Writer by His Longtime Majordomo*. Kent, OH: Kent State University Press, 2009.

White, William, ed. *By-Line: Ernest Hemingway: Selected Articles and Dispatches of Four Decades*. New York: Charles Scribner's Sons, 1967.

Young, Philip. *Ernest Hemingway: A Reconstruction*. University Park: Penn State University Press, 1966.

Articles

Brasch, James D. "Hemingway's Doctor: José Luis Herrera Sotolongo Remembers Ernest Hemingway." *Journal of Modern Literature* 13, no. 2 (Jul. 1986): 185---210. https://www.jstor.org/stable/3831491.

Cowley, Malcolm. "Hemingway's Wound—And its Consequences for American Literature," *The Georgia Review* 38, no. 2 (Summer 1984): 223---239. https://www.jstor.org/stable/41398663.

Hemingway Ernest. "The Dangerous Summer: Part 1." *Life,* September 5, 1960.

---."The Dangerous Summer: Part 2." *Life* September 12, 1960.

---."The Dangerous Summer: Part 3." *Life*. September 19, 1960.

---."The Hemingways in Sun Valley: The Novelist Takes a Wife." *Life*, January 6, 1941.

---."The Old Man and The Sea: A Complete New Book, First Publication." *Life*, September 1, 1952.

---."The Time is Now, the Place is Spain." *Ken*, April 7, 1938.

Hochman, Brian. "Ellison's Hemingway." *African American Review* 42, no. 3/4 (Fall/Winter 2008): 513---532. https://www.jstor.org/stable/40301251.

Manning, Robert. "Hemingway In Cuba." *The Atlantic*, August 1965. https://www.theatlantic.com/magazine/archive/1965/08/hemingway-in-cuba/399059/.

Sarrionandia, Joseba. "Flak Mak." *Erlea-9* (La Habana, 1947). Written in Basque.

ABOUT THE WATERCOLORS

Basque houses have names. Nire Etxea Ohantzea was the
name of the home where I lived in Hendaye. Beltza the dog
always waited for me on the steps, February 1998.

In 1975, on my second trip to Europe with Virginia and no schedule for when we might return, I decided to keep a diary. This bound notebook, ten inches by 7 ⅛ inches was filled with notes on the places we visited. But I also included ink drawings of menacing Guardia Civil from our first trip to Spain, the faces of many people I wanted to remember, fishing boats in Portugal. I discovered later, as photographers sometimes do with the things they shoot, that I did not forget anything that I drew, that my drawings were more lasting in my memory than anything I wrote.

I began to sketch people and places I wanted to remember in my reporter notebooks. After the fall of Communism, I traveled the Trans Siberian railroad from Moscow to Beijing. At the time, Russian trains were full of thieves and I did not dare bring a computer. I reintroduced myself to the pleasure of long hand along with many drawings. Some with color. I had a lot of time.

The real change came in 1991, when I traveled for three months by dugout canoe in the rainforest of French Guiana and Surinam. I wrote all my notes by hand and illustrated them with watercolors. I took one of those pocket-sized packs of color pans and used the water from the river to paint.

Since then there has been no going back. I record all my travels in small books. Sometimes I take watercolor paper to a bindery, and they make books for me. I write very little in these books, but most days I paint one or two or more pictures and write where they are and the day I did the paintings. They are my diaries of all my travels. So far I have 28 color diaries.

ACKNOWLEDGEMENTS

First, I have to thank James Atlas, who first seized on this idea when I mentioned it in passing. I'm sorry he won't be able to see it. But most of all, I want to thank my dear friend Mitchell Kaplan, comrade in arms during most of our careers, for grabbing this book and believing in it with his characteristic enthusiasm and taking it to the wonderful Mango Publishing. I have to thank Mango for a fine job, and especially Yaddyra Peralta for her warmth and skilled professionalism.

I want to thank my parents, Philip and Roslyn Kurlansky, for teaching me to love books and love music. And I should thank everyone in the book, but it would be too long a list. Thank you, Ellen, for the Ferlinghetti, and to the memory of Hank Reynolds, who wanted to introduce us to Spain.

To the memory of Bud Purdy and George Plimpton, and for help from Valerie Danby-Smith and Patrick Hemingway.

Thanks to Sandra Spanier and the incredible Letters project for your five great volumes. Looking forward to the other twelve.

And thanks to dozens of Hemingway biographers—American, Spanish, Cuban, and Basque.

ABOUT THE AUTHOR

Credit: Sylvia Plachy

Mark Kurlansky is the *New York Times* bestselling author of 34 books of fiction, nonfiction children's books, young adult books, and one classic French translation. His books include *Cod, Salt, Paper, The Basque History of the World, 1968, Salmon, The Big Oyster* and *International Night,* among many others. He received the 2007 Dayton Literary Peace Prize for *Nonviolence, Bon Appétit* Food Writer of the Year award in 2006, a 1998 James Beard Award for writing on food, and the 1999 Glenfiddich Award, for *Cod. Salt* was a *Los Angeles Times* book prize finalist. *Salmon* won the IBPA Ben Franklin Award for nature and environment writing, and *The Unreasonable Virtue of Fly Fishing* won the 2021 National Outdoor Book Award. He has been a foreign correspondent for *The International Tribune, The Chicago Tribune* and other newspapers in Europe, Mexico, and the Caribbean. He has written in many parts of the world and has been translated into thirty languages.

Sunset on Socoa from the beach at Saint-Jean-de-Luz, 9:30 p.m., Aug. 5, 2015

View from within the Eiffel Tower, Dec. 7, 1993

Mango Publishing, established in 2014, publishes an eclectic list of books by diverse authors—both new and established voices—on topics ranging from business, personal growth, women's empowerment, LGBTQ studies, health, and spirituality to history, popular culture, time management, decluttering, lifestyle, mental wellness, aging, and sustainable living. We were recently named 2019 *and* 2020's #1 fastest-growing independent publisher by *Publishers Weekly*. Our success is driven by our main goal, which is to publish high-quality books that will entertain readers as well as make a positive difference in their lives.

Our readers are our most important resource; we value your input, suggestions, and ideas. We'd love to hear from you—after all, we are publishing books for you!

Please stay in touch with us and follow us at:

> Facebook: Mango Publishing
> Twitter: @MangoPublishing
> Instagram: @MangoPublishing
> LinkedIn: Mango Publishing
> Pinterest: Mango Publishing
> Newsletter: mangopublishinggroup.com/newsletter

Join us on Mango's journey to reinvent publishing, one book at a time.

ALSO BY MARK KURLANSKY

NONFICTION

The Importance of

Not Being Ernest